THE EVERYTHING®

GUIDE TO CARING FOR AGING PARENTS

Dear Reader,

If you've picked up this book, you are no doubt facing a major change in your life or anticipating the very real possibility in the near future. Getting old is a fact of life. We all hope, by the time we get old, we will have accomplished our goals, realized at least one of our dreams, and still have a little money left to live on. We hope we will have good health, not too much pain, and be able to remain independent. Hopefully, we will still have family and friends who like us and are willing to come around to visit and help us out occasionally.

We certainly don't want to be a burden to anyone. We hope we can manage our own care and that if we need a little help, we hope we still have a little something to offer in exchange or maybe along the way we have paid it forward enough that we aren't asking for too much now. We hope we'll have our wits about us and not be plagued with Alzheimer's or at least be blessed enough to not know.

For now though, we have the new responsibility to learn to help and care for our aging parents. We'll be changing roles and making decisions for them as well as our children. For thirty years, I have worked in home health care and helped families navigate this path, and now I, too, must take this journey with my mother. I hope you'll join us and learn to help your own family. Welcome to the sandwich generation!

Kathy Quan

Welcome to the EVERYTHING Series!

These handy, accessible books give you all you need to tackle a difficult project, gain a new hobby, comprehend a fascinating topic, prepare for an exam, or even brush up on something you learned back in school but have since forgotten.

You can choose to read an *Everything*® book from cover to cover or just pick out the information you want from our four useful boxes: e-questions, e-facts, e-alerts, and e-ssentials.

We give you everything you need to know on the subject, but throw in a lot of fun stuff along the way, too.

We now have more than 400 *Everything*® books in print, spanning such wide-ranging categories as weddings, pregnancy, cooking, music instruction, foreign language, crafts, pets, New Age, and so much more. When you're done reading them all, you can finally say you know *Everything*®!

QUESTIONS?
Answers to
common questions

FACTS
Important snippets
of information

ALERTS!
Urgent
warnings

ESSENTIALS
Quick
handy tips

PUBLISHER Karen Cooper

DIRECTOR OF ACQUISITIONS AND INNOVATION Paula Munier

MANAGING EDITOR, EVERYTHING SERIES Lisa Laing

COPY CHIEF Casey Ebert

ACQUISITIONS EDITOR Katie McDonough

SENIOR DEVELOPMENT EDITOR Brett Palana-Shanahan

EDITORIAL ASSISTANT Hillary Thompson

TECHNICAL REVIEW BY Brette McWhorter Sember, JD

Visit the entire Everything® series at *www.everything.com*

June 14-22

EVERYTHING®

Guide to Caring for Aging Parents

Reassuring advice to help you support your loved ones

Kathy Quan, RN, BSN, PHN

Aadamsmedia
Avon, Massachusetts

To my parents and in-laws,
who have taught me how to deal with this process.

To the loves of my life:
my husband Tim, and my children Amy, Rob, and Becky!

And to all of my former patients and coworkers
who taught me everything I know about home care.

An Everything® Series Book.
Everything® and everything.com® are registered trademarks of F+W Media, Inc.

Published by Adams Media, a division of F+W Media, Inc.
57 Littlefield Street, Avon, MA 02322 U.S.A.
www.adamsmedia.com

ISBN 10: 1-59869-648-3
ISBN 13: 978-1-59869-648-6

Printed in the United States of America.

J   I   H   G   F   E   D   C   B   A

Library of Congress Cataloging-in-Publication Data
is available from the publisher

This publication is designed to provide accurate and authoritative information with regard to the subject matter covered. It is sold with the understanding that the publisher is not engaged in rendering legal, accounting, or other professional advice. If legal advice or other expert assistance is required, the services of a competent professional person should be sought.

—From a *Declaration of Principles* jointly adopted by a Committee of the American Bar Association and a Committee of Publishers and Associations

Many of the designations used by manufacturers and sellers to distinguish their products are claimed as trademarks. Where those designations appear in this book and Adams Media was aware of a trademark claim, the designations have been printed with initial capital letters.

This book is available at quantity discounts for bulk purchases.
For information, please call 1-800-289-0963.

Contents

Acknowledgments

First and foremost, I want to thank my family, my husband Tim, and my children Amy, Rob, and Becky for their unconditional love, devotion, and help throughout the writing of this book. To my mother, who has always been my biggest fan and most honest critic. My parents and my in-laws have taught me a lot about how to deal with aging parents. I hope that I have and will continue to make a difference for all of them. To "the girls," who know who they are. The best friends ever! You have always encouraged me to follow my dreams. You have been there for me and continue to offer support and love. You know this has meant reaching well beyond my comfort zone! Thank you so much.

Thanks, too, to the rest of my family and friends who have encouraged me and supported me in this effort in many ways. You all inspire me always. I must acknowledge all of the many home health-care patients and coworkers I have enjoyed knowing over the past thirty years. You have all taught me how to help others learn to cope and survive this process.

To Barbara Doyen, my agent, who has always helped me all along the way even through emergencies and craziness! Thanks to my editors for all of your patience and help with this book. Thanks so very much to all of you!

Top Ten Things You Need to Know about Caring for Your Aging Parents

1. You are not alone; the Sandwich Generation is growing.

2. You need to learn where to find resources and help and how to navigate the system.

3. You need to organize and delegate responsibilities. You can't do it all yourself.

4. You need to get things in writing.

5. You need to learn how to agree to disagree with parents and siblings.

6. You need to learn to recognize when to change levels of care and act quickly.

7. Your parents may be old and seem childish, but they deserve your respect. You are NOT becoming their parents.

8. Effective communication is essential. Designate one spokesperson.

9. You must take care of YOU.

10. You need to start planning now for your own future care needs.

Introduction

▶ HOW DO YOU know when it's time to start thinking about who's going to care for your parents or other loved ones? If you're thinking about that question, it's time.

Your parents or in-laws will be the main or central characters in your planning process. You need to first discover what their wishes and ideas are for how they want to live out their last years. All decisions have to involve them and, as much as possible, revolve around and incorporate these wishes and desires.

The safety and well-being of your parents should be the most important factor. Helping them live out their lives within the scope of their wishes for as long as it is safe will be paramount in your plan. Financial factors will dictate the reality and success. Planning ahead of time will help to broaden the possibilities. Waiting for a crisis to happen may eliminate choices and make life more difficult.

Take the time to sit down with your whole family and begin this discussion. If it is geographically impossible to have everyone in one place, technology offers many realms of solutions including conference calls, instant messaging, and video conferences.
Begin by encouraging each family member to give this some serious thought, and then bring their ideas together in a brainstorming session. Let your parents speak first, and then give each person the respect of listening to their ideas as well.

Talking about wishes and understanding how each family member feels about them, and what types of responsibilities each person can handle, will help avoid problems in the long run. You must take into account that science and technology will continue to make advances and offer alternatives. These should be incorporated into a plan as life evolves.

Included in the discussion should be whether or not your parents will agree to or are totally opposed to institutions such as a nursing home, board and care, or assisted-living facility should they no longer be able to remain in their own home. Explore whether there are funds to cover these expenses. Can they remain at home, and who will care for them? Additionally, end-of-life issues need to be discussed openly.

Understanding that as adults it is okay to agree to disagree and still be friends is an essential factor in dealing with these decisions. For example, your mother wants to be cremated and her ashes scattered at sea. She wants no funeral and no ceremonies. Your sister thinks it's a perfect idea, but your brother is shocked because this goes against all of your family's spiritual beliefs and upbringing. He thinks she has to be buried, and there must be a viewing and a funeral, with a procession to the gravesite, and so on. You're able to accept the idea of cremation and scattering of her ashes, but you know that you will need to have some sort of closure ceremony. Where do you go from here?

Coming to a meeting of the minds may be easier said than done. Accepting your mother's wishes and agreeing to disagree with her and your siblings may not be an easy task. But understanding you may never all agree to all aspects of these issues, and accepting the fact that you can disagree and move on, is important.

Make informed decisions. Learn where to find information. Learn about the alternatives you have in caring for your aging parents and in-laws, how to get your family involved, how to manage being sandwiched between caring for your children and your parents, and how to avoid burnout.

You will also need to learn to take care of yourself so you can continue to take care of those who need you. Know you will have given this your best effort and you will have made a difference in your loved ones lives.

CHAPTER 1

Defining the Situation

As the population continues to grow and age, more and more people will be in need of some sort of assistance. Shortages of health-care workers such as physicians, nurses, therapists, social workers, and dentists are expected to continue as older workers retire and lower numbers of new health-care workers enter the fields. At the present time, the impact of these shortages places the burden on individuals and their families to meet the needs for care and assistance. This impact is only going to increase as the population grows and ages.

Aging: A Few Statistics

Baby boomers—those born after World War II, between 1946 and 1964—have helped bring about tremendous advances in medicine, science, and technology. One of the results of these advances is that people are now living longer, are healthier, and have access to better diagnostics and health care. Longevity is only expected to increase over the next few decades.

FACT

In 1950, only 12 percent of the population of developed countries (North America, Europe, Japan, New Zealand, and Australia) was over sixty. By 1998, that number had increased to 19 percent, and by 2025 it is expected to reach 28 percent. In absolute numbers, the range is from 100 million people over age sixty in 1950 to over 500 million by 2025.

As each year passes, the number of people over sixty is not the only significant factor; the oldest members of the aging population are also growing older. In fact, the fastest-growing segment of the population over sixty is the segment that is over eighty. This fact alone has a major impact on the health-care industry because, in general, the older the person, the more likely he or she is to need more health-care services. This raises the problem of shortages of health-care workers, especially nurses, to crisis levels.

For a large portion of the older population, the primary caregivers are not children but spouses. However, statistically, women outnumber men. Women are in the majority when it comes to the oldest segment of those over eighty; this means that as they age, most women will need to turn to other family members or to institutions such as assisted living and skilled nursing facilities.

As life expectancies continue to increase, so does the likelihood that middle-aged adults will find themselves caring not only for their growing children but for their aging parents as well. Concomitantly, as their parents age, their needs will become more pressing and more time consuming.

Women are the predominant caregivers. Wives, daughters, daughters-in-law, granddaughters, sisters, and sisters-in-law provide the care to aging family members. Women provide more than twice as many hours of care to their elder parents or in-laws as men do. Often this is due to the type of care provided. Men typically provide assistance with transportation or household maintenance and repairs, whereas women provide more of the activities of daily living and personal care such as bathing, grooming, dressing, and toileting. Shopping, running errands, food preparation, and cleaning chores can be shared, but again, more women than men usually do these chores.

According to several studies from the Bureau of Labor Statistics, 70 percent of these women are forty-five to fifty-six years old and work full time outside the home. The average caregiver is a forty-six-year-old married female who works outside of the home and earns an annual income of $35,000.

Of that number, 20 percent have had to reduce the number of hours they work, utilize flexible work situations, have lost income, and or have had to quit work entirely to stay home and be caregivers to an elder parent or in-law.

ALERT!

In the corporate world, it is estimated that as the population continues to age, most employees will be affected by elder-care issues at some point during their careers. At the present, more productivity is affected due to elder-care issues than those of child care. According to the New York Business Group on Health, Inc., almost $34 billion is lost on elder-care responsibilities in the U.S., and the problems are probably more widespread than any available survey data suggests.

Creative solutions are going to be necessary in order to preserve the valuable work force as it faces the challenges of caring for aging parents. In the U.S., more than 14 million workers have elder-care responsibilities. Of that number, 7–10 million are trying to care for their aging parents long distance. These experienced workers are dedicated employees with irreplaceable knowledge and expertise whose loss can cost companies even more in the long run in terms of corporate operations, competitive edge, and overall financial success and survival.

The Sandwich Generation

The term "sandwich generation" has been around for decades, but it began to appear quite often in the mid- to late 1990s and it has become quite a buzzword in the first decade of the twenty-first century. It now refers to the middle-aged generation known as the baby boomers, those with dependent (or college-aged) children and parents over the age of seventy. The numbers and demographics of how many are simultaneously providing support and care to both generations vary depending upon the breadth of the definition of care and support.

FACT

There are 76 million baby boomers. On January 1, 2006, the oldest of this group turned sixty. By 2014, they will range in age from fifty to sixty-eight years old and either be retired or in the planning stages of retirement.

As baby boomers face elder care for their parents, they should pay close attention and plan for themselves as well. As they age, they will be presented with the fact that the generation following theirs (the baby-bust generation) produced only 37.4 million births from 1965 to 1976. This significant drop in numbers represents a huge shortage in prime-age work force numbers.

This shortage dramatically affects the health-care industry at a time when it will be most challenged by a growing and aging population in need of, and demanding excellence in, health care. This is something to take heed of as baby boomers learn to care for their aging parents and plan for their own elder-care scenarios.

Sandwiched Women

Baby boomers are redefining yet another social aspect as they forge ahead through middle age into the sandwich. Forty-four percent of Americans between the ages of forty-five and fifty-six have aging parents as well as children under the age of twenty-one. In actuality, women are sandwiched more often than men. Surprisingly, they provide coresidence to aging parents as well as their children in only about 1 percent of the cases. This number increases only slightly to 1.2 percent when the children are away at college. It is a much more common scenario for baby boomers to provide financial support to their college-age children and (the women) to devote 500+ hours of time to the dependent parents or in-laws, according to the National Longitudinal Survey of Young Women conducted from 1968 to 2003.

In fact, the Bureau of Labor Statistics estimates the roughly 20 million women in this sandwich generation will transfer $18 billion and devote 2.4 billion hours of their time to their children and their elder parents each year.

In a 1990 article, *Newsweek* reported that the average American woman will spend seventeen years raising children and eighteen years helping her aging parents or in-laws.

As all of the generations age, the sandwich can grow to include a fourth generation, that of grandchildren to the middle-aged caregivers who may also find themselves devoting time as well as financial aide to care for and support the grandchildren.

Challenges for the Sandwich Generation

The sandwich generation has three basic challenges to deal with and try to find balance with in their lives:

- Raising their children and being part of their lives
- Assisting their aging parents and in-laws
- Maintaining their own identity; leading their own lives and careers

Having time to enjoy their lives and the financial ability to do so can be dramatically affected by care-giving needs. Keeping the negative effects and stress level to a minimum will take a lot of planning and organization. Learning to ask for help when needed and knowing where to find it is imperative. Knowing and respecting one's own limitations is essential.

Reversing Roles

Many people have the misconception that they will have to become the parents to their aging parents or in-laws. In fact, this attitude can be dangerous. Your parents are your parents and they always will be. They deserve respect, and it is most important for you to help them maintain as much independence and dignity as possible. Although you may have to take charge in some instances and circumstances, you are not becoming the parent.

ALERT!

The role you are forced to assume may seem very similar to your role as parent to your own children, but there are vast differences. Your parents are adults, and unless they have lost their mental abilities and capacities, they are still capable of making decisions about their care and life. They may need significant assistance from you, as well as supervision, monitoring, and advice, but it is not your role to make all decisions for them.

Depending upon your cultural heritage and the specifics of your upbringing, this may or may not be an easy situation for you to manage. Take it in small steps and enlist the help of family and friends as needed. Even though this may become one of the most draining and stressful times of your life, it might just be one of the most rewarding as well.

Having an opportunity to give back to your parents for all of the love, support, and assistance they have given you during your life can be very special; being forced into a situation to set aside differences and make the best of an awkward relationship can afford you an opportunity to grow and to learn and perhaps mend a few fences before their life is over.

What you have to remember is that you are all adults. The parent-child power struggle is over. That isn't to say that they don't continue to treat you as a child, or that certain looks or phrases don't set off floods of emotions and flashbacks. But don't let old aggravations lead to more frustrations and make this more difficult than it needs to be. Remember that you are an adult and continue to behave as an adult. Resist the urge to revert to childish responses and try to refocus your energy toward the tasks at hand.

Helping your parents regain or hang on to as much of their own independence as possible will help foster this new relationship and help them learn to trust you and accept your assistance. Resist the temptation to take over and do for them. The more they can continue to do for themselves the better; physically and mentally, they will remain in better health and condition. The more you do for them, the needier they will become; in the long run, it will benefit them as well as you to help them remain active participants in their own care and activities of daily life.

Understand, too, that you will differ in what you consider most important and why. Where you may be more concerned about their health and safety, they may be more concerned with independence and continuing to enjoy the things they like to do. Beyond the things that can put others at risk, your parents have a right to continue to make decisions of their own, as long as they are mentally able to do so.

While driving may be out of the question because your parent no longer has the reflexes or dexterity to control the car, it doesn't mean he cannot get out and go to the theater, do some shopping and errands, or visit friends as long as alternative means of transportation can be arranged. He doesn't have to become a prisoner in his home, waiting for you to take him places.

Just because they can't remember to pay bills doesn't mean they have to leave their own home. Sit down with them and pay the bills together. That way the utilities won't be shut off and they won't have to leave familiar surroundings. Your responsibility is to help them make it happen.

Cultural Diversity Issues

The American Association of Retired Persons (AARP) conducted a telephone study of the baby-boom generation in March 2001 that looked at the multicultural aspects of life in America. The study, entitled "In the Middle: A Report of Multicultural Boomers Coping with Family and Aging Issues," provides some interesting information about the extended non-nuclear family as well as the traditional family and how cultural diversity issues affect this sandwiched generation. They used two firms to help them conduct the study: Belden Russonello and Stewart and Research/Strategy/Management (R/S/M).

FACT

The nationwide study of 2,352 Americans aged forty-four to fifty-five revealed that the baby-boomer sandwich has widened to include adults caring for extended family members as well as some nonfamily members. Four percent of the participants were Asian American; 9 percent were Hispanic American; 11 percent were African American; and 75 percent were non-Hispanic whites.

Large numbers of Asian Americans, African Americans, and Hispanic Americans reported having responsibilities for the care of their parents and other aging adults. Additionally, they may have responsibility for not only their own children but also grandchildren, nieces, nephews, and in some instances the children of friends or neighbors.

Most participants said they were being sandwiched, but AARP states it was surprised to note that 74 percent indicated they felt in control and not overwhelmed or extremely stressed by their situation. The other 26 percent indicated they were beginning to feel stressed. This was especially true of those who had direct care responsibilities for older adults and parents.

Those individuals who identified themselves as being in a low-income bracket indicated they were overwhelmed and felt more burdened and stressed by their responsibilities to parents and children. They were also less able to take off time from work to take care of issues for their family members.

The AARP survey also found that 44 percent of those surveyed have children under age twenty-one and living parents, in-laws, or both. Fifty-four percent actually have responsibilities to care for children or parents or both. For 22 percent, their focus is exclusively on elder care for either a parent or in-law.

A few more general statistics from this report include:

- 70 percent have at least one living parent.
- Almost 40 percent have children or adult children living at home.
- 7 percent live in multigenerational households.
- 69 percent do not want their children to have to shoulder the same responsibilities.
- 48 percent feel they should have or should be doing more for their parents.

The vast majority of the baby boomers welcome the chance to care for their parents and most feel they provide more care than their parents expect them to. Seventy-two percent report caring for the parents and in-laws has brought them closer together as a family.

Some of the differences between these racial and ethnic groups include the following:

- African Americans expressed more stress and reported feeling more overwhelmed by their family responsibilities. Of the four ethnic divisions in this report, this group is most likely to have lost both of their parents, especially for the oldest members surveyed, yet 28 percent provide care to their elders.
- Asian Americans have the highest expectations for care of both their parents and children. Forty-two percent provide care to their elders, and they are most likely to have responsibilities that reach across the ocean. They have the highest level of guilt.
- Thirty-four percent of Hispanic Americans are providing care for their parents and in-laws. Much of the care they provide is personal care and assistance with getting medical care. They also provide the most financial assistance to their elders. They have more

children than the other groups and are the most likely to have both parents alive.

- Non-Hispanic whites make up the largest group of participants surveyed by AARP and have the highest likelihood of providing care to elderly parents. However, only 19 percent are actually providing care or financial assistance to their elders. This group was the most adamant that their children should not have to provide care for them.

QUESTION?

What kinds of care did the participants indicate they provide for their parents and in-laws?
For more than 80 percent, the primary answer was social interaction such as making visits and contacting them on the telephone regularly. Forty-six percent transport them to the doctor or take them shopping; 45 percent do housework; 44 percent do the shopping; 33 percent pay bills; and 12 percent assist with intimate care. Only 27 percent indicated having to contribute financially.

Based on these findings, AARP, a nonprofit, nonpartisan membership organization for Americans over fifty, is developing advocacy and educational programs to address the multicultural issues of sandwiching baby boomers face today and in the future.

Dealing with Guilt

It is all too easy not to think about growing older and facing mortality. Does anyone ever really plan for the possibility of having to care for elderly parents? It is a much more romantic notion to think they will age gracefully, and before they become dependent, will go off to sleep one night and just not wake up. The rude reality is that seldom happens. This way of thinking and avoidance of the situation often leads to a crisis situation, with that dreaded middle-of-the-night phone call during a snow storm telling you Dad fell and your mother is panicking because she can't help him up and already pulled something in her back trying. He is injured and bleeding, and she thinks he broke his hip.

FACT

In 2003, there were approximately 14,000 deaths from falls among the population of seniors in the U.S. In fact, accidents are the sixth-leading cause of death for seniors, and falls are the leading cause of death from injury for seniors over age sixty-five. Hip fractures are the cause of the most deaths from falls. Seventy to eighty percent of all hip fractures happen to women

Dad tripped over a throw rug on his way to the bathroom, and no, he didn't take his walker because "he knows his way around the house, and he doesn't need it." He knocked over a lamp and the pile of magazines next to his side of the bed are now scattered all over!

Yes, those are all thing you meant to address with your parents on your last visit, but you thought it could wait. They like their clutter and it really hasn't been a hazard until now. They seem to manage just fine with an occasional visit from you to help with household maintenance. The signs have been there for a while now—they are aging and far less able to do the things they once did. They manage, but their lifestyle is much more casual and slow paced.

It is important to begin planning now, not only for your parents and in-laws, but for your future elder care as well. It's easy to put it off and deny there is a problem brewing just below the surface, but when it hits you smack in the face, you'll be forced to make decisions that might be more costly than if you'd set aside some time to talk with your parents about their wishes for their future.

As the AARP survey found, there is guilt involved in this process; more for some than for others, but each individual case has its own set of circumstances. Everyone wants what is best for his or her parents and loved ones, despite differences along the way. There will be times when you didn't anticipate quickly enough, times when you cannot afford to give more financially, and times when you simply cannot participate personally.

You need to resist the temptation to take over and care for your parents or in-laws simply because you couldn't possibly live with yourself and your guilt if something happened to them and you hadn't made the choice to care for them. There will be times when you simply have to bite your tongue, cross your fingers, and wait and see. Unless the situation is obviously unsafe, you have to let them do as much for themselves as possible.

Learn to understand your own limitations and don't make promises you cannot keep. There are many factors and other responsibilities you will have to take into account, including your parents, children, spouse, and siblings, just to name a few. You also have to consider and protect your job, your own finances, and your health and well-being as well.

If something worries you, speak up, but let them decide how to improve or change the situation. Of course, offering suggestions and advice can be helpful, but don't be surprised if they reject it. Sometimes you just have to plant a seed (idea) and let the idea grow and become theirs. You'll have to be ready to jump in, and quite possibly at the most inopportune time, but in most cases, you should not just take over.

CHAPTER 2

Seeing Their Side

Although you may be changing roles with your parents and find yourself in charge and making decisions, the process of arranging and managing their care will be easier if you take time to understand things from their point of view and learn about their wishes and how all of this is impacting them. Take the time to get to know them again; this time as people, not just your parents. You may have grown up in their house, but just as you have grown and changed, so have your parents. Don't make assumptions; some things indeed will never change, but other things may surprise you.

Communication Is Key

Communication is a fine art, and some people are better at it than others; but in this situation, it is going to be a key player in the success or failure of your efforts. Communicating with your parents can seem like a daunting task, but it is something you are going to have to get really good at. If you have had a good relationship, you are ahead of the game; if is hasn't been, you will have a lot of work to do.

You will also have to have open lines of effective communication with your siblings and other family and friends along this journey. In some instances, this will be an easy task; in others it will be more difficult, but keeping everyone informed will avoid other issues along the way.

Hopefully, you are undertaking this task with your parents before any dementia, short-term memory loss, or even Alzheimer's has advanced to a point where communication is worse than it could be.

FACT

Communication is more than just talking; it is a two-way process in which listening is a major component in addition to speaking. When speaking, you need to ensure your listener has devoted her complete attention to what you have to say. Outside distractions should be avoided, and both parties should be in agreement to talk and to listen.

You need to have your thoughts in order and be ready to discuss matters at hand. Have a clear idea of what you want to say and how best to say it to your specific audience.

On the other hand, when it's your turn to listen, you need to devote your attention to the speaker and listen carefully to what she is saying. You cannot listen if you are speaking, so be sure you have given her the courtesy of hearing what she has to say before responding or commenting.

Nonverbal language plays a key role in communication as well. Body language, hand gestures, sighs, and rolling your eyes can convey much more than words at times. Pay keen attention to nonverbal cues to gage how your message is being interpreted and accepted, as well as how your own nonverbal language portrays your message.

Timing is a key element in communication. Being interrupted during an important task can be a barrier to effective communication. If, for example, you want to discuss important issues with your parents and you call during their favorite TV show, you won't have their full attention. It may seem trivial to you, but in the life of older people, their programs can be a major part of daily life. Likewise, when your mother calls you every day just as you walk in the door from work, you know how distracting this can be.

Take a moment to find out when is a good time to discuss important issues with them. Usually earlier in the day is best to have their full energy and focus, particularly if there are issues of memory loss or dementia. You may need to take a break at work and call them, or schedule a weekend visit or phone call.

QUESTION?

How do you know that you have gotten your point across?
Ask questions. Get them to repeat back what you said in their own words. This will help reinforce the conversation, especially if they have a tendency to forget easily. If it's something they need to remember and follow up with, write it down. Use a white board or chalkboard to keep track of important facts and keep it where they will refer to it frequently.

Another key point in effective communication is verifying the listener has heard what you said. No, this doesn't mean you have to talk louder, it means you have to find out if he understood your message. Just because you told him, don't expect it to be accepted and remembered. Was your information clear? Did he get your point? Is he in agreement, or did he listen politely and promptly dismiss what you had to say?

Effective communication is essential to successfully managing the care of your aging parents. It won't happen overnight. You will have to experiment to find the best ways for your individual situations.

Learn Their Wishes

One of the most important things you'll need to discover is what your parents' wishes are concerning their care as they age and die. This isn't an easy subject to discuss, but it is one that you must address. This information is something you will need to share with your siblings and other key players in your particular circumstances.

Your primary role in caring for your aging parents will be to incorporate as many of their wishes as is possible. Preserving their dignity and respecting them is vital to the success of this new relationship. Listen to their wishes.

Start with the simpler issues to open the lines of communication and build a rapport for discussing such issues. Look at family history. How long did their parents live and what issues did they face in their last years? Sometimes this is helpful and other times completely irrelevant. How did your parents deal with their aging parents? What did they feel worked, and what would they have done differently? Even if your parents won't discuss their own mortality issues, this can give you an idea of what they may expect from you.

Begin a dialog about the what-ifs. Where do they hope to live out their life? Do they want to remain in their own home? What if they can't do it alone? Are they willing to have help from caregivers or a live-in? What if that doesn't work out? How do they feel about nursing homes? Would they consider living in a senior complex or assisted-living facility? Do they expect to move in with you? What if that is not possible?

Understand that they may completely change their minds as their own condition deteriorates. None of us would want to be a burden to family members and would hope we could do something to prevent that from happening. In reality, situations can change rapidly and the best-laid plans get sidetracked. The important thing is to get a feel for what they want and expect.

Put It in Writing

If your parents have very specific wishes, these should be put in writing in a will or other legal document such as a health-care proxy, advance directive, or durable power of attorney for health care. Recording a conversation can be helpful as well, especially for siblings or other relatives who may not like or agree with choices made.

One of these issues could be burial versus cremation. Some people have very strong feelings about one or the other and they can stem from religious beliefs to issues of claustrophobia or fears of being buried alive. Then there is the issue of where to bury or how to handle the ashes. If all of this is set and decided ahead of time, it can be a blessing in disguise when the time comes.

Perhaps the touchiest of all issues is that of heroic measures to be taken (or not) and where to draw the line. When do you consider having a Do Not Resuscitate (DNR) order written? A DNR means that no heroic measures will be taken should your heart stop. It is the simplest form of health-care proxy. However, because there may be different circumstances under which you or your parent would want some heroic measures taken, a more complex document such as a health-care proxy, advance directive, or durable power of attorney for health care should be explored with an attorney.

QUESTION?

Under what circumstances would your parents consider resuscitation measures?
Do your parents expect everything possible should be done at any time and do they expect to be kept alive even on respirators or with other measures? At what point is it okay to give up? If they haven't made out a will, appointed a power of attorney for health care, or signed an advanced directive, start thinking about it now, and get these issues in writing as soon as possible.

Planning for all types of possibilities may not be feasible, but having in writing what the general wishes are is one of the most important issues you can address with your aging parents. It is also something you should consider for yourself. (See Chapter 21.)

Religious beliefs and rituals should be discussed, especially if there are strong feelings or disagreements in the family. Are there specific things they want followed, or not? Perhaps they just want you to do what is important to you and the other surviving family. These are all important decisions to make together and to ensure all key players involved understand and agree to respect your parents' wishes.

Getting Your Parents to Discuss Mortality

Your parents may be very reluctant to discuss any matters about their own mortality. Gently try to prod them along, but you may have to back off and try again another time. You may have more luck discussing a hypothetical situation or one that happened to a friend or other family member. They may be very willing to express opinions about what happened to a widowed elderly aunt who shut herself away in her house with thirty-six cats and left all her money to the ASPCA instead of her children who abandoned her. Or an uncle who just wanted to spend his days sitting in his deceased wife's favorite chair and die at home, but his children had him placed in a nursing home and never went to visit him.

Sometimes it takes a seemingly insensitive situation to evoke emotions and feelings and get them talking. Then you can slowly guide the conversation into how they'd feel if they were in that situation.

Another point for discussion is their needs and concerns for the future. Do they feel that they have accomplished their major goals? What goals or tasks still need to be met? Do they feel they have had a full life, or do they have regrets? What things are important to them now? For example, is playing golf every Wednesday the major focus of their life? What things fill their days and make them happy?

Where once their own personal relationships, work, and hobbies fulfilled most of their needs, being near family and friends can be even more important as your parents age in order to fulfill their need to love and be loved.

Learn Their Present Habits

Once you have a good understanding about your parents' wishes for their last years, you should begin to learn about their present habits. This can be an important issue in making smooth transitions through the remaining years.

If, for instance, your parents wish to remain in their own home with outside help, having a good understanding about their habits can be a big advantage in avoiding problems with caregivers. It can help you in making decisions and in understanding why some things work out while others fail.

If they have always been, and continue to be, early to bed and early to rise, you would want to find caregivers who can adapt to these situations. Say, for instance, they get up at 5:00 A.M. and expect a large cooked breakfast; they will need someone who can come in early to help with this. If you have live-in help, the caregiver has to be someone who keeps these hours well. If you have shift help, this is also an important issue, as the night caregiver needs to be prepared to get them up and cook breakfast before his shift ends. Do they expect to be bathed, groomed, and dressed before breakfast as well?

Older people tend to shop more often. They no longer have a career, household, and family duties to juggle; they have the time to shop several times a week. This can be a problem for those willing to help with the shopping who can't run to the store several times a week.

If your parents are late sleepers and night owls and breakfast is coffee and toast, they wouldn't adapt well to a caregiver who wants to get them up and feed them a large breakfast by 6:00 A.M.

These things aren't always considered or discussed when hiring help, and there can be devastating results. A bad experience can cause all sorts of repercussions.

Your sister may be willing to help with grocery shopping each week when she does her own. This can be a tremendous help, but if she doesn't take the time to learn about your parents' habits and tastes, it can be a disaster. Taste buds change about every seven years, and something your mother loved when you were a child may be something she loathes today. Your parents may be on special diets due to health conditions such as low sodium or low fat/low cholesterol. Where your sister may be buying for a family of five, your parents are only two, or even just one, and they probably don't eat as much as they once did, either. They probably buy the small cans, which may be less economical, but there isn't waste. They might be very particular about brand names and not like her choice of the brand on sale or the one with the coupon.

Cooking, cleaning habits, laundry, and other household tasks can seem trivial, but they can be major issues when the caregiver doesn't do it the same way your mother has done it for years. Suddenly a seemingly adaptable and flexible woman can become someone with all sorts of impossible demands and reasons for telling you the perfectly capable caregiver you hired is totally inept and must be fired right away!

Investing some time in understanding your parents' habits, likes and dislikes, and pet peeves can go a long way in finding a successful caregiving situation.

Helping your aging parents maintain as much of their independence as possible will no doubt be a challenging situation, but the more things they can continue to do for themselves safely, the better the situation will be for all involved. This will not only relieve you of some of the burden but will also help preserve their dignity.

Discuss What Losing Independence Means to Them

Your parents may not be willing to discuss mortality issues, but they may be able to tell you exactly what it would mean to them to become dependent on you or someone else. You may be surprised at what losing independence means to and what it involves for your parents. This will give you some insight into the challenges you may face as they age and begin to require assistance.

The aging process will naturally rob everyone of at least some abilities in varying degrees. From issues of loss of general flexibility and being able to get up from a low couch or chair to loss of bladder and or bowel control, most people fear the embarrassment of these losses as well as becoming a burden or having to have assistance with simple acts of everyday living.

Independence can be defined by many things. Ask your parents what these things mean to them—living in their own home, driving a car, playing golf every day, having good eyesight or hearing, cooking their own meals, having to use a cane or walker—and you'll begin to understand how they perceive their lives and what losing their independence means to them.

FACT

In 2005, the results of a study of women with osteoporosis pointed out that the reason more than half of the women were compliant about taking their medication was that they feared losing their independence. Surprisingly, 74 percent of the doctors surveyed thought the reason their patients were compliant about taking the medication was that they feared breaking bones. While a broken bone could lead to a dependency issue, the women clearly feared the bigger picture of becoming dependent on someone else.

Some will age gracefully and accept change as it happens. Others will fight it tooth and nail and will not accept change without kicking and screaming all along the way. A happy medium would be welcome by most children dealing with issues of aging parents.

One of the challenges for you will most likely be not overdoing it. Let them do as much for themselves as possible. This will not be the most efficient and timesaving method, but it is important. The temptation to jump in and just do it will be difficult to resist, especially at times when you are up against time deadlines.

Time management and organization will become key components in your new life, even more so than when you had three children all playing the same sport on different fields across town. Plan and allow for the extra time it will take them to get ready for the doctor's appointment, but let them do as much for themselves as possible. They will feel in control and you'll feel less stressed.

Get Your Siblings Involved

By default, it is most often the oldest child or the one who lives closest to the parents who ends up with the major responsibility for the care and management of the aging parents. If you are an only child, there aren't many choices, but perhaps there are some cousins or other family members willing to participate with you. If not, perhaps they will at least be willing to let you vent occasionally or offer some welcome advice.

Everyone needs to be kept informed and should have an assignment or some share in the responsibility, and all of the siblings need to have a clear understanding of your role as the leader. They also have to understand that your parents remain your parents no matter how much responsibility you each will assume for their care and well-being.

ALERT!

Be prepared to make moves and step up the care as it is needed. Sometimes that can happen quickly, but learn to be patient when they just need your help to remain as independent as possible. Work together with your siblings to help provide the support necessary, and give each other the opportunity to vent frustrations.

As you come together with your siblings, the first thing you need to agree upon is that your parents need to be consulted and involved in all aspects of the decisions you make from here on out. One of the worst things you can do is make plans and then spring them on your parents.

For example, just because your father recently passed away and your mother is now alone in that big old house doesn't mean she's ready to leave behind the home she loves and shared with your father for many years.

She's not necessarily prepared to leave her friends and neighbors and all that is familiar and comfortable to her for the bright sunshine and happy faces at the senior living complex near your home. This might eventually be the path she'll take, but she needs to come to the decision on her own.

Listen to her needs and wishes, and help her make them a reality. Perhaps hiring a personal driver and arranging for some meal delivery or preparation is all she needs right now. Give her some time to grieve and consider her options. Help her remain independent in her own home for as long as possible. Involve her in making plans for her future.

You will need to establish a new aspect of your relationship with your siblings at this point. Whether you are on the best of terms or the worst, they need to be informed of the situation with your parents and kept up to date as things change. The sooner you can establish this relationship and open the lines of communication as well as set down some ground rules, the better.

It is important for her to be focused in reality. Take into consideration that she will no longer have your father's Social Security checks. Can she afford to continue to live in that house? Can she afford to hire the help she needs to maintain it and to assist her with her own needs? What can you do to help make this possible? Can your siblings pitch in? Does she need to look into renting out a room? Perhaps a college student or a hired caregiver would exchange services for room and board. On the other hand, what are her other options, and can she afford them? What assistance is she going to need?

You and your siblings will have to help her examine her finances and personal situation and investigate some of the alternatives and options with and for her. Remember, though, that she needs to make the final decision. This is not the time and place for you to step in and choose for her.

This won't be an easy process; it will always seem simpler to just take charge and tell them what to do. Think back to your teenage years and struggling for your own independence. How many times did you scream (or want to), "You don't understand me! I'm sixteen; I can make my own decisions"? Cut them some slack. This is not the time for paybacks. They are adults, and they can still make decisions; they just need your help to make them feasible. Of course, if your parents are mentally incompetent, you will have to take charge.

Be prepared for a struggle with your siblings and other friends and relatives who feel you should take charge. Share some of the responsibilities with them and let them see first hand that this is the best way to handle things right now.

From the start, you need to set some ground rules with your siblings. Everyone needs to share in the responsibilities (see further discussion in Chapter 9). Give them a chance to volunteer or to consider what they'd like to take on. Even those who live far away can have an assignment, even if it's just calling your parents daily or weekly or participating financially. There needs to be an understanding that each sibling will participate and at times be responsible to provide some respite to the primary caregiver (you). It is important that you share this "burden" and that no one feels like someone is not pulling equal weight. You have to put aside old sibling rivalries and work together. Organization and clear communication is essential. Not everyone is well-suited to be a caregiver, but you can share in costs and other indirect responsibilities.

It is important to set clear boundaries and responsibilities. Each person will have some supreme authority or decision power within his or her own realm, but all major decisions will be made as a group, which includes your parent.

For example, your sister Sally will accompany Mom to medical appointments and make medical decisions; your brother Tom will take care of household maintenance and yard work; your brother Bob, the accountant, will pay the bills and handle financial matters; and you will be primary caregiver and spokesperson.

CHAPTER 3

Lifestyle Changes and Loss of Independence

Too much change too quickly can have devastating results. In 1967, Holmes and Rahe developed the Life Events Scale, which weighs the probability of life events triggering stress and illness. Moving; death of a spouse, other family member, or close friends; and retirement are among some of the most stressful life events. When too many of these events take place within a year's time, health issues can arise or be significantly affected.

Home Safety Issues

Perhaps your parents have lived in the same house since you were born and never had a problem. Why look for trouble now? As was noted in Chapter 1, accidents are the sixth-leading cause of death for seniors, and falls are the leading cause of death from injury in people over age sixty-five. Most of the falls happen in the place of residence, whether it is their own home, senior housing facility, or skilled nursing facility.

Many seniors use a cane or walker to assist them when they ambulate in the community; however, at home they choose not to use the device. This is often a contributing factor in falls. They feel safe in their familiar environment and "know" where things are, even in the dark. They hang on to walls and furniture and feel secure. One missed step is all it takes. A throw rug, an electrical cord, or oxygen tubing can be some of the most dangerous obstacles in the home.

FACT

Not all deaths from falls are immediate such as from a resulting head injury or broken neck; they most often stem from the complications of the injury. For example, some seniors don't survive surgical interventions to repair or replace a damaged joint, some die from blood clots or clotting complications, or infection in the incision or joint can cause death.

Throw rugs are a primary problem, but getting rid of them is not always so easy. They can conceal a multitude of sins such as worn carpet, which could be even more dangerous, or help to cover up a slippery floor, which left uncovered can be just as dangerous. If they are simply for decoration or to cover up spills and stains, get rid of them. If they are necessary, try to rearrange furniture or tack them down with carpet tape and be sure to use nonslip backings on slippery floors. If possible, replace throw rugs with new carpeting or larger room-size rugs and use carpet tape to secure the edges and nonslip backings as needed to keep rugs from moving.

Clean Out the Clutter

Clutter is another factor. Piles of newspapers and magazines cannot only be fire hazards, they can also block the flow of traffic throughout the home. Hoarding can be a real problem with some seniors. They won't throw them out because of the recipes or articles they haven't retrieved. Yet they will fight to the death not to have them discarded. It can become an issue of trust and betrayal if you try to remove them or have it done while a parent is in the hospital, for example. You need to tackle this issue and make some compromises. Perhaps you can persuade your parents to discard papers and magazines older than one year. You can also suggest they go through a set pile by a deadline. Anything they didn't get through by that time, they agree to discard. Most likely, you're going to have to set aside some time to assist them with this project and be firm about how much they can keep.

If necessary, you may need to contact the fire department and ask for someone to come and discuss the hazard with your parents. Adult Protective Services can also intervene and force some action. You can make a call anonymously to either of these sources and let them be the bad guy.

Too much furniture can be another issue. While they may have it grouped close together so they can hang on to tables and chairs to maneuver through the house, obstacles can be problems in the event of an accident and getting access to the residents. Even though they know exactly where something is, they can still misjudge and trip over the leg of a table or chair. Try to clear out some of the clutter and move furniture to rooms that aren't being used, or rearrange a few pieces to better suit a flow of traffic. Be sure that your parents know where you have made changes so they can make mental notes of the changes and so don't rely on where things used to be. Again, don't make too many changes at one time.

Bathroom Safety

Grab bars in the bathroom can be life savers. Most major home improvement stores and even large chain drug stores carry varieties of grab bars. There are some varieties that can be attached to the edge of the bathtub; others have to be placed on the walls and secured with toggle bolts. If you need assistance in figuring out proper placement, contact your parents' physician to arrange for a home-health safety evaluation from a physical therapist. She can help evaluate the home setting for other safety issues as well as for grab-bar placement and offer instruction on safe use of the bars once installed. The therapist will not install the bars for you.

A variety of bathtub chairs are available to make showering easier and safer. There are sophisticated devices to lower one into the bathtub, and there are now walk-in bathtubs that can replace standard tubs and provide safer tub bathing for the less agile. In a pinch, a resin garden chair can work well to sit on in the shower. Tennis balls cut to fit on the tips of the legs can offer more stability. A rubber tub mat to prevent slipping is a must.

Elevated toilet seats can be easily attached to a toilet to make it easier to get on and off. Some come with handrail attachments for further assistance.

Walking Assistance

Walkers come in a variety of configurations and some offer a handy seat. They can be fitted with trays or baskets or even a plastic grocery bag tied on to help carry things from one place to another. Canes come in single-point and quad-point bases for assistance with ambulation. These devices should be adjusted to the height of the person using them—most have adjustable settings or come in various lengths. Tennis balls can be cut and placed on the tips for easier sliding and better stability.

Oxygen Tanks and Tubing

Many seniors need oxygen in the home and may have miles of tubing so they can move all over the house and not have to haul the tank with them. One issue is the tripping hazard created by the tubing. It isn't always the person using the oxygen for whom this is the greatest hazard but for other household members, especially an elderly spouse. Some of the lengths of tubing could be tacked down with colorful masking tape or have colorful tags tied on to make it more visible to others.

The other issue with the oxygen is cooking and smoking. The oxygen should be removed while cooking. There should be no smoking anywhere in the home while oxygen is in use. In many cases, the oxygen is required because of lung damage from years of smoking. All too often, the patient continues to smoke and, yes, smokes with the oxygen on! This is a tremendous fire and explosion hazard; one the senior is willing to take, but he needs to be reminded that the danger is extended to others as well. Not only could his home burn, neighbors could be harmed or have their houses burn as well.

Transportation and Giving Up Driving

Driving is often one of the last stands in claiming independence. Remember back to when you first got your own driver's license and the feeling of independence you got from having it, no matter what the restrictions your parents put on your driving. Think about having to give up driving and what it would mean to your lifestyle.

Have you ever been stuck in the house waiting for the plumber to come "sometime between 8:00 A.M. and 5:00 P.M.?" You sit and wait all day. Any other time you might not have a thing to do, but suddenly because you can't leave, you have a million things to do. That is somewhat similar to most seniors' reactions to giving up driving.

Usually they are in denial about the reasons they should stop driving. They've always been a safe driver, and nothing has changed. Their eyesight is just fine and their reactions are not slowed. They have no problems remembering where they intended to go, nor how to get there. Then why does it take them seemingly forever just to walk to the car?

Providing your parents with alternative solutions can help them ease into giving up driving, especially at peak traffic times, at night, or when children are most likely to be out playing or walking to and from school.

Senior centers throughout the country can usually provide you with information about such transportation assistance programs as a dial-a-ride, senior vans, and others. Taxi services sometimes offer discounts to seniors. Medical groups sometimes offer shuttle services either from your door to the medical office or from central locations such as senior centers to large clinics. Other medical transportation can often be arranged through the services needed, such as dialysis centers, chemotherapy centers, and organizations such as the American Cancer Society.

FACT

There are courses throughout the country, usually put on by the American Automobile Association (AAA) or AARP, that educate seniors on changes in driving habits they need to be aware of. Using simulators, they can test braking reactions, visual disturbances, and other issues to determine how safe a driver your parents are. Some DMV departments may even offer behind-the-wheel evaluations and driver-safety training for seniors.

Prearranged appointments, shopping trips, and other outings can be easier for family members to assist with transportation issues, but spur-of-the-moment changes and needs can present challenges. Friends and neighbors can sometimes be called upon to assist, but care must be taken not to burn them out or to abuse the privilege.

College students looking for some extra pocket money and nonregular commitments may be a good resource. Check with your local community college admissions and student affairs office to see if there are job postings allowed. Community Internet listings such as craigslist can be a good resource as well. Take care to screen applicants well and to set up safety checks and parameters so no one is victimized.

Guilt is a useful tool for encouraging older parents to give up driving; after all, they wouldn't want to be the cause of anyone's unfortunate injury or death because of their own pride or selfishness would they?

Home Delivery for Groceries, Medications, and Meals

Many major grocery chains have instituted home delivery of groceries. The order is placed online and delivered the next day. There is usually a delivery fee of about $10, but with the price of gasoline today, unless you live quite near your parents, that delivery fee can be reasonable in the face of your time, gasoline, and efforts.

You have to plan ahead, as the delivery is the next day, and it may not work for all of your parents' needs. In most cases, a brand name and size can be stipulated. There is usually a comment section for specifying such things as ripeness, size, and color variations for things such as fresh fruits and vegetables. This may be a hit-or-miss proposition, but it is worth trying. Unless your parents are computer savvy, you may have to assist them in setting up this order. They may be able to handle subsequent orders, or you may have to do this for them.

This could be a job delegated to a sibling who lives out of town, as the ordering can be done on the Internet and the store located by zip code. Your parents could call or e-mail their shopping list and your sibling takes care of ordering. A recurrent list can be organized for staples and paper goods that need periodic ordering and other items added as needed for the week's shopping.

Of course, many older people have grown accustomed to shopping every day or every other day, and getting into a mode of weekly or biweekly shopping can be a challenge. A $10 delivery fee every other day can be a little wasteful. Organization is a key element to handling more than one household, and everyone has to make some concessions to make it work.

Medications

Medications can be set up for home delivery as well. Many HMO medical plans, including Medicare Senior HMOs and standard Medicare drug plans, offer mail-order pharmacy plans that fill prescriptions for ninety days at a price savings and deliver the medications via mail or other delivery services such as UPS. Many small pharmacies offer delivery services for prescriptions as well. A search of the local phone book will usually provide you with this information.

Again, organization is key. Mail-order medications require seven to ten business days to complete and deliver. You can't wait until the bottle is empty to call for a refill. Local-delivery pharmacies may require two to three business days for delivery as well. Be prepared; mail-order pharmacies usually have a phone-in line as well as Internet access for ordering refills. This, too, can be delegated to another family member.

It is important to get the ordering physician or practitioner to order the maximum supply, such as a ninety-day supply, to maximize the cost effectiveness of these pharmacies. Use a local pharmacy first for new prescriptions to be sure they are effective and don't cause side effects. Once it is determined this medication will be used long term, the mail-order option becomes more cost effective.

Meals to Go

Home delivery of meals can be provided in a number of ways. Senior services in most communities have a meals-on-wheels program where volunteers deliver a hot meal at noon along with a sandwich or other similar meal that doesn't require much preparation for dinner. These meals are usually delivered Monday through Friday and not on holidays.

The meals are usually prepared by volunteers or staff in a senior-center kitchen under the direction of a dietitian. Most meals will meet the dietary needs of the general senior population, and some services make special meals for low-sodium or diabetic needs.

There is a fee schedule, and sometimes a sliding scale is available for those who cannot afford it.

Remember that inclement weather conditions can interfere with delivery, so alternative solutions need to be considered and in place. Alternative solutions can include occasional delivery from local restaurants such as pizza, Chinese food, and other take-out/delivery food services. However, if the weather is the issue, they may not be delivering either.

ALERT!

Be aware there can be a waiting list for these home-delivery programs. Be prepared to make alternative arrangements until services can begin. They depend on volunteer drivers, and in areas of high demand, waiting lists can be quite long.

In large metropolitan areas, there are some high-end food-delivery programs, and some that provide frozen prepared meals that can be delivered weekly or monthly. Personal chefs and other food-preparation alternatives are also a possibility. Again, turn to your local community college, or perhaps a local culinary school, to determine if a student might be willing to cook for your parents. Even periodically cooking large volumes of meals that can be frozen and reheated is something to think about.

Cell Phones and Life-Alert Systems

The cliché "I've fallen and I can't get up" scenario is a reality for many senior citizens every day. They may have actually fallen and can't get themselves up, or they may have gotten into the bathtub and can't get out. Whatever the situation, it can be a very dangerous one.

Lying or sitting in a tub for many hours can cause a serious condition called rhabdomyolysis. This condition is caused by the breakdown of muscular tissue from exposure. Lying on a cold floor or bathtub can expose the muscles to cold and cause them to deteriorate. This can lead to organ failure and become a very serious issue.

There are several manufacturers of life-alert systems, which utilize a device that either hangs around the neck or is worn on the wrist like a watch. It has a button that is pushed in case of an emergency, which alerts a central response system. The system then begins a rolling call system to notify a specified number of emergency responders and family members or friends that the system has been activated.

ALERT!

Since falls are a major problem for seniors, being able to summon help is vital to their recovery. If your parent lives alone and no one visits on a regular basis, it could be possible for her to remain on the floor or stuck in the bathtub for days until someone realizes.

Some of these systems offer a two-way radio communication system whereby the response center can actually communicate with the senior to determine the nature of the emergency and to remain in contact until help arrives. These, of course, are more expensive.

A cell phone can mimic this system somewhat if the senior keeps the cell phone turned on and with him at all times. Phone numbers can be preprogrammed and speed-dial services set up for contacting emergency response systems as well as calling specified loved ones. This requires the person to be alert enough to push the speed-dial numbers and to communicate with responders.

There is a set-up fee and a monthly service fee for these monitoring services. The success depends on whether the device is worn or sits in a drawer somewhere. Obviously, it also depends on whether or not the person remains conscious and able to push the button.

A Senior Watch program can be utilized, or simply ask a neighbor to watch for signs of trouble and notify you. If they don't see or hear from your parents in a couple of days, have them contact you. Piled-up newspapers or mail can be telltale signs something isn't right as well. Don't forget to say thank you. Send them a gift basket occasionally, or make a financial arrangement with them so they remain a willing participant.

FACT

While some signals can be used to alert you to trouble, they can also alert criminals that the house may be an easy mark. Telltale signs of disrepair or lawns and gardens not kept up or manicured are usually a good indication that an elderly or infirm person lives there. Hiring a gardener and keeping up with house maintenance issues can go a long way in keeping your loved ones safe.

Enlist the assistance of your siblings to make regular phone calls or visits to your parents to keep tabs on them to make sure they don't end up lying on the floor for days. A daily phone call can be delegated to a sibling who lives far away or claims to be too busy to help with other tasks.

Energy Conservation

For many older persons, just walking across a room can delete them of all their energy for the day. In hot weather, they may not even make it out of bed. Learning to conserve energy is not a complicated process, yet it can make a world of difference in regards to remaining independent. It can be the difference between continuing to live at home or having to move to an assisted living facility.

Learning to perform tasks efficiently and to minimize energy expense requires mental organization. Before an elderly person gets up and does something, she needs to stop and think about what else she can do at the same time.

For instance, getting dressed in the morning could require several trips to the closet. She should stop and think about all of the things she needs to gather from the closet such as clothing, necessary accessories such as a belt, and shoes. She should gather them all at once instead of getting clothes out, putting them on, then going and getting a belt and looking for shoes. Going in and out of the closet several times, sitting down, standing up to get something else, and then sitting again to put on shoes requires a lot of activity and energy; gathering all of the items at one time and dressing in order can take a few simpler steps.

Grooming can be scattered by first brushing her teeth, then getting dressed, then going back to the bathroom and washing her face and combing her hair. She can then go eat breakfast and return once again to the bathroom to apply some makeup, for instance.

They should perform all tasks in one location and then move on to the next area and tasks. Make sure they take a break and rest sufficiently between tasks. When cooking, they should gather supplies at one time, perform the prep work, and then put away what is no longer needed. They should cook the food, sit down to eat, and then clean up. Multitasking may be a time saver, but it may not always be the most energy efficient way to go.

Anyone who has to use oxygen should learn energy-conservation techniques. Postoperative patients should minimize their expense of energy as they recover. Each action or task takes on a new purpose: What else do you need from the kitchen when you go for a glass of water?

There are many other aspects of energy conservation, including breathing techniques and rest and relaxation tips. Rearranging space such as kitchen-cabinet contents and household furniture can be helpful in making energy conservation work more efficiently. Occupational therapists (OT) are experts in the field of energy conservation. Along with a home safety evaluation from a home-health physical therapist, an energy-conservation evaluation and instructions from an OT could be quite helpful as well. This can be ordered by their physician.

Bill Paying

Your parents could possibly manage on their own if your father could just remember to pay the bills on time and not end up having the electricity shut off once or twice a year for failure to pay. But when your mother depends on the electrical power to run her oxygen, you don't think you can take that chance any longer. Or perhaps your father died recently, leaving your mother alone. She is capable of caring for herself but has never been involved in paying bills and wouldn't know how.

Helping your parents remain independent and able to live in their own home sometimes takes some skill at supervising them without them knowing about it. And sometimes it simply means taking over some tasks they are incapable of handling, but that doesn't prevent them from living independently. Paying the bills or being notified when they are left unpaid is one of these tasks. Even from across the country, you can help out with these tasks. (Again, this task can be delegated to a sibling who cannot partake in the other aspects of care for your parents.)

While most bills can be redirected to your address for payment, not all are willing to notify others if the bill isn't paid. Utility companies are probably the most cooperative at helping set up a plan for notifying a relative in the event of nonpayment of a bill. Credit card companies will require a written letter of approval. Be sure to keep copies. It's probably easier just to take over paying these bills and having them sent directly to your home.

An alternative is to sit down with your parents once or twice a month and helping them pay the bills. This keeps them actively involved, and you have the piece of mind of knowing the gas or power won't be shut off anytime soon.

The tax assessor is usually cooperative with notification arrangements as well but isn't going to advertise it, whereas many times the utility bills have information on the bill or in fliers accompanying bills that tell you how to set up notifications.

CHAPTER 4

Taking Charge

The thought that Mom and Dad are getting older and seem to be a little forgetful, and have less energy and more complaints about getting old, has probably been rolling around in the back of your mind for a while now. You make a mental note that one of these days, you're going to have to make some decisions about their care, and then you dismiss it for another day. Actually, this is when it would be best to intervene. Avoid a crisis and start talking to your parents about their wishes and expectations. Find out where their important papers and all their financial information are while they can remember and aren't .overly stressed.

When Should You Intervene?

It's human nature to want to put off things that are uncomfortable, and dealing with mortality issues is never a comfortable situation. The obvious time to intervene is when you have no other choice, but a lot of stress and heartache can be avoided if you begin to get things organized long before it becomes a crisis. As you begin to note that your parents are getting older, this is the time to begin to intervene and plan for the future.

One way to broach the situation, especially if your parents are very private, is to make a list of your important information and provide them with this list in case something was to happen to you. Then suggest they reciprocate with their information.

Talk about their wishes and their fears. Let them know that you are here for them and that you expect to participate in their elder-care issues; you want to help them remain as independent as possible for as long as possible and you will help them do this. Express your own feelings to them about your fears and expectations regarding their care. Discuss the issue of being a burden, and try to relieve their guilt. They raised you, and perhaps even helped to care for your children while you worked—now it's time to return the favor.

Encourage them to begin to rely on you for some assistance, as needed, now. Perhaps your husband is handy like your father always was, but now your father is not able to fix things. Have them keep a list, and each time you visit plan for some handyman tasks.

Perhaps your mother used to love to embroider when she watched TV at night, but she seems to have lost interest lately. Maybe she can't see well enough to do it anymore. There are a lot of new lights and magnifying devices available that would allow her to continue with her favorite hobby. She may not know this or be able to afford them. She would never tell you she can't see well; she'd rather you think she's just lost interest. You may have to probe into a situation and make it a special-occasion gift.

Help Them Get Organized

Think about all of the things you might need to know or find if your parents suddenly died or were incapacitated. Are your parents neat, orderly, and organized? Do they have a filing system that makes sense to you? Do you know where to locate the information? Are they secretive and have they hidden their jewelry and valuables? Would you know where to begin to find them all?

These are questions you should begin asking yourself long before a crisis happens. You need to help them organize their information and share it with you. Some of the most important information you need includes:

- Bank accounts, including checking accounts, savings accounts, CDs, mutual funds, 401(k) and IRA accounts, stocks, and bonds. You'll need names of institutions and account numbers. Don't forget PIN numbers for ATM cards.
- Internet accounts and passwords
- Life insurance policies and homeowner's or renter's policies
- Car and other vehicle insurance policies
- Real estate deeds, mortgage information, and property tax information
- Social Security numbers, passports, driver's licenses, and other forms of ID
- Credit card account numbers—photocopies of the front and back of the cards is advisable
- Burial-plot information, prepaid cremation plans, mortuary arrangements, as well as any funeral requests
- Health insurance policies, including copies of cards
- Safe deposit boxes, including passwords, keys, combinations, locations, and any other specific information for access
- Wills, advance directives, living wills, power of attorney, durable power of attorney for health care
- Hiding places in the house, yard, garage, and car for money and valuables
- Contact information for friends and neighbors

- Contact information for health care (doctors, dentists, chiropractors, pharmacies)
- Keys, location, and combinations to house, vehicles, gates, lock boxes, and safes
- Titles and pink slips for cars, boats, and other vehicles
- Location and information about jewelry, artwork, and other valuables
- A complete medical history and list of current medications and allergies

Depending on your parents' particular situation, some of these things may not apply. There may be many other forms of information you need, such as immigration documents or employee paperwork if they are still working. Prepare your own list and make sure you have what you need while they are still able to provide it.

You don't need to probe into private financial matters and specifics at this point; it is just important to be able to find the information should it become necessary. Certainly, a checkbook would lead you to a bank account, but your parents may have several accounts. Does your mother have a secret separate account? Make sure you get all of their information.

Your parents should have all of this information in one place, and you should have a copy of it. If there is a family attorney, she should have a copy in her files. It should be kept up to date.

Making a Smooth Transition

Having a loving, trusting relationship with your parents can make it easier to transition to assisting them with their daily activities and care or making decisions for them. Even so, it may not always be smooth sailing. If your relationship hasn't been good, it can be difficult at best. If you have issues with your siblings, this can be a rough time as well.

Changes can bring out the worst in people, and even the closest, trusting relationships can become strained as you move into new and uncharted territory. Be prepared to hit bumps in the road and even to be blindsided. Be realistic that you are not going to change your parents. The same traits they had that annoyed you growing up are still there, and may even be amplified by aging and illness.

ALERT!

Old sibling rivalries that you thought were long dead and buried can rear their ugly head at the most unexpected times. This can come either directly from something your siblings say or do now, or through something a parent says or does to remind you of those rivalries.

You may have been spending every free moment taking care of your father after a minor surgery, only to have him say how wonderful it was for your sister to come and visit last week. She just showed up and then went outside and cleaned up the dog poop and the leaves that had accumulated on the porch from the recent windstorm. He was so impressed because she just did it without being asked.

You've been cooking and cleaning and changing his bandages and helping him bathe every day for three weeks and he never even says thank you, but your sister shows up one day and she's the big hero. Ouch!

He undoubtedly appreciates everything you've done as well, but it's something he's grown to expect, and unfortunately, take for granted. Your sister is not his primary caregiver and he sees her visits in a different light. Instead of getting angry, use this to your advantage. When things get to be too much for you, take a break and get your sister to visit more or to call more and distract him. You'll know he's okay, and you can take time to replenish yourself.

If you had a strained relationship with your mother and now you have to care for her, you're going to have to let it go. You may be able to talk to her about your feelings, but you don't want to make things harder for yourself. She did the best she could under the circumstances. Now you have the opportunity to take the high road and provide her something better than she gave you. Perhaps through the experience you'll have a chance to get to know each other in a different way and gain insight into why things were they way they were. Don't expect miracles, just take a deep breath, and do the best you can.

As she faces the last years of her life, try to find some common ground and develop a new relationship. If not, think of her as a friend or neighbor and not your mother.

Remember that your primary goal is to help your parents and in-laws remain as independent as possible and not to just take over and do. This will definitely take time and more patience than you ever thought you had. Help them do for themselves; make them a part of all of the tasks you do for them.

Your dad may not know how to cook, but he can set the table or perhaps do some of the prep work under your supervision. Mom might need some help with the laundry, but she can sit on the couch and fold the clean clothes or match up the socks. Don't do it all. Yes, indeed it will go faster if you do, but the more you do for them, the more dependent they will become and the more you will have to do.

Dealing with Resistance

Don't expect your parents to enter into old age and dependence willingly. Just as you may feel you don't ever want your children to have to take care of you and change your diapers; they too want to be independent and never become a burden. You may also expect to meet with resistance from your siblings, which can take on many different faces from struggles over who's in charge to refusing to take part in any way, shape, or form. Facing more changes and losses is not high on their wish list. Allow them to grieve and express their feelings. Realize that you, too, are grieving for the loss of your parents as they once were: strong, vital, and independent members of society.

They may be very resistant to talking about, much less cooperating with, changes that affect their daily living. No matter how urgent and necessary the changes may be, you will most likely meet with at least some, if not a lot of, resistance.

You will most likely have to try different approaches to getting them to discuss issues and open up to you about matters they consider private, such as their finances and personal files and information. They may change the subject every time you try to discuss end-of-life wishes.

FACT

As parents age, they will face many losses. These include the loss of a job, friends and colleagues, financial security, independence, and perhaps the loss of control over some bodily functions, as well as the loss of mobility. These losses, along with more tangible losses through the death of friends and family, will all have a grieving process.

It may be easier to discuss how friends or family members feel about such subjects with them, or discuss past experiences that worked well or were disasters in order to know what they don't like or want.

Mentioning someone's lavish funeral arrangements and being buried in their pink Cadillac might evoke a response such as, "Just cremate me and sprinkle my ashes in the ocean and have a big party to celebrate my being out of your hair finally." Or "I just want to be buried next to your mother. Put me in my best blue suit in a fine mahogany casket. Raise a toast to my life and move on."

Mentioning to your parents that you and your spouse have made a will and appointed a durable power of attorney for health care in case you can't make decisions might prompt some discussion of whether or not they have made any such decisions and where such documents might have been filed.

Asking if they know of a good lawyer to set up a will or living trust for a friend may also give you a clue as to whom they used for such papers and where to begin to search for answers if you can't get any from them.

Resistant Siblings

Dealing with resistant siblings could take even more creativity than dealing with resistant parents. It can be almost more important to have cooperation and assistance from your siblings than from your parents. With parents you can take it one day at a time, play it by ear to see where things go, but having to fight your siblings on another front can be disastrous.

While having everyone on the same page at the same time would be ideal, this may never happen. It can be better to have them refusing to participate than having them disagree with and criticize every move you make.

Getting your parents wishes in writing, especially in the form of legal documents, can be an absolute necessity if your siblings disagree. This can diffuse arguments and help you uphold your parents' wishes.

Creating a plan with your siblings that outlines each person's responsibilities and appoints one spokesperson can save a lot of grief. This can be done in person, over a conference phone call, through e-mails, or arranging an online chat. If no one can agree on who's in charge, simply drawing straws can solve the problem. Delegating responsibilities and putting it all down on paper can help define roles and avoid arguments in the long run. Making sure each person shares in the responsibilities is important. Equality probably won't be achieved, but sharing and having someone to vent frustrations to can be just as important.

Organization and open, effective communication are both key elements to making these situations work. Being flexible and understanding that circumstances can change without warning will make this an easier process as well. Nothing can be completely set in stone.

The more urgent the situation, the harder it may be to pull everyone together. Discussing ahead of time what you each can do and expect can be a huge step in the right direction when the time comes to make hard decisions.

Make Sure They Still Have Some Control

No matter how dire the circumstances get, it is important to remember your parents are adults and need to be part of the decision-making process.

Unless they are totally incapacitated or mentally incompetent, they need to have a voice in what happens to them. Walk a mile in their shoes—would you want someone making decisions about your life and not asking for your input?

Just as you need to preserve their independence by keeping them involved in their own care, you also need to preserve their dignity. For example, while they may not want to move to an assisted-living facility, there may be no other safe choice. Letting them be involved in choosing the facility provides them the opportunity to retain some control over what happens to them.

For example, your mother was the primary caregiver for your father. She died last week, and now you have to make decisions about your father's future care. He can't continue to stay with you. He wants to remain in his own home, but he cannot be left alone. He is forgetful and needs assistance with all aspects of his daily activities such as dressing, grooming, walking, eating, and even toileting. He needs access to assistance twenty-four hours a day, which your mother has provided for years.

You tried to hire help several times, but your father is rigid and prejudicial. He was rude to the caregivers you hired and told each one of them to leave and not come back. Although they were knowledgeable, competent, and provided excellent care, your father wouldn't accept their help. He doesn't want any help now and says he can manage on his own. Realistically, he won't make it until dinnertime without falling. Nor can he cook for himself, or get himself into bed without assistance.

You have tried repeatedly to hire help he would find acceptable but have not been able to. There is a small facility near your home where he can be cared for, and you can visit every day. It won't be home, but he can move in some of his own furniture and belongings.

There is another facility further from your home. It is larger and has more potential for group activities and socialization for your dad. He could have more of his furniture there, but you might not be able to visit as often.

You will also entertain the possibility of letting him remain at home, but he has to be willing to accept care from the agency you had before. He would have to be more tolerant and cannot be rude. He could not fire the aides.

You and your brother present him with all of the information and brochures on the two facilities. You can take him to visit them tomorrow and then make a decision. Although none of the choices please him, your father still has the control to decide which one he's willing to try. He's angry, but he knows he can't live alone. He is, however, still capable of making decisions for himself. By not making the decision for him without any input from him, you have hope that he'll be more cooperative and willing to make the best of the situation.

CHAPTER 5

Medical Care

Whether your parents or in-laws are healthy or not, at some point they are going to need some form of medical care. Annual checkups are vital to continued health and wellness as well as an annual visit to the dentist for teeth cleaning or evaluation of any dentures or prostheses. An ophthalmologist and audiologist might also be needed for vision or hearing deficits. As your parents age, they will statistically require more and more health care. Accessing care, finding transportation, and understanding the care may require assistance from you as well as other family members.

Finding Quality Medical Care

In the best of circumstances, your parents or in-laws will have a family physician with which they have established a rapport and see at least annually. However, this may not always be the case. If you have had to move them nearer to you, for instance, they may have to find a new physician. There may be a variety of other reasons they need to find a new physician.

In some instances, due to reimbursement cuts and other issues with Medicare, physicians may discontinue servicing patients under Medicare. If the Medicare is an HMO plan, you may never see the same physician twice as physicians don't tend to stay in these organizations for long periods of time. If your parents have had a physician for a long time, they may lose him to retirement.

In many of these circumstances, the physician may have arranged for another physician to take over his practice and will transfer records. These situations don't always work out because older people in general have greater difficulty with change. But they may feel stuck because their physician handed their care over to this new person.

FACT

It is important to note and remember that no one is ever stuck with a physician. Even in an HMO, you can request to change your primary care practitioner. You can request to see another specialist if you don't like the one you've been to. If you live in a very small or rural community where access to health care is very limited, you may have few choices, but otherwise, you always have a choice.

Personalities and bedside manner are important factors. Gender and English as a first language may play an important role as well. This can be important if there are strong feelings of bias, modesty, and even difficulty hearing. It is important that your parents trust and are be able to communicate with their physician and other health-care team members.

Quality of medical care is also important. This is not always so easy to judge. Medicare has adopted policies for reimbursement as well as reporting quality issues for hospitals and home health-care agencies. Medicare is exploring the ability to rate and report on quality issues with physicians.

Unfortunately, some of the best practitioners are not always the most warm and friendly human beings. Many times this is due to having very busy practices. Time is money and Medicare and most insurance companies reimburse at rates that have driven physicians and other practitioners to limit their time with patients to only a few minutes. This makes it hard to get to know, trust, and connect with the practitioner.

Finding a quality physician can be a challenge. Word of mouth is often the most common factor. Either a physician recommends or refers your parents or a friend, neighbor, or coworker does. If the Medicare plan or other insurance has restrictions, you may have to investigate to find a member or network physician. This information is usually available on the Internet or by calling the Medicare or insurance-plan office.

You can find information on your state government's website regarding the licensure of a physician. Most also list whether there have been any malpractice issues or other medical-care issues with this physician. Your state's website address is usually the two-letter abbreviation for your state followed by ".gov." For example, *www.ca.gov* is the California website. Then search for licenses and follow the links.

ALERT!

Not all physicians will accept Medicare. If they do, they have to accept whatever rate Medicare will reimburse them at. They can only charge an additional 20 percent, which most Medicare supplemental plans will cover. If your parents have an HMO plan, they may have a copay of approximately $10–$20 per visit.

Other ways you can find a physician include asking your own physician for a recommendation. You can also call your local hospital and ask for the physician recommendation or referral department. Again, word-of-mouth contacts such as your local senior center can be good sources.

It is important to establish a medical-care connection as soon as possible, especially if you have relocated your parents or in-laws. Don't wait until they have a need to try to find a physician. It can take weeks to get an appointment with a good doctor if you are a new patient. Set up an appointment just to get acquainted and get medical records transferred. Then if the need arises, you have someone you can call. Should there be an emergency, there is a physician of record for the hospital to contact.

One thing to be aware of is whether or not the physician has a policy of not allowing the spouse or other family members to come into the office with the patient. Some physicians think that others create a distraction and take up more time. While this can be a valid point in some instances, it should be something to handle on an individual basis. Older patients often need someone in there with them because they don't hear well, they have memory issues, or they just don't always understand what the doctor said.

This kind of health-care illiteracy is an issue for more than 50 percent of the population. It is a bigger issue for the elderly. If this is the case with your physician, either find another physician or make arrangements to have a longer appointment time, but don't give in to being shut out of the office.

As health-care costs increase and the shortage of physicians grows, it becomes more and more commonplace for a physician to use a nurse practitioner (NP) or physician assistant (PA) to assist with patients' care. These are health-care practitioners specially trained to assess and treat patients. They work with the physician to provide quality care. In some instances, your parents may always be seen by the NP or PA and never or rarely see the physician. As with choosing a physician, if you don't like or trust the NP or PA, you may have to choose a different physician.

HIPAA and Privacy Issues

In 1996, Congress enacted the Health Insurance Portability and Accountability Act, known as HIPAA. The original intent of this law was to protect workers with the ability to continue their health insurance if they left or changed jobs. It prohibited employers and insurance companies from imposing preexisting condition clauses. This act also provided the government the power to deal with fraud and abuse issues in health care that were plaguing the Medicare system.

HIPAA imposed strict privacy clauses on all health-care providers from physicians and nurses to pharmacies, DME (durable medical equipment) companies, and insurance companies. Part of the intent of this law was to form the foundation for electronic health records (EHR). This issue is still being debated today.

FACT

It took five years for HIPAA to become effective on April 14, 2001, and another two years before compliance became mandatory on April 14, 2003. HIPAA has been costly to implement and will continue to be so as Congress catches up to the fact that costs weren't factored into the policies.

HIPAA may only have influenced your life so far by the lines in pharmacies being set far back from the counter to provide an air of privacy to the person being served. You may have noticed a different format for signing in at your physician's office or laboratory facility. You were probably given a pamphlet to read about your privacy rights.

As you begin to deal with family members' health issues, you will delve deeper into the throes of HIPAA regulations. For instance, if a family member is having surgery, you may be given a code number or word to present at the information desk before anyone can give you a status update. And that is only if the patient has designated you to receive that information. Upon admission to the facility, patients have to designate whether family members can be told about their condition or given any information about their health issues.

If you wish to be able to speak to a physician about or on behalf of your loved one, the information should be on file with the physician's office. This is something you need to discuss with your parents or in-laws and have the necessary forms signed as soon as possible. It can also be designated in legal documents such as a power of attorney for health care or advanced directives. (See Chapter 8 for further discussion of these documents.)

It is important to pay attention to HIPAA regulations now so you are not inadvertently eliminated from access to information about your parents. There may come a time when you have to be the spokesperson, and you need to be sure you have the authority to do so. These laws are subject to interpretation and may vary from one health-care setting to another. You need to know your rights; as technology advances, the laws will be tweaked. As compliance issues are monitored and infractions noted and fines issued, there will be more stringent attention paid to the regulations. You can keep up with the latest information about the laws and your rights from the U.S. Department of Health and Human Services. Their website is *www.hhs.gov/ocr/hipaa.*

Privacy Issues

Confidentiality and protecting a patient's privacy have always been important issues to health-care professionals. In addition to HIPAA, patients have other rights to privacy. Some of the biggest problems that come to light in this category include the patient's right to keep a diagnosis or prognosis from his family, and conversely, the family who wants to keep a diagnosis or prognosis from the patient. It can become even more complex if there are only certain people who are or aren't to be told.

Everyone has the right to discuss matters confidentially with his or her health-care practitioner and to keep information private. When an outcome can be compromised or severely affected by this choice, the practitioner will discuss the issue with the patient and recommend a different course of action. If the decision puts the patient's life in jeopardy, the physician may have to break that confidence to protect the patient from harm. As long as your parents or in-laws are competent to make decisions, they have the right to privacy in medical matters. The medical community will expect you to respect those rights.

Attend Medical-Care Visits

As you assume responsibilities for assisting and caring for your parents, it is important that you meet their health-care team. With the understanding that your loved ones still have their rights to privacy, you will probably want to begin attending medical visits with them. You can step out if they need to discuss something private, but you should begin to become aware of their health-care issues and give input where needed.

While it may take weeks to get an appointment, the wait to see the doctor (or other health-care practitioner such as the nurse practitioner or physician assistant) on the appointed day may seem even longer. Medical offices are often overbooked and emergencies happen. Some patients take longer, and phone calls and other interruptions set even the most organized office back. Be prepared to wait. Bring a book to read or something to help pass the time. You might even want to bring a snack.

When visiting the doctor with your parent, try to keep other distractions to a minimum. Don't bring young children along if you can possibly avoid it. Teenagers aren't big on waiting rooms, either. Plan for the worst possible scenario. If for example, your parent has bladder- or bowel-control problems, consider using an adult diaper for the day and bring wipes and extra diapers. A change of clothing can be kept in the car. Use the bathroom before you leave home, and ask to use the restroom when you get to the office as well.

It's important that the few short minutes you spend with the health-care practitioner be centered around the reason for the visit and not on social graces and small talk. You should be focused on why you are there and what needs to be done. Be prepared to ask questions, listen, and then ask questions for clarification. Bring a notepad to write instructions or other notes.

One of the most common problems starts with the greeting. The practitioner usually enters the room and asks the patient she is. Most people automatically answer, "Fine, thank you." Okay, so why are you at the doctor's office? Patients should learn to lead with the primary complaint, saying something like, "Not so good today" or "I've been better," and continue to tell about their problem. They can also get right into it with something like, "I've been having these terrible pains in my stomach lately" or "This cough is driving me crazy!"

You only have a few minutes of the practitioner's time; make the most of it. Be prepared with a list of your parent's symptoms. When did they start? Does something make them worse? What makes them better? Do they affect her life by affecting how she sleeps, eats, drinks, breathes, or moves?

In addition to the information provided by the patient, the practitioner is probably going to ask for or expect you to comment on the problem from your perspective. Can you add something? Perhaps you notice something your parent hasn't or she's left out an important component. Listen carefully to the response and any instructions from the doctor. Jump in if you have reason to think something won't work or has already been tried. Ask questions if you need more information, and be sure your parent understands or asks questions.

Questions to Ask

It is a good idea to keep a small notebook handy to write down questions you need to ask the practitioner or, as things occur, that you may have reason to question or need advice on. Review the questions before the appointment and transfer them to an index card that you can put in your wallet or purse. Have your parents or in-laws do the same so when you get to the appointment you are both prepared with your questions as well as any signs or symptoms that need to be reported.

FACT

If you use a list of symptoms or questions as a guideline for the focus of appointments with the MD or other health-care practitioners, you will find you have a better understanding of your parents' health-care status and prognosis as well as more control over the effectiveness of the visit. This will also serve to improve the quality of the health care provided.

Physicians and other health-care practitioners are not mind readers. If the patient doesn't tell them how she feels or reacts, they aren't necessarily going to discover something unless she has obvious outward signs. These signs could include bleeding, bruising, or other dramatic visual signs; abnormal lab values; or other obvious findings upon general examination such as an elevated blood pressure or very slow or rapid heart rate.

The patient is the central character in health care. The patient has rights and responsibilities to uphold and is responsible for the ultimate status of his outcomes and wellness. The practitioner can only diagnose (with the help of the patient) and prescribe treatment. She can't force the patient to take a medication or to comply with a diet or exercise routine, and she cannot guarantee success in all instances even if he follows all instructions exactly.

Some of the typical questions to ask the health-care practitioner include:

- How long does she need to continue to take this medication?
- What kinds of side effects should we look for? Do we report them to you?
- How long will it take for this to begin to work? What results should we expect?
- What causes this condition?
- Is this medication safe to take with the other medications she takes?
- When will she feel better?

In Appendix C, there are some sample forms that you or your parents may wish to use to keep track of information to be shared with health-care providers. These include forms to help keep track of all current medications. Along with these will be typical forms for medical history, names of all health-care providers with contact information, as well as medication administration records for use by your parents and others, specifically for caregivers to use.

This kind of information is valuable to primary health-care providers as well as any specialists or emergency-care providers you may come into contact with. It is particularly useful to have a complete list of any medical conditions, surgeries, medications, and allergies in the event of an emergency when it may be difficult to remember all of the names, dates, and dosages.

PCP to Coordinate All Medical Care

The PCP, or primary care provider, is your primary physician or health-care practitioner. This may be a family-practice doctor or a specialist your parents or in-laws see regularly. They may each have a different PCP. The point being, someone has to be designated as being in charge of each person's medical care.

Statistically, as people age, they require more health care. This can mean that several different doctors as well as other health-care services can be involved. As a result, there can be duplications of services as well as medications, treatments, tests, and procedures that are in direct conflict or contraindicated.

Sometimes, a physician will refer a patient to a specialist and not send copies of recent lab, X-ray, or other test results with the patient or to the new physician. Instead of asking for them, the new physician orders the same tests to be repeated. This is not only time consuming and stressful for the patient, it is not cost effective. Insurance companies have begun to crack down on this type of duplication by refusing to pay.

Without a complete list of current medications, the new doctor may order something similar or even prescribe a duplicate of a medication already being taken. Patients and family members may not even detect this if a different pharmacy is used to dispense the prescription and the pharmacist doesn't catch the duplication. If a different manufacturer of the drug is used by the new pharmacy, the pills may look very different. If a name brand is ordered and the version already being taken is the generic version, or vice versa, the duplication may not be caught either.

A specialist may be treating only a specific condition such as cardiac disease, diabetes, cancer, or kidney disease and may not be concerned with any other conditions. There could be several doctors involved in the care of your loved ones. Don't expect them to talk to each other about your loved one or even to consult in the event of a serious problem. They will most likely expect you or the patient to be managing the overall situation and informing each doctor what is being done.

The patient is ultimately responsible for his own health status and advocating for himself. It is important to discuss this situation with the primary-care practitioner and involve her in the process of overseeing all care. Copies of all aspects of care should be sent to the PCP for inclusion in one complete medical record. The PCP should be consulted for all new orders as well.

Some physicians may balk at this responsibility, but others have had to learn this role through managed-care processes, where all requests for care must be authorized by the PCP. HMOs have gotten a bad rap for this type of scenario, and rightfully so in far too many instances, but the basic philosophy that the PCP takes charge and manages the care has excellent merits in preventing errors.

All Communication Must Go Through You

In the same vein as having all care coordinated by the PCP, it is beneficial to officially designate a spokesperson through whom all communication involving health-care matters should go. You will need to discuss this matter with your parents or in-laws, and you should involve all siblings as well. You may also want to broaden this beyond issues of health care, or not, as the situation presents itself.

If there is a family member who is a health-care professional, perhaps this duty could be delegated to him or her, and this person should also attend health-care appointments to maximize efficiency and accuracy.

Under HIPAA regulations, you will need expressed permission from each individual for health care information to be divulged to you. This can be accomplished by having each parent sign a letter giving you expressed permission that can include any parameters or restrictions you determine jointly.

Permission could be formatted something like this:

To Whom It May Concern:

I, _____, being of sound mind, hereby designate _____ (my daughter [or whomever]) as my official spokesperson for health-care communications with all health-care professionals including, but not limited to, my practitioners, pharmacists, insurance companies, nurses, therapist, and DME companies. Any and all inquiries or information should be communicated to my spokesperson.

Signed this day _____ (date).

_____ (signature)

(print name) _____

_____ (spokesperson)

(print name) _____

Witness_____

NOTE: This is a copy for your files. Please request to see the original, which is in my spokesperson's possession.

This form is being provided to _____

on _____ (date).

You should have the signatures witnessed by someone outside the immediate family if possible; it could also be notarized. Make several copies and provide them to health-care professionals as the need arises. Keep the original in a plastic glassine sleeve. You should have it with you when presenting copies to health-care professionals so they can make note of having seen the original. It's beneficial to keep a log of the persons you have given the copy to, along with the date.

By designating and using a spokesperson, it helps ensure information is current, as accurate as possible, and that it isn't being processed by several people before getting to the patient and primary caregivers.

CHAPTER 6

Activities of Daily Living and Other Issues

Activities of daily living, or ADLs as health-care providers may refer to them, include bathing, grooming, dressing, sleeping, mobility, and eating. These are self-care tasks people perform for themselves each day. The ability or inability to perform any of these ADLs provides a measure of the effect of a disorder or disease's process. With aging, many ADLs naturally become more difficult to perform. As individuals loose the ability to perform ADLs, the higher the level of assistance they may require, if only to be safe.

Hygiene

It is well known that the better you look, the better you feel. Cleanliness is essential not only to health in preventing skin infections or breakdown of the skin such as bedsores, or decubiti, it is also essential to maintaining self-esteem.

The skin is the largest organ of the body. As a covering, the skin helps maintain the integrity of the body. Therefore, keeping the skin clean and intact is very important.

FACT

Keeping the skin clean and moisturized is important to maintaining its integrity. With age, the skin needs more moisture. The best time to apply moisturizing creams is after drying off from a bath when the skin is still slightly moist. However, the skin should not remain wet.

Prevention of skin breakdown is an essential part of caring for any individual who is bedbound, restricted to a wheelchair, or spends long periods of time sitting or reclining in one position. Good hygiene and clean sheets or clothing are important to this process. Changing position frequently, even just shifting weight slightly from one hip to the other every few minutes while sitting, will help improve circulation and reduce pressure.

Bathing

Bathing and showering can be difficult for your parents or in-laws. Many of the women especially are still of a generation where baths were more popular than showers. Agility is affected by aging, and getting into the tub and out again can be impossible. A warm, relaxing bath may have been a ritual for your mother, and now she is unable to do this even with help. This is a loss that may affect her more than even she knows.

Grab bars and bath benches or chairs are important safety devices to aid in bathing and showering. Nonslip mats in the tub are advised. Shower curtains should be hung by rods that are screw mounted.

There are a number of devices available to assist with lowering and raising a person into the bathtub. There are now bathtubs that can be installed with a sealable door that allow the elderly to enter the tub without climbing over the edge. A new company even makes a door that can be installed on an existing bathtub. A search through durable medical equipment catalogs and even the Internet can reveal a growing number of devices to assist with hygiene care for the elderly and disabled.

Sponge bathing at the sink, or in bed if necessary, can be just as effective as bathing or showering. Be sure to rinse off soap well, as it can be very drying to the skin. Thinner skin also means a greater sensitivity to heat; be sure to set hot-water tanks so water temperatures don't go above 120°F.

Cooking for One or Two

Proper nutrition is essential to maintaining a healthy lifestyle. It is also essential to healing and preventing any skin breakdown. If you ask an older person about the difficulties of growing older, he will often include learning to cook for one or two people. After rearing a family and sometimes being a short-order cook, learning to cook for only one or two can be quite a challenge.

ALERT!

Too much sodium can lead to retaining water even in the healthiest person. This is most obvious in swollen feet and ankles. Anyone with cardiac or kidney conditions should not consume too much sodium. This can include those with high blood pressure, congestive heart failure, or chronic or end-stage renal disease. Many other conditions can also be exacerbated by excessive sodium intake.

It is easy to fall into the habit of not cooking. Relying on processed foods and frozen TV dinners is often the choice of the elderly. There are many healthy choices in the frozen and canned food aisles, but nutrition labels need to be read carefully. Many prepared foods, both frozen and canned, contain a large amount of salt or sodium. (The chemical compound for salt is sodium chloride.) There are many low-sodium choices, and they can be enhanced by adding other herbs and spices before or after cooking. Some of the most popular items for adding flavor include lemon, lime, and a variety of black or white peppers. There are also a number of salt-free herb blends in the spice aisle of the grocery store that can add flavor.

Kitchen Safety

Safety in the kitchen is another issue. There are a variety of counter-top appliances that can make cooking small amounts of food an easier and healthier task. These include panini grills and some of the more popular George Foreman grills. A frozen hamburger patty or chicken breast, for example, can be prepared quickly on these, and the excess fat cooked off. Steamers, microwave ovens, rice cookers, and slow cookers are all quite useful in cooking smaller amounts of food.

Sometimes food just tastes better when it is prepared in large portions. So go ahead and fix a family size dinner, and then freeze portions. Be sure to carefully label and package the foods. Include the date, and don't keep for more than two to three months, or as recommended according to the contents.

Older people are acutely sensitive to food contamination and can become quite sick from foods that are undercooked or have not been properly stored. Always remember to use separate cutting boards and utensils for meats and other items. Wash surfaces with hot soapy water and rinse well. Keep hands clean. Don't forget to wash off the spice bottle after spicing meats as well.

Leaving the stove on is a common problem with older people. Many household fires have started in the kitchen. Something as simple as a sign hung over the sink or posted on the refrigerator can serve as a great reminder. However, the sign itself as well as the location should be changed regularly, as it will be ignored after a couple of weeks.

A smoke alarm is an essential item in every home. Having one in the kitchen can be bothersome, as some of them are too sensitive to heat and sound off too often—these tend to get removed or disarmed. Placing one outside the kitchen and another over bedroom doors can be a lifesaving device.

It may also be helpful to rearrange kitchen drawers and shelves so the most frequently used items are within easy reach. This will not only help conserve human energy (see Chapter 3) but can be a safety factor as well. Try to eliminate the need to climb on a stool or chair or having to stoop too low.

Exercise and Mobility

Unfortunately, the need to exercise does not go away as you age. Mobility is important to proper functioning of many parts of the body such as digestion and maintaining integrity of the skin as well as the bones and muscles. The heart is one of the largest and most important muscles in the human body and it needs proper conditioning to continue to work properly.

Painful arthritis can be worsened by not using the joint. Stiffness and progressive loss of motion can result, which leads to even more pain. Maintaining range of motion in all joints is important. Flexing and extending muscles helps keep them in shape and functioning properly. This can greatly affect balance and help to prevent injury and falls.

Pumping iron is not required, but gentle activity involving as many muscles and joints as possible is. Even sitting in a chair, your parents can exercise most of the muscles of the body by following a simple range-of-motion routine. Check with your health-care practitioner first, especially if your parents have had any injuries or an illness that restricts their activity.

There are several gentle exercises you can try with your parent. First, make sure she is sitting straight in a chair with her feet flat on the floor. Then try the following exercises:

- Begin by relaxing, then, using your head and neck muscles, slowly bend your head forward to touch your chin to your chest, then lean your head backward. Turn and look over one shoulder and then the other. Then slowly rotate your head in a circle from your chest to one shoulder, leaning back, and then to the other side, and finally back to the chest.

- Shrug your shoulders together a few times. Then raise one and then the other.
- With your hands resting in your lap, raise one arm over your head and then return it to your lap. Repeat with the other arm.
- Resting your arms at your side, make small circles in the air with your wrists. Stop and reverse direction.
- Touch your thumbs to the base of your little finger. Repeat several times.
- Close your fingers into the palm of your hand and open again. Repeat several times.
- Raise your feet off the ground slightly and point your toes like a ballerina. Then flex your toes up toward the ceiling and push downward with your heels. Repeat several times. Alternate your feet for variation.
- Draw circles in the air with your big toe and then reverse direction.

These exercises can be done together or separately throughout the day. It may be best to do them early in the morning if your parent is easily fatigued.

Walking is great exercise for everyone. Get up every hour and walk around the house. Rise slowly and take a deep breath if you tend to get dizzy or feel lightheaded.

Incontinence

Exercises can also help with incontinence. Losing control of bladder or bowel function is not a pleasant thought, but age as well as other conditions can cause or exacerbate incontinence of urine or feces. Incontinence is one of the major reasons families place their loved ones in nursing homes or skilled nursing facilities.

To help prevent or forestall incontinence for yourself or your parent for whom it is not a problem, you can begin to exercise the pelvic muscles. This can be especially important for women but has been shown to work for men as well. Known as Kegel exercises, the purpose is to improve the tone of the pubococcygeus and other pelvic-floor muscles. This most simple demonstration of this is squeezing the sphincter muscle to stop the flow of urine. Relax and let the urine flow freely and then stop it again.

Once you understand how to do this, squeezing and relaxing this muscle can be done multiple times a day without urinating. In fact, it is not recommended to do this during urination, as it could lead to a urinary tract infection. Kegels can be done without anyone else knowing and should become part of your daily routine.

Constipation or a fixation about bowel movements is a common problem for older adults and may have an influence on bowel control and or retraining. (See the discussion on constipation later in this chapter.) The PCP should be consulted at the onset of any incontinence to rule out infection or other medical reasons for the incontinence.

Sleeping Habits and Changes

As people age, they typically require less sleep. However, they also don't sleep as deeply as they did at a younger age and are more likely to be awakened easily and frequently through the night. Consequently, they may not feel like they sleep well and are tired all the time. The best judgment of how well they sleep is to determine if they feel well rested and refreshed upon arising in the morning.

FACT

There are many factors that can affect normal sleep habits, including stress, depression, lack of activity, medications, pain, diet, and hormonal changes. These factors can be even more pronounced as people age.

Alcohol, tobacco, and caffeine also affect sleep patterns. Many believe that having a glass of wine or shot of whiskey before bed will relax them. Most often, this is not the case. In fact, it can have the reverse effect and wake them up as the effects wear off. It also prevents them from reaching deeper levels of sleep. Caffeine should be restricted to the morning hours.

Remember that many carbonated drinks also contain caffeine, sometimes even more than coffee. But a glass of warm milk can be quite helpful in making a person sleepy.

Medications can cause disruptions of sleep patterns. Diuretics are one of the biggest culprits because they induce frequent urination. They need to be taken very early in the day. Other medications such as decongestants, steroids, antihypertensives, and anti-Parkinson's drugs can also play havoc with sleep. Some antidepressants, pain medications, and asthma medications can also affect sleep patterns.

Boredom is often a big factor in sleep-pattern problems. If Dad spends more time in bed or napping on the couch because he has nothing else to do, he's not going to sleep well at night. If he goes to bed too early, he may not sleep as well as he thinks he should either.

Help him find something to occupy his time. If he isn't interested in finding a hobby, get him to do some chores for you. Think about things you never have time to do, such as clipping coupons, recipes, or articles. Matching socks and folding laundry may not be an interesting chore, but it is something he can do while watching TV. If he's not living with you, take the items to him. Make him feel wanted and that he's doing something to help you.

ALERT!

Sleeping pills are not the answer but are all too often the Band-Aid offered. They should only be used for a short time, if necessary, to break the new habit of insomnia. In older people, sleeping pills can take much longer to clear the system and can mimic signs of dementia and depression.

Over-the-counter (OTC) sleep aids such as "PM" products like Tylenol PM usually contain about 25 mg. of diphenhydramine, which is the active ingredient in Benedryl, an antihistamine. Antihistamines cause drowsiness, and when mixed with ingredients such as Tylenol or ibuprofen, they can help induce sleep. Other OTC meds for sleep contain ingredients such as melatonin. All OTC medications should be cleared with a physician before taking. They can have serious side effects when mixed with some prescription medications or illnesses. Again, these medications should not be taken for long periods of time.

The body has its own internal clock, and sometimes it needs to be reset. Going to bed at the same time each night and getting up at the same time each morning will help reset this clock. Regardless of whether Mom slept well or not, have her get up at the same time. Staying up later and getting tired can help. Tell her to resist napping, or set limits of no more than forty-five to sixty minutes each day—that includes nodding off while watching TV. Napping around 2:00–3:00 P.M. is the best time of the day to nap; later in the day will interfere with sleeping habits.

A light dinner that isn't too spicy or fatty is best. Eat several hours before bedtime and sit up to allow for proper digestion. A light snack before bedtime may help if they are likely to awaken because of hunger in the middle of the night. Exercise in the afternoon such as a walk can help encourage normal sleep at night, but don't let them exercise right before bed.

The bedroom should be just for sleeping or sex. (And yes, your parents are probably still sexually active.) Bed is not for reading or watching TV for hours before falling asleep. If you have moved your loved one, make sure she has some familiar items in the bedroom to make her feel at home and safe. These could include photos and other mementos.

Bedtime rituals such as a warm bath, good book, and soft music can lead to a restful night's sleep. Meditation, deep-breathing exercises, or other relaxation techniques may also help induce sleep.

Socialization

Human contact and human touch are essential parts of life and wellness. As people age, they can become more and more isolated, and that isolation can lead to problems. It's important to find ways to keep them involved.

Once they are thrust into the situation, most find it a pleasurable experience and are willing to continue. It's getting them over that first hump, kind of like taking your child to his first day of school. More than likely, this isn't something they are going to initiate on their own; you will probably have to do some research and even offer to take them or go with them the first time.

Your local senior center is just one place to look for opportunities to share common interests. Volunteer opportunities may be another avenue to explore, such as a local hospital, nursing home, library, school, or church.

If they are able, your parents or in-laws may be interested in finding a part-time job. Fast food restaurants and some large home-improvement retailers are some of the more popular employers for older persons. They might find an opportunity helping a self-employed person such as a real estate agent with some of his duties, such as filing or bulk mailing.

ALERT!

Even the most outgoing, natural-born leader may resist and find it difficult to make new friends or join a new group. Senior centers are the perfect outlet for seniors to find socialization, but getting them there may be more difficult than just finding transportation. The typical reaction is that old people don't like the idea of being with other old people who remind them they are old.

Other opportunities for socializing and keeping busy include taking an adult-education class. These classes offer instruction in a variety of avocations such as needlework, pottery making, stained glass, feng shui, digital photography, or even how to write or record family history information. They could also take computer classes from the basic to how to use a multitude of software. Perhaps they could even teach a class.

Dealing with Depression

As people age, they face increasing numbers of losses. Not only do they have to deal with loss of a spouse, siblings, friends, and neighbors, they also have to deal with everyday losses as well. They may have to contend with issues such as changes in vision and hearing. They may have to learn to use a cane or a walker as they lose the ability to walk unassisted. They may have given up driving or lost the ability to do something they love such as playing golf or painting. All of these things are losses and require time to grieve.

Apathy, irritability, malaise, and sadness are not just part of growing old, they are signs of depression. Depression is treatable. It is not a weakness; it is not something you can just snap out of. It is an illness just like diabetes, cancer, heart disease, and Parkinson's. It requires medication and often counseling.

FACT

Grief comes in five stages: anger, denial, bargaining, depression, and acceptance. They don't always come along in that order, but all stages must be passed through in order to complete the process and heal. The more important the loss, such as a death, the more obvious the grief.

Clinical depression is common among older people. Unfortunately, it still carries a stigma, and therefore it isn't always identified and dealt with as the health-care issue it is. Depression is characterized by mood changes, but it is not just a mood. Depression is an illness caused by a chemical imbalance in the brain. Many factors contribute to it, such as loss, stress, boredom, and loneliness, as well as diet, medications, inactivity, hormones, and other physical illnesses.

Some behaviors that can be signs of depression include:

- Sadness or dejection without obvious cause
- Change in eating habits and or a change in weight without cause
- Change in sleeping habits or insomnia
- Feelings of hopelessness and/or worthlessness
- Loss of interest in hygiene and grooming
- Loss of interest in favorite activities
- Crying for no apparent reason
- Increase in the use of alcohol or tobacco
- Thoughts of suicide

If your loved one exhibits any of these signs for more than two weeks, you should seek medical evaluation and treatment for depression. Any talk of suicide should be taken seriously, and if the person says he has a plan, immediate action should be taken.

Depression is not something older people have to suffer with, but more than 75 percent of them will because depression is something they were taught to be ashamed of. Your parent or in-law may be very resistant to discuss depression or see a health-care practitioner for evaluation. You may have to be very firm and insist that he be seen, for your piece of mind.

Depression can also be mistaken for dementia. Confusion and forgetfulness can be signs of Alzheimer's as well as other forms of dementia, but they can also be the result of depression. Only a medical evaluation can make the distinction.

Left untreated, depression will not just sap his energy and make his life miserable, it also leaves him vulnerable to complications and other conditions such as stroke. It reduces his ability to bounce back from illnesses and infections or to recover from any necessary surgery.

Constipation and the Obsession with the Bowels

There will no doubt come a time when each of your parents will become obsessed with their bowels, and life will revolve around whether or not they have had a bowel movement today and what can be done about it if they haven't. Nothing else will seem to matter until the bowels have been moved. Daily conversations will revolve around whether they were able to have a normal bowel movement today. Discomfort, constipation, gas, and indigestion will all become a major part of their vocabulary.

Constipation can cause abdominal distention due to a buildup of gas. This is uncomfortable. Passing gas can present an embarrassing moment for anyone, but older people have weaker sphincter muscles and therefore less control over when and where they release their gas.

Old people generally have fears about losing control of bodily functions, and when they can't or don't have a bowel movement at their normal time each day, they worry about having an accident.

As people age, muscle tone decreases. The intestines depend upon a series of large waves of muscular contraction to move the bodily waste along its way. When this slows down with age, daily bowel activity may slow to every other day or even every three days. This would be perfectly normal, but the average older person won't have it!

ALERT!

This may seem comical, but it is a fact. Almost all old people will become obsessed with their bowel movements at one time or another. Grocery shopping will become focused on bran cereals, prunes, and fiber as well as the inevitable forms of laxatives, suppositories, enemas, and antidiarrhea medications for times when they have overdone the combinations.

Most older people consume smaller amounts of food and therefore generate smaller amounts of waste to be disposed of. They also tend to drink less water, which is needed to keep the waste softer and more mobile. When they try to fix the situation by increasing the fiber, they actually form hard waste. Compare this to making cement and you'll have a better understanding of why they are now more constipated than before.

When introducing more fiber, it is essential to increase the fluid intake. Old people generally don't like to drink liquids because it makes them have to urinate more. Frequent urination can involve other problems such as incontinence, urgency, and being up all night running to the bathroom. Diuretics that promote urination to rid the body of excess fluid have a natural side effect of causing constipation because they pull the liquid into the kidneys before it can be absorbed in the intestines. Other medications can affect the absorption of water by the intestines or slow bowel motility and cause constipation.

Older people tend to be less active physically. This inactivity tends to slow down the intestinal activity even more. Remind them to get up and walk around at least once an hour to help promote better intestinal motility.

Like most other issues, the more they worry about it, the worse the situation will get. Worrying and obsessing about constipation and bowel movements will only make the situation worse; unfortunately, obsession seems to breed obsession.

Constipation can be managed; dietary measures can help. Unless otherwise restricted because of chronic diseases such as kidney or heart disease, five or more servings of fruits and vegetables as well as plenty of noncaffeinated fluids will help establish a healthy system. Plenty of fiber from grains will help as well. Low-fat food choices will make a difference, and keeping salt to a minimum will reduce the body's temptation to retain water in the tissues of ankles and feet instead of absorbing into the intestines.

Laxatives and enemas should only be used as a last resort, as they can quickly become a habit and eventually the bowel won't work without their use. Stool softeners and fiber supplements can be used more readily but should not become a daily habit unless recommended by a physician.

Increasing activity will help as well. And finding something else to think about will reduce the obsession and stress.

CHAPTER 7

Aging and Medical Issues

The body is an amazing thing, but as it ages, it wears down. Aside from the obvious external changes such as wrinkles, sagging skin, and gray hair or baldness, the insides also tell the toll of age. If the owner has taken good care of herself, hopefully the aging process has been kind. But when a lifetime of abuse or other illness has wreaked havoc, the aging body will be pretty-well beaten and battered.

Common Diseases, Medications, and Treatments

Vision and hearing often begin to fail long before one is considered old. The need for reading glasses and hearing aids can begin in middle age, but by the time a person reaches seventy-five or eighty, other problems compound these issues. Osteoporosis and arthritis may have begun to show signs in middle age, especially if they are due to injuries, but now can have a profound affect on daily life for your loved ones.

Digestive disorders can produce a variety of issues. Muscles weaken and bowel and bladder incontinence becomes a real issue for many. The heart muscle may begin to show signs of weakening and failure. And the largest organ in the body, the skin, becomes thin and vulnerable to an assortment of imperfections and problems.

Vision Problems

Aside from presbyopia (which makes reading difficult because the eye has become more rigid, causing a degree of farsightedness), some of the more common eye disorders include cataracts, glaucoma, and macular degeneration. With the increasing instance of diabetes, diabetic retinopathy is also becoming more prevalent. Each of these is treatable, but the earlier they are diagnosed, the better the prognosis.

FACT

Surgery can correct cataracts and has a 95 percent success rate. The procedure has been perfected over the years and is now a simple, painless procedure that can be performed in an outpatient setting such as the doctor's office or a clinic. This is not the same surgery your grandparents may have had that required them to be flat on their back for days or weeks.

Cataracts affect about 95 percent of people over the age of sixty-five. The thin, transparent lens of the eye becomes cloudy. The world begins to look like they're wearing fogged-up glasses. This can be a gradual process and your parents may not even notice anything has changed, except that they have difficulty accomplishing small tasks or they bump into things more than usual with no other apparent cause. Sensitivity to glare or bright lights at night may make driving at night difficult. This can be due to cataract formation, and it may be one of the earliest symptoms. An annual eye exam can determine if cataracts are developing and when it's time to correct the problem.

The symptoms of glaucoma don't usually appear until at least some damage has been done. This is why it's important to have an annual checkup to have the pressure in the eye read by a professional. This is even more important if there is a family history of glaucoma. Glaucoma is more common in African Americans, those with a family history, and those with diabetes. Eye injury can also predispose a person to glaucoma.

Glaucoma is caused by a build up of fluid inside of the eye that presses on the optic nerve. As it does this, the peripheral vision is lost. With surgery, this fluid can be drained and the pressure reduced, but the vision is not usually restored.

ALERT!

Glaucoma can be treated with eye drops. It is critical that the treatment continues uninterrupted and that periodic checkups be made to evaluate the effectiveness. Partial to complete blindness can result if glaucoma is not properly treated.

Macular degeneration is characterized by the fine details in the center of the field of vision becoming curved or distorted. The macula, which is the part of the eye that distinguishes the fine details, is failing or degenerating.

A fuzzy or blind spot appears in the center of the field of vision, which usually affects both eyes at the same time. Over time, this blind spot enlarges until, while trying to read, your parent will be unable to see several words at one time. These symptoms should not be ignored. They will not go away and will only worsen with time.

When caught early, low-vision aids can help restore the ability to read and enjoy other activities that have been affected by the loss of this central field of vision. There are also several promising medications available and others under development and review that can help slow and possibly prevent macular degeneration.

For diabetics, one of the major side effects of poor blood-sugar control is blindness. Most often, this is caused by diabetic retinopathy. The retina is the light-sensitive area at the back of the eye. Diabetic retinopathy is primarily caused by the accumulation of new blood vessels on the retina, or leakage of the blood vessels that feed the retina, due to swelling. Blood fills the center of the eye, causing a blurring of vision. Left untreated, blindness can result.

Like other eye ailments, by the time there are symptoms from diabetic retinopathy, major damage has most likely been done. An annual eye exam with dilation of the pupils can detect retinopathy before symptoms and damage appears. This is an essential part of diabetic care and recommended for anyone with a family history of diabetes or retinopathy.

FACT

Diabetic retinopathy is treated with laser surgery called scatter laser treatments. The physician introduces 1–2,000 laser burns along the retinal arteries to cause them to shrink. Some peripheral or side vision may be lost due to these treatments. Most importantly, vision lost due to the bleeding associated with the retinopathy is not usually restored. This is why it is important to have an annual eye exam with dilation before any damage occurs.

Hearing Loss

Hearing loss is usually a gradual process that may begin in middle age. It is estimated that over 30 percent of the population over sixty has some form of hearing loss, but far fewer than that have addressed the situation. This may be because of the stigma associated with hearing loss, or it may be that the loss has been so gradual it has been ignored.

It is easier to turn up the volume on the TV or radio than to question whether there is a reason for not hearing so well. Asking someone to repeat what he said is simple enough, but when your father yells at you that he's not deaf when you repeat something louder, he may have a sensorineural loss of hearing rather than a volume issue. This involves losing the ability to clarify what is said rather than not actually hearing it and is one of the most common forms of hearing loss in the elderly.

Understand that hearing aids do not mimic the human ear. All sound will suddenly be created equal, and background noises will seem to become amplified because the hearing aid can't tune them out. This will require an adjustment and should be given three to six months before giving up on the hearing aid.

One of the prime reasons people tend to toss aside hearing aids is their hearing loss is the result of presbycusis, or sensorineural hearing loss. This is nerve deafness and involves the loss of the ability to distinguish certain sounds such as consonants. The sounds for "z," "s," and "f" can often be indistinguishable. Sounds at certain levels can be harder to understand, such as the more high-pitched tones. After a while, the brain forgets how to distinguish between these sounds, and hearing aids simply amplify the problem.

It is very frustrating to carry on a conversation with someone who cannot hear. The person with the hearing loss often gives up and withdraws. Any change in hearing should be evaluated by an otologist or otolaryngoligist. These are doctors who specialize in ear disorders. If there is not a physical reason such as a buildup of wax or infection in the ear, she should refer your parent to an audiologist for evaluation. The audiologist can evaluate hearing loss and fit for hearing aids and train your parent in how to use them.

There are a number of other devices to help amplify for use with telephones, in theaters, or with the TV. Sometimes these provide a better hearing experience than the hearing aids do. Experimentation is important; support and encouragement are essential.

Osteoporosis

The bones and joints of the human skeleton are vital to the function of the body. They provide the framework and structure to support the other organs as well as the ability to move. If a bone or joint is broken or injured, that framework is compromised and can profoundly affect the rest of the body.

If your mother breaks her hip for example, she can find herself having to have major surgery to repair or even replace the hip joint. Surgery itself is a huge risk to older people. The aftermath can present even more problems such as infection, blood clots, circulatory problems, bedsores, and pneumonia.

Osteoporosis is a disease that diminishes the density or hardness of the bones. Over time, the bones can become very brittle and snap easily. The vertebrae can be especially susceptible to compression, due to this decrease in density causing painful compression fractures.

FACT

Osteoporosis can be prevented, but this has to begin at an early age. Exercise, a diet rich in calcium and vitamin D, and taking estrogen hormone replacements can help prevent osteoporosis. Hormone replacement therapy has become very controversial of late, due to the risks of cancer, heart attacks, and strokes, an issue to be discussed with your parent's primary care practitioner.

Arthritis

Arthritis is a group of more than 100 diseases that cause pain, stiffness, and swelling in the joints. Osteoarthritis is a degenerative disease that destroys the cartilage and joints as a result of injury or wear and tear. It usually affects only a few joints such as the knees, hips, hands, or spine. Rheumatoid arthritis (RA) is an autoimmune disease whereby the body attacks the cell lining (synovium) in its own joints. RA can affect many or all of the joints throughout the body at one time.

Arthritis is painful, and the most common reaction is to rest a joint and not use it. While rest during an acute phase can help, inactivity can be quite detrimental in the long run. It is important to reduce or alleviate the pain and swelling and increase mobility to prevent stiffness and eventual loss of movement.

Heat, ice, exercise, passive range of motion, massage, and other forms of nonmedical treatments can be quite effective in managing arthritis. Adaptive devices can be helpful with activities of daily living such as jar openers, reachers, long shoe horns, and devices to assist with buttons and zippers. Canes, walkers, splints, and other devices to assist with safe ambulation can help alleviate fears of falling.

Medications such as aspirin, acetaminophen, ibuprofen, and NSAIDS (nonsteroidal anti-inflammatory drugs) can be helpful in controlling pain and inflammation. Be aware that "arthritis strength" versions of these over-the-counter medications are simply a larger dose and don't have any special ingredients in them. All OTC medications should be discussed with your parent's health-care practitioner before taking them.

Stronger prescription medications such as corticosteroids may be needed for brief periods of time to relieve symptoms. These have many side effects and should not be taken for long periods of time, if possible. If these medications are needed, close medical supervision is necessary.

Surgery may also be needed to replace a severely damaged joint such as a hip or knee. This is a major surgery and should be considered carefully.

Digestive Disorders

These can include a variety of ailments from gas, heartburn, and indigestion to ulcers, hemorrhoids, diverticulitis, and difficulty swallowing. Constipation and diarrhea also commonly plague older people.

FACT

Taste buds change every few years, appetite and eating habits change with age, and even a change in water or environment can affect the function of the digestive system for anyone. As your parents age, many of these factors will influence the function of their digestive system.

Spicy, rich, and fried foods and chocolate are among some of the more common culprits of heartburn and indigestion. Smoking and alcohol consumption can exacerbate the situation. Overindulging at a holiday meal or eating too fast also contributes to the heartburn, bloating, nausea, and general discomfort. An antacid or a glass of ginger ale or 7Up can often help. Sitting upright or walking around can also help relieve symptoms. Changing diet and avoiding the trigger foods can help to prevent the problem. If it persists or worsens, consult the PCP.

ALERT!

Older people have less control over the sphincter muscle in the anus and therefore can't hold in gas as well as they used to. Although gas is uncomfortable, it's usually their ego that gets hurt from embarrassment. Gas is a part of life, and all you can really do is joke about it and not make a big issue about passing it.

Gas comes from swallowing air while eating and drinking or chewing gum. It also develops as food digests and bacteria are produced in the bowels. Older people often develop a lactose intolerance or sensitivity, and dairy products produce excessive gas. Other foods such as beans, broccoli, cauliflower, cabbage, bran, raisins, and fiber can also form gas. Avoiding these foods will help reduce the gas. Antigas antacids can help, but make sure they aren't contraindicated with other medications they may be taking. Some contain large amounts of sodium, which may also be contraindicated.

Ulcers are usually caused by bacteria in the stomach. Production of normal acids in the stomach is stimulated, and these acids eat away at the stomach lining producing raw, sensitive, openings. These sores are aggravated by spicy and acidic foods, alcohol, tobacco, and caffeine. Medications such as aspirin, NSAIDS, and many prescription drugs can also cause or irritate ulcers. Stress can influence ulcer formation as well.

Ulcers are treated with a bland diet of small, frequent meals, medications to reduce acid production, and antibiotics. Treatment regimen must also include eliminating foods, tobacco, alcohol, and other contributing culprits.

Hemorrhoids are caused by putting pressure on the veins of the anus. The veins protrude and become small, soft, nodule-like appendages about the size of grapes. This happens most commonly because of straining to move the bowels. It can be the result of sitting for long periods of time as well.

Hemorrhoids can itch or be painful. They can make sitting quite uncomfortable. There are a variety of creams and ointments that help shrink them and address the pain and itching.

FACT

Ice packs, sitz baths, and cold witch hazel can also help alleviate pain and itching from hemorrhoids. Fluids, fiber, and stool softeners can help alleviate constipation and straining; this will allow the hemorrhoids to shrink and disappear. Minor surgery may be necessary if these don't help.

Difficulty swallowing can be the result of other illnesses such as Parkinson's, cancer, stroke, dementia, or brain injury. These factors usually cause interference with the brain's ability to control the swallowing process. It can also be the result of dry mouth—with aging, the production of saliva is decreased. Some medications may also have the side effect of reducing saliva. This dry condition makes it difficult to swallow.

Diarrhea and constipation can be caused by many factors. Stress and change in environment can disrupt regularity. (See Chapter 6 for a more in-depth discussion of constipation.) The overuse of laxatives can also play havoc with normal bowel activity. Additionally, medications and a slowed mobility or activity level can affect bowel function. Diarrhea can be the result of overuse of laxatives or too much fruit or fiber. The water and sodium loss should be replaced. Gatorade is one example of a solution used to replace sodium and water. Diarrhea can also be the body's means of ridding toxins, so antidiarrhea medications should be used sparingly. These can cause constipation and create a vicious cycle. Consult your parents' or in-laws' PCP if diarrhea or constipation lasts more than five days, worsens, or at anytime is accompanied by pain, fever, confusion, or bleeding.

ALERT!

Swallowing difficulties should be evaluated, as they can lead to choking, malnutrition, and pneumonia by allowing fluids and food particles to go down the wrong pipe into the lungs instead of the stomach.

Incontinence

Weakened sphincter muscles decrease the body's ability to hold in urine and feces. Dementia, confusion, and illness also contribute to incontinence issues. There are solutions to the problem; however, they are not all without side effects or consequences. And not all of them will be long lasting or permanent.

Diapering and the use of incontinence pads, which are similar to sanitary napkins, can be used to catch accidents and prevent the soiling of clothing, furniture, and bed linens. Larger incontinence pads, also known as CHUX, help to protect bedding and furniture. They must be changed when they become wet or soiled and appropriate hygiene care given to avoid rashes, infection, and skin breakdown. This is essential if your loved one already has a bedsore that is trying to heal, as it will complicate or retard the healing process.

Another way to avoid incontinence is known as bladder or bowel training. The process is to visit the bathroom routinely every one to two hours.

Encourage your parent to make a conscious effort to empty the bladder or bowel and avoid accidents from urgency.

FACT

A balanced diet is essential to general good health. Green leafy vegetables, whole-grain breads, pastas, and cereals, fresh fruit, plenty of water, and exercise are all elements needed to maintain normal bowel activity. Routines and daily rituals are important as well. And when the urge hits, don't hold it. Laxatives and enemas are habit forming and can become a necessary part of life if used more than occasionally.

The bowel pattern may be harder to establish, but most adults have established a pattern of elimination over their lifetime. Sometimes a cup of coffee or other hot liquid may stimulate the bowel, and then making a visit to the toilet a few minutes later will be successful.

Some medications can help with incontinence issues, especially if the incontinence is due to urgency issues, an enlarged prostate, or previous prostate surgery. These medications don't work for everyone and most shouldn't be used for long periods of time, but they can work well with bladder-training efforts.

A Foley catheter can be placed in the bladder and attached to a plastic bedside or leg bag. These can increase the chances of bladder (or urinary) infections and can be contraindicated in some. An external, or condom, catheter can be used for males and can also be attached to a bedside or leg bag. The infection rate is not as predominant, but these can be uncomfortable and not all fit well, so some leaking is likely.

Unfortunately, for bowel incontinence, unless bowel training works, diapers are the best choice. There are a few devices that plug the rectum like a cork, but they are not well suited for lay public use.

Sometimes incontinence is a symptom of infection or other underlying medical conditions. Sneezing or coughing can cause stress incontinence, where a small amount of urine or feces leaks with the cough or sneeze. These events should be evaluated by the PCP. Some medications are helpful in reducing stress incontinence. Sometimes a device such as a pessary is needed. This is a rubber ring inserted into the vagina to hold up a sagging or protruding uterus pressing on the bladder, causing the incontinence. In males, the prostate gland may be enlarged and causing bladder irritation and promoting incontinence.

ALERT!

Bowel incontinence, surprisingly, is usually the result of constipation. Liquid leaks around the blockages. A high-fiber diet can help control bowel incontinence by restoring regularity and allowing for routine toileting.

Heart Failure

Heart failure is a common ailment in the elderly. It can result from other heart disease or just from age. The heart muscle begins to wear out and is no longer as effective at pumping blood through the body. In basic terms, this causes a backlog of blood in one of the chambers of the heart and results in fluid retention (most notably evidenced by swelling of the feet and ankles), fatigue, and shortness of breath. The body actually tries to compensate for a reduced flow of blood by increasing the blood volume, which only serves to create more of a backlog and worsening congestive failure.

This is a progressive disorder, and when other factors such as kidney disease, diabetes, and/or hypertension are present, the condition can become even worse.

Medications such as lanoxin to control the heart rate, and diuretics to reduce the fluid volume, are used to control heart failure. Sometimes a pacemaker is needed. Oxygen is sometimes needed either periodically or full time. A low-sodium diet is usually prescribed as well.

Heart failure can't be cured, but it can be controlled. It is progressive, and periodic evaluation and adjustment of medications and other treatments is essential.

The Skin

The skin is the largest organ in the body. The body is made up of at least 55 percent water (varying by age and fat content); skin is essential to maintaining fluids necessary for other organ function. It also helps maintain body temperature.

Aging affects the elasticity and thickness of the skin. Older people have very thin skin that can bruise and tear easily. It is vulnerable to pressure, accidental contact with objects such as walls and furniture, and to friction such as moving about in bed against the linens.

These skin tears can become infected and be difficult to heal. The use of bandages may be necessary, but the very act of removing the bandage can cause another skin tear if special care is not taken.

The skin is a good source of information about the body. It is easily reddened or flushed with a fever, it becomes taught and stretched over areas of swelling, and it can become very dry, pale, and rigid in case of dehydration.

Pressure over bony prominences such as elbows, knees, ears, hips, and buttocks can reduce circulation and cause the skin to break as well. Underlying tissue can be damaged and infection or microscopic organisms can eat away at the tissue. This causes bedsores, or decubiti. If not treated quickly, these sores can rapidly worsen and can even be fatal.

Pressure should be avoided and alleviated by frequently changing position (every fifteen to twenty minutes), which can alleviate pressure sufficiently to avoid decubitus formation. In changing position, care should be taken not to pull too hard, bump against something, or cause friction by sliding or rubbing along material such as bed linens. Gently massaging the skin over bony prominences helps increase the circulation and reduce damage underneath the skin. Applying cream while massaging helps reduce any friction caused by rubbing.

Mobility Issues

Poor balance and the fear of falling as well as pain with movement are the most common reasons elderly people don't move a lot. They may have a routine of getting up, fed, and groomed and then spending the day in a chair watching TV. Then they'll eat dinner and go to bed.

There are a lot of exercises that even bedbound patients can do (see Chapter 6), and anyone who is fearful of falling can do these from the chair. Pain should not be a reason to avoid movement. Lack of movement can cause stiffness and even more pain, especially if arthritis is the underlying cause. If pain is keeping your parents and in-laws from being active, talk with the PCP about pain management.

FACT

Inactivity can lead to bedsores, constipation, increased pain and stiffness, loss of appetite, depression, and boredom. Exercise has been shown to improve and prevent these conditions and improve overall quality of life and health.

Movement and exercise can help improve balance issues and mental outlook. Using appropriate assistive devices such as walkers and canes can help increase confidence and reduce fears. Poor balance can also be due to such factors as a build up of ear wax or inner-ear infections or disturbances. This issue should be evaluated by the PCP.

Nutrition

Proper nutrition is necessary to ensure proper tissue growth and repair and to slow or prevent progressive diseases and disorders. Appetite dwindles with age, and as activity levels decline so will the appetite.

Protein and vitamin C are essential to the repair of tissue such as wounds or fractures. Fiber is necessary for bowel function. Calcium and vitamin D are needed to maintain and improve bone strength. Other vitamins and minerals are essential to maintaining heart health and preventing diseases such as cancer. Proper nutrition provides brain food; memory, cognitive thinking, and decision-making skills require fuel.

According to the Harvard School of Public Health, a healthy diet includes:

- Whole-grain foods at most meals, such as oatmeal, brown rice, and whole-wheat bread
- Healthy unsaturated fats from plant oils like peanut oil, canola oil, olive oil, soy and sunflower oils, and omega-3 oils from such sources as salmon
- Fruits 2–3 times a day and an abundance of vegetables
- Fish, poultry, and eggs up to two times a day for protein
- Nuts and legumes 1–3 times a day, such as almonds, walnuts, pecans, hazelnuts, pistachios, black beans, navy beans, and garbanzo beans
- Dairy or a calcium supplement 1–2 times a day, preferably from non-fat or low-fat substances
- Red meat and butter should be eaten sparingly due to large amounts of saturated fats
- White rice, potatoes, white pasta, soda, and sweets should also be eaten sparingly due to the fact they easily break down to sugar and cause spikes in blood-sugar levels
- Alcohol in moderation, 1–2 drinks a day. For instance, red wine has been shown to lower risk of heart disease (if not contraindicated).
- A daily multivitamin can help supplement any holes in nutrition.

Small, more frequent meals or frequent small snacks can help older people meet nutritional needs. Swallowing difficulties, poor condition of teeth and gums, and minor digestive ailments can adversely affect the ability to meet nutritional needs. Cooking foods to a soft stage can destroy the nutrition; however, food can be chopped in a food processor to aid in chewing without having to be overcooked. An electric knife or meat slicer can be used to slice foods thinly to aid in chewing and swallowing as well.

Falls, Wounds, and Fractures

Thin, fragile skin can easily tear by brushing against even the softest surfaces, bedsores can cause breakdown, and peripheral edema can cause the skin to ulcerate. These wounds can all be slow to heal and a tremendous challenge to treat. Balance issues and not using walkers and canes when needed can lead to unnecessary falls and fractures.

Injuries can be prevented or avoided with a little extra care and attention to detail. A conscious effort to protect skin and prevent tears and other injury means making slow, careful movements. Preventing falls and injuries such as fractures requires compliance with safety practices such as turning lights on, using assistive devices, and removing throw rugs and other safety offenses such as clutter.

Skin tears, bedsores, and ulcerations require cleansing and various forms of bandaging several times each week to daily. Sometimes the dressings themselves can cause more damage to fragile skin; tape can remove skin if not removed carefully and dressings that have dried can become stuck to wounds and damage new healthy tissue as they are removed. An ounce of prevention truly can go a long way in maintaining quality of life and preventing other complications such as infection. Ulcerations can be much harder to prevent because they result from poor circulation and edema, which may be very difficult to manage, especially in this typically more sedentary population.

Fractures and other injuries can require surgical interventions that put older persons at risk. Casts and postoperative precautions can lead to decreased mobility and other complications including blood clots, pneumonia, infection, constipation, and bedsores.

Dementia, Alzheimer's, and Other Cognitive Behavior Issues

One of the saddest and most devastating issues in dealing with aging parents is watching them lose their memory and cognitive abilities. All too often, they lose these mental abilities without other physical or mental changes. It can rapidly become a frustrating day-to-day situation with seemingly no light at the end of a long, dark tunnel.

Dementia and Alzheimer's can affect a person without any other warning or physical symptoms or ailments. Dementia is a symptom—of Alzheimer's, Parkinson's, or Huntington's disease. It can also be a sign of dehydration or depression. Dementia is a decrease in intellectual capacities including memory, the ability to reason, and mood or behavior changes.

FACT

Sixty-four percent of all dementia is due to Alzheimer's. Alzheimer's is a disease that presents with a list of symptoms such as loss of memory, loss of the ability to perform life skills such as ADLs, loss of language skills, disorientation to time and place, behavior and mood swings, personality changes, and the inability to reason things out.

Other factors such as stroke and neurological illnesses can affect cognitive abilities. Speech may be affected as well as the ability to do simple math, make decisions, and perform simple everyday tasks.

All of these symptoms can be helped by early diagnosis and treatment with medication and physical, occupational, and speech therapy to retrain the brain. The extent of success depends largely on early diagnosis and intervention as well as the underlying disease entity. Discuss symptoms with your parents' PCP and seek early intervention.

Support Groups

Almost every major disease known to man has a foundation or other support group associated with it to raise awareness and funds for research. An Internet search will most likely reveal at least one or two such groups somewhere in the world. With this global capability, information, support, and other levels of assistance can be found from your living room.

ALERT!

As far as whom to believe and trust, it is best to stay with national organizations and large research facilities. However, there may be message boards, chat groups, and other support sources that have risen from grassroots efforts that can offer personal experiences and emotional support.

Before jumping into anything, consult with your parents' PCP. Understand that anyone who claims he can cure a disease with traditional or nontraditional medicine may have had some dumb luck once or is a terrific con artist. If he truly could cure a disease, it would quickly be a proven fact, and he would become a candidate for a Nobel Prize.

Nontraditional treatments can be dangerous and should be evaluated for appropriateness for your parent first. Some may help alleviate symptoms and indeed offer some relief, if only for a short period of time. But care should be taken not to make a situation worse. Good common sense can go a long way in keeping you from parting with your hard-earned money for some snake-oil treatment. Some of the most well-known support groups for memory and cognitive issues include:

- The Alzheimer's Association, *www.alz.org*
- The Alzheimer's Foundation, *www.alzfdn.org*
- Dementia.com, *www.dementia.com*
- National Stroke Association, *www.stroke.org*
- Parkinson's Disease Foundation Inc., *www.pdf.org*
- National Parkinson's Foundation, *www.parkinsons.org*
- Medline Plus (*www.medlineplus.gov*) is sponsored by the National Library of Medicine and the National Institutes of Health. Health on the Net Foundation (*www.hon.ch*) is a nonprofit, nongovernmental organization that offers accreditation to medical websites that meet their criteria for providing factual information and education. Look for the HON CODE icon on a website.

CHAPTER 8

Legal Issues

Most people think if they don't have millions of dollars in the bank, multiple investments, and property they don't need to set up a will or any sort of estate planning. Therefore, they may not have an attorney, financial planner, tax advisor, or other such advisors. Regardless of the health or wealth of your parents, there are several legal documents they need to sign to protect their health-care decisions and wishes as well as their property and estate from taxes.

Wills, Living Trusts, and Lawyers

Many people assume that because their house is paid for and their child's name is listed on the deed as well as all as on their bank accounts, they don't need to bother with legal documents. Their children all know who gets what and all agree. Why should they go to the expense of having a lawyer draw up complicated documents?

Unfortunately, things aren't that simple. Even if your siblings all agree with what goes to whom and how everything gets divided evenly, the government is going to take a huge chunk of taxes out of the estate if proper financial planning isn't done ahead of time.

ALERT!

Without a health-care proxy or directive or a durable power of attorney, you may have to go to court to be able to make decisions for your parents. You may find yourselves trying to act in the interest of your mother who has suffered a stroke and is no longer able to communicate or your father's dementia, which has taken a turn and made him incompetent to make decisions. Without the paperwork, your opinions don't count and you may have to sit idly by while they suffer through procedures and treatments they never wanted.

A will is a legal document that typically lists and describes a person's assets, property, and personal belongings and how they are to be distributed after her death. It names a person to execute the will, pay taxes and debts due, and make sure that items are distributed according to the will.

A simple will can be drawn up by a lawyer for about $200. Anyone who owns a house or other assets, has children, or has a savings account should have a will. Each of your living parents or in-laws should have a will of their own, as joint wills can be complicated. Wills should always be kept up to date.

Codicil and Letter of Instruction

A codicil is an amendment to a will. Often when someone is cut out of a will, it is through a codicil. When a child marries or a grandchild is born, a codicil can be used to add them in, as opposed to rewriting the entire will.

A letter of instruction can be used along with a will (and codicils) to provide information about your parents' wishes such as what to do about their pets, family photo albums, business files and equipment, funeral and burial wishes, and an inventory of personal items that weren't included in the will. This inventory could include jewelry, furniture, diaries and personal letters, collections, and instructions on who is to receive these items.

This letter, although not binding, could include instructions to family members about how they should spend or invest their inheritance and what to do with items if there are disagreements between siblings.

Probate

Probate is the legal process of settling an estate and includes such things as paying off debts and taxes, inventorying assets, and distributing them according to the will and codicil. This process has a reputation for being lengthy and costly. The clarity of the will and the size of the estate have a lot of influence over the length and fees for probate. Most states have now streamlined the time and expenses for small estates for this process. You may need an attorney to assist with probate; however, it is possible to do this yourself in some states with assistance of the probate clerk.

Without a will, based on the laws of that state, the probate court will decide how to distribute any property and will appoint an administrator to oversee the closing of the estate. This could end up costing you a lot of money, as this administrator may charge up to 5 percent of the total value of the estate.

The will, along with codicils and letter of instruction, should be stored in a safe place and you should know where it is. It is not a good idea to put it in a safe-deposit box, as this may be sealed at the time of death. The lawyer could keep it, or it could be kept in a safe or strong box in your parents' home or with a state registry office.

Living Trusts

A living trust is set up in addition to a will. The trust cannot encompass all assets, and thus a will is still a necessary document. There are two types of living trusts. One is revocable and the other is irrevocable. These are both set up while the grantor is still living.

FACT

A will only covers assets that will be placed in probate. It does not cover items owned jointly by a surviving spouse, anything listed in a trust, or anything given directly to a beneficiary such as from a 401(k) or life insurance policy.

Living trusts have become much more popular because they can be set up to save the heirs by reducing estate (inheritance) taxes and possibly time and costs of probate. A living trust also protects privacy because assets are not passed through probate.

The revocable trust can be changed or cancelled at any time during the grantor's lifetime. The grantor manages the trust until such time as he becomes incapacitated or dies. At that point, the trustee steps in and manages or distributes the assets according to the grantor's wishes. The trustee in this type of trust is often a bank or other financial institution. Unlike a will, the terms of a revocable trust cannot be contested; courts have no control over them.

An irrevocable trust is a serious step because it cannot be changed or cancelled. Estate taxes are usually significantly reduced by this type of trust. However, beneficiaries are still subject to gift and capital gains taxes on assets, but these are usually far less than estate taxes.

The grantor specifies the terms of the irrevocable trust including appointing the trustee(s). This type of trust also protects the privacy of assets, as they don't pass through probate. It can also protect the assets from creditors.

Lawyers

Lawyers usually specialize in certain aspects of law such as criminal law, malpractice, tax law, contracts, or mergers and acquisitions. When choosing a lawyer to draw up a will, living trust, health-care proxies, or any DPOA (durable power of attorney), you need a lawyer who specializes in estate planning and wills and trusts. Just like you wouldn't see a gynecologist to take care of your heart condition, you need a lawyer well versed and qualified in wills and trusts to handle this task.

If you have a good friend who is a criminal attorney, don't ask him to help write a will. Instead, ask him for a recommendation of someone qualified to draw up trusts and wills or to point you in the direction to find a qualified estate-planning attorney.

For additional help see Appendix C. The IRS also has publications available on probate and estate taxes. Call 800-829-3676.

Advance Directives

In addition to learning a whole new vocabulary of medical jargon, you also need to learn some legalese to help you cope with and manage your parents' and in-laws' final years.

Everyone has the right to accept or refuse treatment. Usually a person does this after hearing about the risks and benefits of the treatment or procedure as well as alternatives, including no treatment at all. This is known as informed consent. Sometimes they may choose to refuse treatment without any further information; this is still their right. People have the right to appoint someone to act on their behalf should they be unable to make their wishes known. This is known as an advance directive.

Advance directives are legal documents used to enable your parents and in-laws to spell out in advance exactly what their wishes are concerning their medical care and treatment. They are used in the event that they become too ill, too confused, or otherwise unable to communicate their wishes.

There are two types of advance directives. One is a living will and the other is a health-care proxy, which may also be known as a durable power of attorney for health care or durable health-care power of attorney. These terms and the forms necessary for them vary by state and region.

The Living Will

A living will deals primarily with end-of-life decisions and focuses on questions about sustaining life if there is no hope of recovery. These are open-ended questions and should be answered as completely as possible.

For example, it could be stated in the living will that your father wants to be kept comfortable and pain free, clean and warm, and to be offered food and water. He does not want anything done to intentionally end his life.

Further, he should answer the following questions about whether he wants any of these and under what conditions he wants them:

- To receive food or fluids through a feeding tube or IVs
- To receive mechanical respirations (via a respirator or ventilator, also known as a breathing machine)
- To be resuscitated (CPR)
- To receive transfusions of any form of blood products
- To begin kidney dialysis
- To stop any life-sustaining treatments if they have been begun

The living will needs to be signed and witnessed. It should not be witnessed by family members. If at all possible, it is advisable to have these legal documents prepared by an attorney to ensure that rights are protected and the documents meet your state's laws.

The Health-Care Proxy

This is a durable power of attorney for health care and is broader in scope than the living will. It empowers the agent, or proxy (which is most likely you, as their primary caregiver), to make health-care decisions for your parent at any time she becomes incompetent or unable to make deci-sions. The agent can make decisions about matters other than life or death.

He can make decisions regarding issues such as:

- Accessing or refusing physical or mental health-care or treatments
- Admission or discharge from hospitals, nursing homes, or other health-care facilities
- Home health care
- Organ donation
- Access to medical records

The durable power is only invoked when your parents are incompetent or unable to make decisions, such as under anesthesia. As long as your par-ents and in-laws are capable of making decisions, this power of attorney is irrelevant.

Your parents and in-laws can change their minds about any of these decisions at any time, as long as they are competent. The documents can be changed and old ones discarded. This would be particularly relevant to revisit and possibly update these in the event of a significant change in their health status such as a terminal diagnosis. Be sure that you make sev-eral copies of the documents and distribute them to all practitioners and hospitals. Each family member should also have a copy and understand the decisions made.

If a practitioner or hospital knows of a family member who disagrees with these decisions, especially if he wants life-sustaining treatment con-tinued, the hospital may decide to err on the side of caution to avoid any lawsuits or litigation. Therefore, it is important to discuss these intentions and decisions openly with your family members and understand why they have been made to avoid problems and disagreements down the line. A shouting match in a hospital corridor is not the time to be discussing your mother's end-of-life wishes with your sister.

In 1991, Congress passed the Patient Self-Determination Act, which requires any health-care facility that receives federal monies to inform patients of the right to accept or refuse medical care and treatment in advance. Since almost all facilities receive some form of federal monies, they are required to ask about advance directives, living wills, and health-care proxies and to explain their policies regarding these documents.

Durable Power of Attorney

This general power of attorney is a document that provides you with certain powers as defined in the document to act on behalf of your parents. This could be for paying bills and handling financial matters if they are out of the country for a few months or more; it does not pertain to health-care matters. This is a document that needs to be carefully drawn up with a lawyer, and everyone involved needs to understand exactly what is expected and allowed. You will also need to file this document with the appropriate institutions, such as banks or other financial institutions.

ALERT!

In case of an emergency or admission to a hospital, you should have a copy of these documents with you for the hospital to file. Once they have been filed, they can be accessed at the next admission. If you don't have a copy handy to take with you, it's a good idea to know where to find it quickly should it be needed.

Determining Competency

An event such as a massive stroke or an illness such as Alzheimer's may progress to a point where your parent or in-law is unable to make safe and competent decisions. She is unable to understand information as it is given to her or evaluate choices. There is no clear line defining competency, and just because she disagrees with a choice, such as refusing treatment, does not make her incompetent.

Determining competency is a complex matter and will most likely involve the physician as well as a lawyer, and quite possibly even a judge and jury, to determine what matters she is incapable of handling and to what extent she needs guardianship or assistance.

Having a health-care proxy or other durable power of attorney can help expedite decisions in this matter, or at least not delay treatment of medical matters. In fact, a health-care proxy may be all that is necessary at this point to keep your parent safe. However, if these documents don't give you enough power to control the situation for him, it may be necessary to go to court to have him declared incompetent, but this should be a last resort.

FACT

Every state has its own laws about guardianship and they are very strict. Being declared incompetent strips your parent of certain rights, such as the right to vote, buy or sell property, drive, handle financial affairs, and make medical decisions.

If determined to be incompetent, a guardian is appointed who must report back to the court periodically on the status of the person and her affairs. You or another family member might be the appointed guardian, or it can be an outsider. The extent of the authority the guardian is allowed is determined by the court and your parent's abilities.

Delegating Responsibilities Legally and Financially

Helping assume care for your parents will have an impact on your life in regards to time, emotions, and finances. This can range from minimal to a significant amount of time and money as well as the emotional toll it takes on both you and your immediate household. There may be legal issues and ramifications as well if ground rules aren't clearly laid out from the beginning.

Just stopping at the grocery store to pick up a few items for your mother on your way home from work can begin the financial impact of care giving. You need to save time, so you don't want to take the time to go and get her to shop with you, nor do you get her credit card to use. It's just a few items and you need a few things as well. The bill comes to less than $50, and you tell Mom not to worry about the money. You don't have time right now to wait for her to find her checkbook, much less to deposit a check. Time is worth more to you right now.

However, after five years of picking up things from the market two to three times a week you feel entitled to reimburse yourself from Mom's checking account before you divide up the balance with your siblings now that Mom has passed.

Your brother sees it quite differently and objects. Mom paid for your groceries when you shopped together and she paid for lunch or dinner at a restaurant whenever you took her shopping, to the doctor, or to run other errands.

Factor in the fact that you had to cut back to part time at your job in the first year you took on the responsibility for Mom, and by the next year you had to quit entirely before they fired you because you had taken off so many days when she broke her hip. A few groceries and an occasional lunch or dinner out don't come close to making up for lost salary and benefits for the past four years.

If necessary, an outsider such as an accountant can be put in charge of reimbursement purposes. In some instances, without benefit of agreements in writing, allegations of elder abuse may arise. It is best to put it all in writing and distribute the agreements to all parties. Keep everyone updated, aware, and honest.

Your brother paid the burial fees when your father died and never got reimbursed for them. Your sister has flown in three times from out of state to give you some respite when your son graduated college, your daughter got married, and your grandson was born. No one reimbursed her for her airfare. They have a strong sense of entitlement and seem to think that you being the oldest and geographically nearest child had an obligation to provide the care whatever the cost. They both feel the money needs to be divided equally.

Without the benefit of some form of agreement, your arguments can go on forever. Or you can take them into a court of law and risk losing even more. It is important to delegate responsibilities up front and to put it in writing, no matter how informal. Whether financial responsibilities are going to be reimbursed partially or in full should be agreed upon up front. Receipts should be submitted and payments made as bills come up.

If, on the other hand, financial responsibilities will be included in your contribution to the care, that should be agreed upon and noted as well. Ideally, everyone should share in the responsibility. There should be an accounting for all contributions whether it be time, money, or expertise, and these matters should be included in the ground rules as you begin this process. As things change and other obligations, expenditures, and sacrifices become evident, they should be discussed and your ground rules amended in writing and disbursed to each member involved.

For those who are not directly involved, financial matters may be a complete surprise. Your brother didn't shop for mom and didn't see how much time and money you spent each week. Nor did he realize that she only occasionally bought you any groceries, the meals out barely matched your gasoline costs, and no one has considered how much money you gave up in salary and benefits. In fact, they see it is a positive that you got to quit your job and become a stay-at-home mom.

While you would do it all over again, fighting with your siblings over who gets how much money is a hurtful process. Laying it all out on the table in the first place and updating each other as things transpire can help avoid such issues.

CHAPTER 9

Family Communication and Delegation of Duties

One of the most important aspects of establishing a plan to care for your parents or in-laws is to make your best effort to ensure all of your siblings and other family members have the same information. You need to streamline communication and avoid rumors and miscommunications whenever possible. Each person needs to feel important and to have a role.

Primary Contact Person

To avoid miscommunications and rumor mills, using one person as the primary contact person can be helpful. All communication should go through this person, and all information should be disseminated by this person. This can be especially important when establishing new situations as well as during a crisis.

As the primary contact person, it is your job to present information to your family members. To avoid issues, you should keep the information honest and brief, and be sure to tell each person the same thing.

Think of the primary contact person in terms of the White House secretary calling a press conference. She calls together all of the important members of the press and disseminates information to them all at one time, sometimes reading from a written document. This way everyone hears the same information at the same time.

In terms of Dad's care, following the recent death of your mother you are now the official caregiver and spokesperson for Dad. He will remain in his own home and have meals, groceries, and medicines delivered. You and your children will take him out at least once a week for dinner or some other outing.

The cleaning lady will now come weekly instead of every two weeks. She'll assist with laundry, changing linens, vacuuming, and other house-cleaning chores your mother had been helping with. A gardener will be hired to take care of the lawn and flower gardens.

Dad can take care of himself at this point and does not want to move out of his house. The plan is to help him remain there as long as he can. You cannot provide for all of his needs, especially in terms of your time, but you will organize a plan to involve all family members, and as things come up you will ask for help from the most likely person. For instance, handyman items will be referred to your brother, the carpenter; medical questions will be referred to your sister, the nurse; your niece who loves to sew may be asked to help make some new curtains for the kitchen.

The family should call Dad as often as they can. If he mentions something he needs, ask the family to please let you know so things don't get duplicated. They should also let you know if he has concerns or questions.

What if Mom Gets Sick?

If something changes radically, such as Mom gets sick and has to have care at home or is hospitalized, it's time for another press conference. If need be, delegate this role temporarily to someone else. Alert everyone and let them know that you'll be in touch again as soon as you know more.

You might use a phone-tree system whereby only a few people are called directly by you and then they call their immediate family and so on. But stress the importance of only giving the information as it is given to them, and to direct questions back to you or the temporary spokesperson.

Using notebooks, e-mail bulletins, and family blogs can also help keep the information streamlined and dispel myths, rumors, and other untruths.

Who Does What

If you are an only child, the answer is simple—you get to do it all. However, if you have siblings, the job should be shared. It will likely be difficult to avoid some of the old tensions and power struggles you had growing up, but if you can remember to keep the focus on establishing and continuing care for your parents, it will be easier.

Sometimes you may find you need to bring in an outsider, such as having the medical social worker call to moderate a family meeting and let each person express his or her ideas, opinions, needs, and concerns. If not an outsider, then the spokesperson needs to call a meeting, whether it is in person, over the phone, or both. Be sure to involve your parents.

It can be perfectly natural for the oldest child to take charge because that was his role growing up. Other roles will come back to light as well and may cause struggles over who does what or who gets stuck with what. Try not to let these influence the quality of care you need to provide. Any power struggles or resentments over childhood issues are all irrelevant now; there is a job to be done. Each person brings a unique perspective that needs to be heard and considered.

ALERT!

Establish a few ground rules such as setting a time limit for each person to speak, listening without interrupting, no pointing fingers or using the word "you" to begin a sentence, staying focused on the subject at hand, and not reverting to old sibling or family issues.

Everyone can help in some way. It may be easier to let people volunteer, but each sibling should have some role in the care of the parents. Make a list of all of the things that need to be done and either volunteer or delegate responsibilities. No one should take on the whole burden alone as it will be increasingly difficult to recruit help later.

Some of the duties or responsibilities could include such things as:

- Help with paying bills
- Transportation to medical appointments
- Grocery shopping and errands
- Filling out insurance forms; following up on insurance payments
- Investigating future housing such as assisted living, board and care, or nursing homes
- Finding community resources as needed
- Meeting with lawyers and handling legal matters
- Housework and cooking
- Handyman chores

As time progresses and circumstances dictate, more responsibilities may be added to the list and some eliminated. Always keep your parents in the loop. Don't make decisions without consulting them first.

Siblings who live far away can still help with the responsibilities. They can make regular phone calls to check in with your parents or help provide occasional respite. They can participate in a number of ways and should not feel left out or that they have left the burden entirely to others. At the same time, other siblings shouldn't feel that those who live out of town have skipped out on helping.

Once you have the duties delegated, make a master list of who is doing what and distribute it to all involved. In a couple of months, you should evaluate how well the system is working and call another meeting to discuss any problems or changes that should be made. Again, involve your parents and let all family members express their opinions, ideas, and concerns.

It may be a good idea to involve spouses so they understand that everyone is pitching in to help and there may be some time sacrifices and compromises to be made in the care of your parents. Time may have to be devoted to caring for the parents that takes them away from their own family. Strong, supportive relationships with your spouses will be important to the success of your plans.

Using a Notebook for Forms and Communication

One of the most successful means of communicating with others who rarely gather in one spot at the same time is to use a notebook, which is left in a central location in the house or at the bedside, especially if your parent is now in a facility. It maintains a written record of information shared and affords everyone an opportunity to participate.

FACT

Home health-care professionals use this format to leave instructions and information for other members of the home health-care team, caregivers, and family members. This could include instructions for a new aspect of care, information about progress, any new issues that have been noted, or requests for information.

The notebook should contain some very basic forms for information such as emergency contact information for your parents, caregivers, health-care team members, and other family members.

It should contain a list of current medications, allergies, and basic medical history. Other information pertinent to the current situation can be added. For instance, if your parent is a hospice patient it could include the DNR form (Do Not Resuscitate) and information as to the mortuary and others to contact in the event of the passing of your parent.

The notebook should be divided into sections to make information easier to access. The forms discussed above could be kept in the front or in the back and noted by an index tab. A section specifically for information that should be given to a physician should be included. A separate section could be devoted to communication between family members only or it could be included in a larger section devoted to communication among all persons involved in the care or visitors.

As an example, your sister has visited and has a question about how much Mom is eating at lunch time. She would start a thread in the notebook and the caregiver who is there at lunchtime would answer. If the home-health nurse was visiting and noticed that the calorie count was low, he might leave some instructions for the caregiver to try adding a supplemental shake midmorning. Your brother comes later in the day and adds that he'll bring Mom some of his wife's special custard pudding to see if she'll eat that. It's full of eggs, milk, and not too much sugar. Mom always liked it; maybe she'll eat it now.

Turns out Mom likes the pudding, eats it every day now, and is getting her appetite back and building some strength. In real time, this information was being missed; by using a notebook, Mom's needs were expressed and met.

E-mail and Etiquette

E-mail can be an easy way to distribute information to family members quickly and ensure the same information is given to all. It's easy to build a distribution list in most e-mail software and with one click send the same note to everyone without having to rewrite or resend it several times.

If you have difficulty building a distribution list, you can usually easily add contacts to the "To" section by scrolling through a list and checking off each person as you go through the list. (See Chapter 20 for further instructions.)

You can add photos and other documents to your e-mail as needed. Photos go a long way in telling a story and letting others see how loved ones are really getting along. If you want to send copies of documents such as a DPOA, health-care proxy, advance directives, or a medication list, you can scan it and add it to an e-mail. Most scanner software now has the capability of saving a document as a .pdf file, which is easy for the recipient to open and to save or print as needed.

Because you can save considerable time by only having to write one e-mail to send to several recipients, perhaps you can write a more detailed message and even include a personal message from Dad to all. It is important, however, to read over what you have written before you send it out. Perhaps you should have another family member look it over as well, especially if there is any sensitive information included.

Written documents are open to interpretation and can be easily misread or misinterpreted. Sarcasm, for instance, doesn't translate well into written words. Be sure to add a few asides if you are being funny, sarcastic, or downright silly so everyone gets it and no one takes offense. Using all capital letters usually indicates shouting or other extreme emphasis.

If you have something sensitive or difficult to communicate, e-mail may not be the best choice. You could send an e-mail to your list, calling for a family meeting or phone conference, or just telling them all to call or visit you at their convenience.

It's also important to set some ground rules if you're going to use e-mail as a means of communicating family business. Remember, this is a written format, and it can be printed or read by other eyes, with or without your knowledge. Keep this in mind, and caution your siblings to maintain privacy. If you don't want someone to know something, don't put it in an e-mail.

Keep a positive tone to your e-mails. Don't badmouth or criticize others; e-mail should not be used to solicit sides in an argument or disagreement and then to spread rumors or ill will. If you have differences of opinion, you should have a family meeting and discuss them openly when everyone has an opportunity to participate.

If you can't get together, you should have a conference call over the phone. Face-to-face discussions or at least phone conversations can be more helpful under these circumstances, as voice inflections and tones can tell a lot more than written words, and perhaps cause others to reflect on what they are saying and how it sounds.

A Family Website or Blog

For those who are more Internet savvy, a family blog or website can be very useful to help keep everyone in touch. In addition to being the primary care-giver, however, writing and maintaining a blog or website could put you over the top, so be careful how much responsibility you bite off. This could be a great job for one of your children or a sibling who is close to the situation.

FACT

The blog or website can also be a way for your parents or in-laws to share some of their most memorable times. It's a great way to encourage them to talk about their childhood, college years, how they met their spouse, and to share some other family history. Old family photos can be posted for your siblings and cousins to download and share; comments back can keep everyone interacting and connected.

A family blog or website can be a great place for families to keep in touch and interact. Posting and reading blurbs about the latest births, grad-uations, marriages, and happy family news can also help keep up the spirits of your parents or in-laws. Seeing a few great photos from a family mem-ber's European vacation can be a nice way to share the adventure.

It's a great way to post invitations, photos, announcements, and bulle-tins. Should your parent or in-law have a sudden health episode, it's also an easy way to post updates on her condition and even a few photos to help ease the minds of those too far to visit.

Keep in mind that the Internet is very public. There are ways to keep your blog or website more private by using passwords and other means of limiting access, but again, it's a written format that can be printed or read by others without your knowledge. Used appropriately, a family blog or website can be something to enjoy for years to come.

CHAPTER 10

Levels of Care

There are many different levels of care and variations within those levels. Caring for your parents and in-laws can involve some or all of these, and you can find yourself going from one level to the next very quickly. Being prepared, knowing when to make a move, and understanding your options will help divert a crisis and ease the transition for all. These levels of care range from assisting your loved ones in their own home to moving them to a skilled nursing facility or nursing home. Safety and appropriateness of care are key.

How to Know When It's Time for More Help

Obvious events may make it quite apparent it's time to move your parents or in-laws to a different level of care, but the more subtle the situation, the easier it is to miss or remain in denial that something has to be done.

One fall does not necessarily mean your Dad is no longer capable of caring of caring for himself or living alone, but it should be a loud warning and should not be ignored. A second fall means you really have to look carefully at the situation and make some changes. You may just need to get the grab bars installed now, remove obstacles and throw rugs, or add an alert system or make sure he has a phone with him at all times. You may also need to examine other possibilities such as in-home care or a move to a higher level of care.

ALERT!

Certainly if an event has caused an injury or frightened your parent, you need to sit down and discuss how to improve the situation and what the options are. The severity of the situation will dictate how drastic a measure you need to take. You have to be alert to the cues and willing to accept the fact your parents are aging and are going to need more and more help as they get older.

It's common to ignore signals or to minimize them, especially if you are overwhelmed with other responsibilities or are having a particularly difficult time coping with the fact that your parents are aging. Facing mortality is not a pleasant experience, but it cannot be avoided.

If other responsibilities have you overwhelmed, perhaps it is best to call in reinforcements from your siblings or other family members to give you a more objective opinion of the situation.

Besides obvious falls, other clues can include increasing forgetfulness or confusion, changes in eating habits or personal hygiene, household chores being left undone, bills going unpaid and utilities shut off, or pets being neglected or unkempt.

Changes in mood and sleeping habits can also signal a need for change. Everyone can have a bad day or two, but ongoing issues should not be ignored. These signs can also indicate a change in condition that could warrant medical attention and should be evaluated by the PCP.

Try Something Different

Some solutions can be simple and may work for a while, or they may be short lived but help buy some time to make other changes. Using a newspaper to make note of the date or a daily calendar to cross off the days and make note of what day it is can help reorient your parent to time and reality. Wearing a watch may help your parent remember what time it is and be more based in the present moment. Using a loud kitchen timer can help remind Mom the food is done and to turn the stove off, as long as she remembers what the timer was for and to turn it on.

Post-it notes, memos on a calendar, signs, and even a banner can be helpful to remind her about simple daily tasks. Again, remember that after a while the brain will ignore these reminders, so they should be changed or moved to improve the effectiveness.

FACT

A new habit can take three weeks to develop, and an action must be repeated at least twenty-one times before the brain recognizes the pattern. Telling Dad to cross off the days on his calendar each night is not going to sink in as a new pattern of behavior right away. You're going to have to remind him several times before evaluating whether this can be a helpful tool.

If all of your best efforts are failing to help, a change in level of care may be necessary. This could be temporary, or it could be the start of a series of progressive changes.

Part-Time Versus Live-In Care

The cost of care can be prohibitive even for minimal levels of care, so you need to evaluate what your parents need and when they need it. For example, a companion who provides supervision, cooking, and some light cleaning but no hands-on care can cost $9–$15 per hour. A certified nurse's aide or home-health aide trained in hands-on care can run about $19 per hour. A licensed practical nurse will cost at least $32 per hour, and an RN in excess of $50 per hour. Expect your parents or in-laws to balk at the idea, so if they don't need live-in care, start with something short term and only as often as necessary.

A friend or neighbor might be willing to stop in daily for a few dollars a week or an exchange of favors. Someone to bring the newspaper and check to see that Mom is up, knows what day it is, and has taken her daily medications may be all you need right now. You may need to add a daily phone call later in the day to make sure she has eaten and fed the dog.

From there, you might have to progress to the wake-up bath or put-to-bed visit from a nursing aide. Or you may have to hire a layperson to come in and help cook and clean and spend a few hours a day with them to make sure they've gotten themselves up, bathed, groomed, and fed. If they need assistance with personal care, you'll need a trained person to assist with this—either a nurse's aide or a layperson you have trained.

Start with a few hours a few days a week if you can, and let them get used to having someone in. If you need to add more time, they will be more comfortable if the process started slowly.

Older people are usually at their best in the morning and fade as the day progresses, so it may be that you need to look into having someone come in later in the day and help them with an evening meal and getting ready for bed. Hiring someone to arrive in the morning would be a waste of money and not solve the problem.

It may be that your parents are just fine during the day but have difficulty during the night. Most falls occur during the night when an older person gets up to go to the bathroom and doesn't turn on a light or use a walker or cane.

Having someone there at night can be a big comfort. And perhaps that's all you need for now, but it may come to a point where someone is needed

24/7. You can choose to staff that situation in several ways. Shift care can sometimes be less costly because a live-in caregiver must have eight hours of sleep. If your parents are up all night and need help during the day, you'll need to hire someone to relieve the live-in so she can sleep.

Shifts are typically eight or twelve hours. For most older people, the fewer the changes the better, so twelve-hour shifts may be the best choice.

Whether you hire privately or go through an agency, always ask for references and check with agencies such as the Better Business Bureau and even your local police department before hiring anyone.

Board-and-Care Homes

A board-and-care home is a residential care home usually licensed to house two to six individuals who require intermittent nonmedical assistance throughout the day and night. They are usually for seniors, but some are set up as group homes for children or adults with various physical or mental disabilities, or developmental problems such as autism or Down syndrome.

Board-and-care homes are typically converted single-family homes, but they can also be small apartment houses converted to a larger board-and-care facility. Residents may have a private bedroom or share one with another resident. Usually they share bathrooms. Communal meals are provided. Assistance with activities of daily living is provided as needed, such as bathing, grooming, toileting, dressing, and feeding.

Residents cannot be bedbound; they must be able to ambulate. They may use a walker or cane, and they may require some minimal assistance to walk. In some instances, they can be in wheelchairs, as long as they can assist with the transfer to and from bed and wheel themselves about the facility. When a person requires moderate to maximum assistance, he needs to move to a higher level of care such as a skilled nursing facility.

Licensing agencies make periodic visits to ensure standards are being met, but these visits are often infrequent. It is suggested family members make unannounced visits to confirm conditions are sanitary and services are being rendered as promised. No medical care is provided by the staff in a board-and-care home. Home-health agencies may visit residents to provide intermittent nursing care such as treating wounds or providing physical, occupational, or speech therapy. Some homes allow residents to have a Foley catheter as long as a home-health nurse comes to change it regularly or in case of blockage or accidental dislodgment.

FACT

Many board-and-care homes are licensed and regulated by government agencies, but there are also some mom-and-pop homes that aren't licensed. Licensure status can be verified with your county or state government licensing office. Licensing helps ensure standards of care are being followed and that substandard care can be reported.

Some licensed board-and-care homes can accept government assistance payments for residents who receive government assistance such as SSI. Fees for care range $350–$3,500 per month depending on the location, facilities, and amount of assistance needed. Other than those who may qualify for SSI assistance, these fees are an out-of-pocket expense. Some long-term-care insurance policies will cover these costs. Check with your policyholder for more information.

Retirement Homes

In true fashion, retirement homes are not assisted-living facilities, although they may have attached or associated facilities that offer higher levels of care for those who need and can pay for it. Retirement homes and villages are simply apartments, condominiums, single-family residences, or large neighborhoods for those fifty-five and over.

Some of these retirement homes and communities are very private, not necessarily community oriented, and serve to offer only a place for seniors to live away from children and families.

Sometimes in these retirement communities the homes are specifically designed to meet the needs of an older population, such as being equipped with grab bars and railings, wheelchair ramps and wider doorways, and raised toilets.

On the other hand, some of these facilities and residential areas are more community oriented and may offer centralized shuttle services to local venues such as grocery stores, pharmacies, medical centers, theaters, malls, and senior centers.

These apartment buildings, mobile-home parks, condominiums, and single-family residential communities strictly for those fifty-five and over are communal living areas for seniors who can live independently. They are usually tight-knit communities where neighbors keep an eye on each other and possibly share responsibilities such as shopping.

They may also offer social activities either in a community meeting room or through day field trips. They may have exercise classes, craft events, and card and board games. They often have a large recreational room for communal TV viewing, and perhaps a music room with a piano.

These are usually private residences, and the costs will vary according to the local real-estate market and rental rates. As such, usually there is no government assistance for this form of residence, and long-term-care insurance policies don't cover them either.

Continuous-Care Retirement Communities

Some retirement homes are run by various nonprofit professional or religious associations and provide continuous care from independent living to skilled nursing care under one roof, so to speak. In some instances, residents deed their own homes to the association when they move into these facilities and remain in the care of this association for the rest of their lives. Others have buy-in fees and monthly fees according to housing and levels of care provided for the duration of their lives.

Costs can range $400–$2,500 per month and have buy-in fees from $20,000 to over $400,000. The costs and monthly fees vary by location, amenities, services needed, and whether the space is owned or rented. This is a binding, lifetime contract and should be considered carefully and reviewed by an attorney or financial advisor before signing. Most of these CCRC facilities are accredited through the Commission on Accreditation of Reha-bilitation Facilities (CARF). Their website is *www.carf.org.*

Assisted-Living Options and Added Services

Assisted living is an intermediate step between independent living and skilled nursing care. Residents typically require some personal or custo-dial care, but limited or no medical care. They cannot be permanently bed-bound or require extensive medical care. In some instances, assisted-living facilities can apply for a waiver from state licensing agencies to allow hos-pice to provide end-of-life care to a resident who arranges for a private pri-mary caregiver.

Assisted-living facilities currently house about 1 million Americans. They typically house 25–150 residents in small, one-room studios or one-bedroom efficiency apartments or units with scaled down kitchens. They provide communal meals three times a day. In some facilities, these meals are served restaurant style, with menus and salad bars. Others are cafeteria style or sit-down, with a fixed menu with variations to accommodate spe-cial nutritional needs. Most will provide meals to the resident's room, but not for long periods of time. Residents have to be able to get to the central dining area with or without assistance.

FACT

Assisted-living facilities provide twenty-four-hour supervision; assistance with personal care such as bathing, grooming, dressing, and eating; some assistance to and from the dining room or to and from transporta-tion; and minor medical care such as assistance with medications. They also provide housekeeping and laundry services; transportation services to local shopping, medical centers, adult day care and senior centers; and some social engagements such as theater outings.

All of these services are usually included in the monthly fees, but some facilities charge extra for anything beyond twenty-four-hour supervision and meal services. Be sure to discuss services and fees up front and get it all in writing. If ownership or management changes, you may need to renegotiate.

For additional fees, some facilities can provide personal supervision and assistance to residents in their rooms on an hourly or shift basis. Most assisted-living facilities charge extra for those who need special supervision such as Alzheimer's patients who require a locked unit to avoid wandering. Most also charge extra for diapering and toileting services. For Alzheimer's residents, these toileting/incontinence fees are usually included.

Some facilities have a nurse on duty to assist with taking pulses and blood pressures and addressing first-aid issues, but assisted-living facilities aren't licensed to provide medical care to residents. As with the board-and-care homes, home-health agencies can provide intermittent nursing or therapy to assisted-living residents.

Assisted-living facilities usually have community cultural, social, and educational activities and may provide health and exercise programs. Some of these may be at additional costs.

Typical costs for assisted-living facilities range $850–$4,000 per month depending upon the location, amenities, and services. These fees are usually out-of-pocket expenses, but there may be some government assistance to those who qualify for SSI.

Skilled Nursing Facility

Skilled nursing facilities are also known as a SNF (pronounced "sniff"), or nursing home. They provide two basic levels of care: custodial and skilled care. Residents may be temporary or long term. Temporary stays are usually for rehabilitation purposes after a major surgery, injury, or illness. Long-term stays are usually for those who can no longer live alone and require a higher level of care than can be provided at home or in assisted-living facilities or board-and-care homes.

Skilled care in a SNF is usually short term and continuous only so long as measurable gains are made. However, some circumstances require ongoing skilled care such as those who require a ventilator or other tubes or mechanical means for nutrition and life support. An episode of illness or injury may also be cause for skilled care on a temporary basis in a SNF for those who usually just require custodial care.

FACT

Skilled care can be provided by a nurse or physical, occupational, or speech therapist. Licensed physicians prescribe and supervise all skilled care in a SNF. This may be your parents' PCP or physician supervising all care at the facility. Registered nurses supervise a staff of licensed practical or vocational nurses who provide twenty-four-hour medical care.

Custodial care in a SNF is also supervised by the licensed physician and a registered nurse, but it is usually provided by nursing assistants. An RN or LP/VN manages and dispenses medications. Custodial care consists of activities such as bathing, dressing, feeding, grooming, transferring and assistance with ambulation, and toileting or incontinence care. If the resident needs some skilled care as a result of illness or injury, or develops a decubitus or bedsore due to immobility, skilled care will be ordered and provided.

Who Pays for Skilled Care?

Skilled care is covered by Medicare and most private insurance using Medicare's guidelines. Under Medicare's guidelines, the skilled care must be preceded by a minimum qualifying hospital stay of three days. Admission to the SNF must be within thirty days of the qualifying hospitalization. The first twenty days are paid at 100 percent; after that, there is a daily deductible. (This may be covered by Medigap insurance.) There is a maximum of 100 SNF days for a qualifying hospitalization and diagnosis.

The patient must show measurable gains, also known as rehab potential, toward independence in the documentation by the RN or therapist. If at any time before the 100-day maximum stay the measurable gains or skilled-care need ceases, reimbursement will end. Custodial care will be included and covered during a skilled-care stay.

Long-term-care insurance policies may provide coverage of care in a SNF. Read the small print, as there may be restrictions. Some Medicare Advantage or HMO plans advertise they will cover long-term care in a SNF. Again, read the small print, as there are restrictions.

ALERT!

Those who qualify for Medicaid may also qualify for coverage of long-term care in a SNF. Not all SNFs accept Medicaid, and those who do usually have a limited number of "Medicaid beds."

Costs can average $192 per day for a private room in a SNF (over $70,000 per year) and $169 per day (over $61,000 per year) for a shared room, according to a MetLife survey in 2004. These costs showed an increase of $4,000 over the previous year and are expected to continue to increase. These are for basic custodial services; additional services can increase total costs, and costs can vary by location.

With the advent of assisted-living facilities, the number of long-term nursing-home residents has declined in recent years. Those who become increasingly frail and need more care than caregivers can provide at home or in an assisted-living facility may need to move to a SNF. This includes those who require twenty-four-hour care and supervision, become bedbound, or require maximum assistance to transfer to and from a wheelchair.

CHAPTER 11

Setting Up Home Care

There are several different aspects of home-health care and day-care options that should be investigated as possible resources to help your parents and in-laws remain as independent as possible in their own home for as long as possible. Some require skilled needs and orders from a physician, and others are self-referral agencies and services that can provide a variety of assistance on a fee-for-service basis.

Skilled Intermittent Home Care

The key point is that this is skilled care and it is intermittent; therefore, it is not custodial or long term. A skilled need is defined as being something that takes the skill of a registered nurse or physical therapist to perform. In many cases, the nurse or therapist will be instructing the patient or caregiver how to perform these duties for the patient and reducing the frequency of visits to supervise, evaluate the care and outcomes, and revise the care to meet the ongoing need. These duties are provided under the direction and orders of a physician.

The visits are intermittent and last for an average of thirty minutes to an hour. The frequency of visits usually ranges from once or twice a week to once or twice a day as the skilled need dictates.

In the majority of cases, the object is to get the patient or family independent in the care as soon as possible and to reduce the frequency. Home care is, in general, thought of as a bridge between an acute level of care such as a hospitalization and complete independence as far as health-care issues go. It is not meant to be an intense and long-term service, nor does it meet custodial needs.

Medicare (both standard and managed-care plans), Medicaid, and private insurance provide reimbursement for home care for patients who qualify. For Medicare there is no copay from the patient; however, for share-of-cost Medicaid patients there may be a fee, and most private insurance providers have copays for home-care services. Medicaid, HMO Medicare plans, and most private insurance plans usually require prior authorization for home care and may have set limits on the number of visits a patient can have in a given time period. These numbers are cumulative, so from one episode of care to another, the limits can be reached quickly if not carefully planned out.

Medicare reimburses home-care agencies in a lump sum based on a number of factors including diagnosis and functional limitations of the patient. Medicare requires the patient to be homebound. Homebound means that it takes a taxing effort for the patient to leave home, and therefore he could not go to the doctor, clinic, or other outpatient setting for this care. The patient doesn't have to be bedbound, and the homebound status can be temporary due to this spell of illness. It does not mean that the patient doesn't drive or has no means of transportation; lack of transportation does not equal homebound.

FACT

Besides being homebound, Medicare requires the care to be skilled and have a specific ending point. The patient must demonstrate the potential to make measurable gains such as significant rehabilitative progress, and the care must be ordered by a physician. The care must be provided by a Medicare-certified home-health agency.

Medicaid and private insurance companies don't always require the patient to be homebound, but they usually expect the other guidelines to hold true. In fact, in many instances they will pay for more visits because it is more cost effective than being hospitalized or going to an outpatient setting for the care, even if the patient is not homebound.

Home care is often initiated after a hospitalization, but it can be ordered at any time by a physician. The discharge planner or case manager at the hospital will recommend the physician order home care at discharge for follow-up care and will make the referral. If not hospitalized, a patient can make a request for home care from his physician or the physician may suggest the care so the home-care nurse or therapist can provide her with a bird's-eye view of the home situation.

Most commonly, home care is ordered if the patient is going home with surgical or other wound dressings that need changing, requires intravenous antibiotics, or continues to need a pain-management device such as a PCA pump. Diabetics newly on insulin might need a home-care nurse to visit daily for a few days to instruct in glucose testing and insulin administration.

Physical therapy visits are usually ordered for patients after joint-replacement surgery or fracture repairs. They could also be ordered for patients who need home-safety evaluations and instructions, especially anyone who has been significantly weakened by the hospitalization or the underlying disease or has a reported history of falls with or without injury.

Other home-care services include:

- Occupational therapists
- Speech therapists
- Home-health aides
- Medical social workers

Occupational therapists provide such care as education in energy conservation, home safety issues, and adaptive equipment for assistance with dressing, grooming, bathing, and other activities of daily living. This would include such things as long shoehorns, reachers, and devices to help button clothing. They can also help designate proper placement of grab bars.

Speech therapists typically work with patients who have impediments from such things as strokes. They also work with patients who have cognitive-thinking issues that can result from strokes, early dementia, or the after effects of chemotherapy and other treatments.

Home-health aides primarily assist with bathing and grooming services, but they can also provide some limited personal laundry services, meal preparation, bed-linen changing, and assisting with ambulation or exercises prescribed by the physical or occupational therapist. A home-health aide is a certified nurse's aide who has additional training to work in the home.

Medical social workers provide services such as assistance with short- and long-range planning by providing community resources and assisting with applications for Medicaid or other medical or financial assistance programs. They can also provide counseling services for coping with life changes and loss. In instances of neglect or abuse, they can assess and make appropriate reports as well as assist families in correcting such circumstances.

Hospice care is another branch of home-health care and will be discussed in Chapter 16.

Anytime there is a significant change in condition or a new care-giving situation, a home-care referral can be beneficial to instruct the patient and caregivers in safe care, medication safety, and other safety issues. If the situation doesn't meet reimbursement guidelines, most home-care agencies offer the services on a fee-for-service basis. One visit from a physical therapist could provide sufficient education to prevent a novice caregiver from suffering a back injury, and the cost is worth its weight in gold.

Adult Day Care

For many families, adult day-care services provide the same kind of respite and ability to continue to work as day care for their children does. Whether it is full time, part time, or for occasional periods of respite, adult day care can be the answer to your needs. Three-quarters of the adults attending day care live with their spouse or adult children or other family members; others live alone.

Adult day-care centers provide supervision as well as group exercises, activities, and even field trips for attendees. Some centers are set up specifically for persons with special needs such as Alzheimer's or other dementia or cognitive issues, and the activities are specific to their needs. Advanced Alzheimer's patients may need to be in locked facilities to prevent them from wandering off. This care requires specific training for the employees and licensure for the centers.

Some centers provide very general services and can only serve clientele that don't require locked units. Many may be in diapers, but some centers require their adult clients to be continent (have bladder and bowel control) and able to be taken to the toilet at regular intervals to prevent accidents. Almost 60 percent of consumers require assistance with two or more ADLs (bathing, eating, dressing, grooming, toileting, transferring, or ambulating). Just over 40 percent require assistance with three or more ADLs.

The vast majority of adult day-care centers are affiliated with other health-care organizations such as skilled nursing facilities, home-care companies, medical centers, or organizations such as Alzheimer's, Stroke Recovery, or senior citizen centers.

Care is usually available for extended hours, 6:00 A.M. to 6:00 P.M., Monday through Friday. Some offer pick-up and take-home shuttle services and others require a drop-off and pickup. More information on these services is available from your local area agency on aging (AAoA). Check your local phone directory or call 1-800-677-1116.

FACT

There are more than 3,500 adult day-care centers in existence in the U.S. today. Two-thirds of adult day-care consumers are women, and the average age is seventy-two. While the national average daily fee is $56, according to the National Adult Day Services Association (*www.nasda. org*), this is about half the cost of a day's care in a skilled nursing facility.

Private-Duty Care

Private-duty agencies offer twenty-four-hour live-in care, or live-out shift and partial-shift care in your home from several levels of providers ranging from unlicensed sitters to registered nurses. In most instances, this is an out-of-pocket expense; however, some insurance policies and long-term-care policies cover some or all of the cost. Medicaid may also cover the costs if significant skilled care is needed and the cost savings over being placed in a skilled nursing facility can be demonstrated.

Some agencies offer short-shift wake-up services, which can include bathing, grooming, dressing, and breakfast preparation. They may also offer a put-to-bed service that can include bathing and diapering. However, most require a four-hour minimum, which is primarily to meet their staffing needs. This is a highly competitive business and employees will often opt for the best deal they can get each day by working for more than one agency. In order to compete, an agency needs to provide eight hours of shifts. These can be split shifts, but this is why the four-hour minimum is often required.

It is often difficult to maintain a staff of registered nurses in private duty, so most skilled nursing services will be provided by licensed practical or vocational nurses under the supervision of an RN.

An issue often cited as a disadvantage is that because it is a licensed agency, it has to adhere to regulations such as requiring a licensed nurse to dispense medications or to change even simple dressings. Hiring privately means you could instruct the person in how to dispense your parents' medications and perform simple treatments or have a home-care nurse instruct them. Hiring an aide or even a layperson you train can be a cost savings over hiring a licensed nurse.

If the client requires medications to be administered or skilled procedures such as dressing changes or tube feedings, a licensed nurse will be needed. On the other hand, if he just needs to be reminded to take medications at a set time and a family member has dispensed the medication in a marked paper cup, a certified nurse's aide or other unlicensed employee could provide the care.

Hiring Help Using an Agency or Not

There are advantages and disadvantages to using a private-duty nursing agency for hiring help in the home. The most obvious advantage is the agency pays the salary, taxes, Social Security, and worker's compensation. The agency usually provides background checks and health screenings and bonds the employee. However, don't assume this to be the case—ask, and get it in writing.

Most agencies have policies against customers hiring employees away from their agency, but some will work with you in a manner similar to how a temp agency works. They screen the applicants and you can try them out for a set period of time, then hire them permanently and pay the agency a fee for this service.

The employees are usually trained in CPR and how to handle an emergency. They have a supervisor to contact for help and advice. That supervisor can act as a buffer to mediate issues for you as well.

As discussed earlier in this chapter, there are rules and regulations licensed nursing agencies have to abide by. These are set by the federal, state, and local government to protect the public. Government agencies oversee the continued compliance with the rules and can intervene on your behalf if a legitimate complaint is filed.

ALERT!

Using a private-duty agency may be more expensive, but there are advantages, such as it's role and responsibility to find a replacement if an employee calls in sick or otherwise does not show up. The agency will also find others to staff your case when an employee needs time off for vacation or holidays.

These rules dictate the level of care provided by unlicensed caregivers as well as licensed nurses. Again, these rules are meant to protect the public. In hiring an agency to provide care, you will need to discuss all tasks you might expect the employee to perform. Unlicensed caregivers cannot perform any hands-on care, including grooming, dressing, bathing, and feeding. They can only provide care such as meal preparation, light housekeeping and laundry, and companionship to ensure if your parent falls or needs further assistance someone can call for help. They may or may not be allowed to transport your parent in a car or on a bus or other public transportation. Shopping and errands may not be something they can provide either, so be sure to ask.

Certified nurses aides can provide hands-on care but cannot dispense medications or perform medical tasks. Transporting patients is an issue that varies from state to state and even agency to agency, depending upon liability-insurance issues.

Hiring someone privately can eliminate some of these restrictions but can create other headaches for which you need to have a backup plan. The most obvious is if the person is ill or doesn't show up. You have to be the employer and withhold and pay taxes, Social Security, and provide a worker's compensation plan in case this person gets hurt on the job. You have to carefully check references.

If you have a community college or university in your vicinity that offers nursing programs or other health-care education, you may have an opportunity to find a pool of students willing to provide quality part-time care, but you still need to check them out carefully. Word-of-mouth advertising through a social network such as coworkers, church, school, and other personal contacts should be used first, as you'll have personal references to rely on. Local and throwaway newspapers can be your best bet, as opposed to the more expensive metropolitan publications potential employees cannot afford. Don't take short cuts: Screen your applicants carefully, and if you find a gem, reward and praise them.

Home-Care Equipment and Furniture

The basic durable medical equipment (DME) you may need to assist your loved one safely includes items such as a walker or cane, raised toilet seat (with or without arm rests), a bathtub seat, a bedside commode, a wheelchair, and a hospital bed.

FACT

If your parent has been in the hospital, the discharge planner or case manager may have asked you about what DME you have and arranged for items to be sent to your home or taken with you upon discharge. If you're having home-health care, the nurse or therapist can assist you in obtaining this equipment. You can also call a DME provider yourself.

Walkers, canes, raised toilet seats, commodes, and bathtub seats are purchase items by virtue of the personal nature; they are not rentable from durable medical equipment companies. They can be purchased from DME companies as well as through catalogs and drug-store chains. Medicare may reimburse for some of these, but they have restrictions. Your DME provider can advise you, as the rules change frequently. Usually you get one in a lifetime for seniors. Younger disabled persons on Medicare may qualify for more than one depending on their age. This is why it is important to find space to store the items if they are no longer presently needed but might be needed again.

The purpose of durable medical equipment is to provide safe assistance where needed, not only to the patient, but to the caregiver as well. These items should be used only as directed. Be sure you understand all directions before the delivery person leaves; if you have questions or the equipment malfunctions, call the DME company immediately.

Walkers and Canes

Walkers come in two basic styles: one that roles or wheels and one that has to be picked up and set down with each step. They are named accordingly—wheeled walker or pick-up walker. Some people slide the pick-up walker as opposed to picking it up and setting it down. Pick-up walkers are often seen with tennis-ball covers on each of their four tips. This helps give them a little more stability but also makes them slide easier. Walkers can be outfitted with trays, baskets, or bags to help carry items.

Canes can be single-point, tripod, or quad canes. The multipoint canes have a single shaft leading down to either 4' or 3' and extending from the shaft 6"–8" above the ground. These multipoint canes are adjustable in height, offer more stability, and are a step down from a walker. This means that either the person is becoming weaker but has not progressed to the point of needing more stability of a walker, or she has significantly improved in her rehabilitation to leave the walker behind and progress to a cane. Single-point canes come in various lengths and can be sawn off to be made shorter. A physical therapist or DME specialist should adjust the cane to the proper height for greatest safety and effective function.

Toilet and Bathtub Seats

There are several types of raised toilet seats and they come in a variety of heights. Some clip on to the toilet with the regular toilet seat in the upright position. These can be removed and replaced with each use so others don't have to use the raised seat. Others are more permanent, as they are attached to the seat-bolt area. Those with arm rests may or may not have legs as well and rest on top of the toilet. For most purposes, the toilet seat must be removed.

Bathtub seats or benches come in a few sizes and configurations as well. There are smaller, rectangular ones that fit inside the tub and triangular-shaped chairs that fit in the corner of a tub or stand-up shower. There are also larger ones that are set both outside and inside the tub, so the person can sit down or transfer from a wheelchair and then slide over into the tub. She would slide back over to get out and stand or transfer back to the wheelchair.

These seats and benches are made from thick molded plastic and have holes to allow water to flow through. The legs are heavy-duty aluminum and have pushbutton adjustments to raise or lower the seat.

Most often raised toilet seats are used for persons who have difficulty sitting on or rising from a standard-height toilet. They might also be transferring from a wheelchair and require a higher toilet. Handicap stalls in public restrooms often have a taller toilet to aide wheelchair patrons in transferring to and from the toilet. People who have had hip-replacement surgeries also usually require a raised toilet seat.

A bedside commode is a portable toilet that looks somewhat like an armchair and has a bucket underneath that slides in and out for emptying. The purpose is to set it near the bedside so your parent does not have to travel to the bathroom. This can be especially useful at night or if he is ill. With the bucket removed, most bedside commodes will sit on top of a toilet to provide a raised toilet seat and armrests. It is advised to put about 1" of water in the bucket so that solid matter doesn't stick and to help dilute urine. There are a number of odor-reducing products your DME provider can recommend; a little baking soda in the bucket can work quite well.

Wheelchairs

Wheelchairs can be standard, manual-push type or they may be electric and run off a battery that looks like your car battery. They should be sized to the person by height and weight. If the person sits in one for long periods of time, she should have a cushion that is specifically designed to reduce pressure and help prevent pressure sores. Wheelchairs can be rented for short-term use or purchased if the need is long term. Medicare, Medicaid, and private insurances often cover rental or purchase fees for wheelchairs, but there are many rules and regulations. Diagnosis and prognosis are important factors in determining reimbursement issues. Work with your DME provider to understand what your best options are.

ALERT!

Medicare is notorious for changing the rules about DME. Of course, these changes are usually dependent on rules and funding issues set by Congress in the annual budget and other legislation. Pay close attention to how your legislators vote on the issues that affect Medicare, Social Security, and other funding regarding the elder population. Listen to candidates' platforms on eldercare and health-care issues. This now directly affects you and your family. Make your vote count and your voice heard.

Hospital Beds

Hospital beds can be rented or purchased as well; again, reimbursement is tied into diagnosis and prognosis issues and your DME provider can best advise you. In general, a manual crank-type bed is the basic version and usually the one that will have the greatest reimbursement. Electric beds are more costly, but the costs should be considered carefully in terms of the type of care your parent needs.

If your parent is bedbound or requires a lot of assistance while in bed, your body is best protected by a bed that moves up and down easily so you are not bending or providing assistance at a level that places additional strain on your back.

Who Pays for This?

Surprisingly, the vast majority facing this situation for the first time have the notion that Medicare will pay for all services needed, and if not, the supplemental policy will cover it. It can be quite a rude awakening to discover custodial care is not covered. This is an out-of-pocket expense and can be quite costly.

While skilled care may be covered, in most instances this is intermittent and only for infrequent visits. Not even all long-term-care policies will cover all forms of custodial care. If they do, they will most likely have financial limits that may not cover all expenses.

FACT

National averages for custodial care are staggering and increasing at a constant rate. A skilled nursing facility can cost an average of $6,200 per month. An assisted-living facility runs about $3,000 per month for the basic housing fee. Assistance costs are added on to this. For instance, if your parent needs assistance with bathing, medication dispensing, special meals, or getting to and from the central dining area, you'll pay for this.

It is also important to understand that they have to be able to walk to live in most of these facilities. A walker or cane is okay, and you can usually pay for someone to walk with them, but they can't be in a wheelchair even if they can transfer themselves. If they are confined to their bed or room or need a wheelchair except for a very short term, they'll have to be moved to a skilled nursing facility.

The national average fee for a private certified nurse's aide or home-health aide is $19 per hour. A licensed practical nurse can run you about $32 per hour, and if you need a registered nurse, be prepared to pay about $50 per hour.

The cost of long-term-care policies can be frightening, but when you consider what they will cover and how much out-of-pocket expenses can quickly add up to, they can be a necessity. The younger you are when you purchase a policy, the less expensive it will be.

CHAPTER 12

How to Avoid Scams

You may be quite surprised to learn that your parents, who have warned you about scams and not talking to strangers all of your life, are suddenly victims of schemers themselves. Sometimes it's because they have become forgetful or have some form of dementia, and sometimes it's out of the genuine goodness of their heart that they have fallen prey to the latest ploy to steal money from the elderly.

"You've Won a Million Dollars"

Even the most highly educated have been known to fall for one of the best advertising gimmicks from the big magazine-subscription agencies. No purchase is necessary; simply return the multitude of documents with the stamps you have to hunt for placed in specific locations. The hope is that you'll be tempted to purchase at least one of the special rates for a subscription as you look for all the special stamps. Even though there is no purchase needed, they hope you'll feel you have better odds of winning if you do purchase at least one subscription.

FACT

The saddest part of all with this type of contest is that so many people, especially the elderly on fixed incomes, have fallen for the fact that it says in huge print that they have already won. Believing this to be true, many have been known to run up tremendous credit card or other debt thinking they'll soon have the funds to cover these purchases, only to find they have been fooled.

While there is nothing wrong with spending the time to hunt for all of those specific stamps to place on the entry forms, and even ordering magazines they can afford in hopes of being picked as the next winner, the elderly need to understand the odds are not in their favor, and no, they have not already won.

Next time those contests arrive in your mail, be sure to check up on your parents and in-laws; don't assume they won't get caught up in the hype. Remind them that there is no easy way to get rich, and that because they are older they are going to be sought out by scammers.

Phone Scams and Door-to-Door Scams

These can be some of the most dangerous scams because the con artists are very good at this and their edge is in catching people off guard. They can sweet talk the elderly right out of their Social Security numbers, date of birth, and credit card numbers, and before they even realize what they've given out, the scam artist has stolen their identity and spent $5,000 on their credit card.

It's easy to say just don't open the door to any strangers or don't give out information over the phone, but these scammers are clever. They can claim to be your bank, your credit card company, or even a utility company. There is usually some problem with your account or perhaps they're trying to track down some fraudulent activity. That seems legitimate, so why not give them the information they need?

Even just providing a partial number can be dangerous. A recent scam involved the caller claiming to be from a utility company who is going to shut off your service for nonpayment. That situation sets up some panic, to say the least. Now he needs you to verify the last four numbers of a Social Security number so he can access the full account. This seems to be a normal procedure, so you oblige. Then he wants to verify that the first five numbers are "such and such"; well of course they're not, and before you realize what you've done, you've corrected him. With the correct number, he sees your account is not in trouble and he's so sorry to have bothered you. In reality, you just handed this thief your identity.

ALERT!

Never give out your numbers. If there is an issue, get the caller's name or other identifying information and call the company back yourself. Don't rely on any number the caller gives you, as this may be a set up as well. Find the number yourself and call and talk to a customer service supervisor.

Door-to-door scams can be easily avoided by not answering your door to strangers. This was always a hard-and-fast rule your parents told you growing up; now it's a rule for them to follow as well. But if they do, or happen to be outside and can't avoid the sales pitch, they have to firmly say, "Thank you, I'm not interested."

A screen or storm door is helpful to keep the person from sticking his foot in the way so your parent can't close the door. A screen door can also make it more difficult to see directly into the home.

Watch your neighborhood newspaper for news about door-to-door scams in your community. Read the newsletters your city or county government sends out—they usually have alerts about the latest scams in your community as well.

Many communities require any door-to-door salespersons to obtain a permit from the city or county before campaigning. They are required to show you this permit. Ask to see it. If they don't have one, close the door. If they have one, be sure it has your city or county name on it and a current date. Check with your city or county office to see what this type of permit looks like.

A common scam is for two people to come to the door together, and after a moment or so, one asks if he could use the telephone or bathroom. It's usually an urgent need. The first person distracts the homeowner while the other person quickly rifles through personal belongings, drawers, purses, and billfolds. They are usually long gone before any missing money, jewelry, or valuables are noted. Hopefully, the Social Security card wasn't in the wallet next to the credit cards!

Tell your parents and in-laws never let anyone in their home. They will beg or try to intimidate them, but your parents have to be strong and firm. If the person really needs to use a phone, they can close the door, go get the phone, and bring it to them to use outside or direct them to a nearby public place for a restroom stop.

You have to be firm with your parents and remind them they need to be suspicious and not overly trusting of people. It's not easy to say no to someone, especially if she seems to need help, but they have to protect themselves.

E-mail Scams

When you worked so hard to teach your technophobic parents to use e-mail so they can keep in touch and receive pictures, you may not have thought about the spam they'll be getting eventually. Can you just picture their faces when they get their first e-mail about how to enlarge or enhance some part of their body? It's bound to happen, so you'd better warn them. No matter how many filters you set up, some spam or scams are bound to get through.

Can you even count the number of times you've received an e-mail offering you a unique opportunity to assist someone from a remote part of the world in settling an estate for a late husband or other relative whom they can't seem to claim as their own for various reasons? If you would just respond to this e-mail and agree to pose as some long-lost relative you could possibly receive a large sum of money for your help.

Of course, there are strings. They need your bank account number to transfer the money to or some earnest money from you to help pay the fees to get this money, or there is some other elaborate scheme to separate you from your money or to steal your identity.

There are also any number of other e-mail schemes designed to obtain personal information such as bank account numbers, PIN numbers, passwords, credit card numbers, Social Security numbers, or any combination of these in order to access accounts or identity.

Many of theses scams appear to be very real. They use logos from legitimate banks, credit card companies, and other online financial or retail services; right down to the tiniest details, they look real and legitimate. Most, however, don't address you by name, or the name under which you might actually have an account. That is usually the first clue that they are fakes.

The next most obvious clue is that while you may have an account with the company they claim to be, you have never given them this particular e-mail address. For that reason alone, you should have only one e-mail address that you provide to businesses, financial services, and credit card accounts. This makes it easier to determine these e-mails are phishing for your information.

Phishing e-mails are usually requests for updated information on your account. They may claim your account has been suspended for some reason or will be soon if you don't login and update your information. Of course, the information they ask for includes such things as account numbers, passwords, PIN numbers, or other identifying information.

Always exercise caution when using the Internet to conduct financial transactions. Most legitimate banks and retailers have a customer service area set up to handle inquiries about phishing scams. They may have an e-mail address to forward any suspected phishing e-mails to, or other instructions for determining how to distinguish legitimate e-mails and websites. When in doubt, contact the corporation by phone or letter.

QUESTION?

What is "phishing"?
Phishing refers to a scam seeking (fishing for) information from the reader. The scammer has set up an authentic-looking website that appears to represent a real corporation or financial institution. The purpose is to get the reader to input personal information such as PIN numbers, passwords, or account numbers into a nonencrypted system in an effort to steal this information

While many legitimate financial and retail operations utilize the Internet safely and securely every day, there are breeches of security from time to time. There are precautions to take, and you must remind your parents to be wary and scrutinize.

Rumors, Urban Legends, and Hoaxes

In addition to the phishing scams, there are a collection of e-mails that can ruin your parents' computer. Despite your best efforts at virus and spyware software solutions, something is bound to get through and pique their curiosity. You may never be able to fully explain a computer virus to your parents, so just remind them never to open an attachment or an e-mail from someone they don't know.

How do you know what is real and what is a hoax? There are a couple of websites devoted entirely to checking out the latest in a never-ending supply of e-mails purporting to help causes, cure diseases, and impart essential information about frauds and scams. Next time you get one of these e-mails, check to see if it has been evaluated by one of these sources before you send it on to everyone in your e-mail address book. There are a number of legitimate e-mails worth forwarding, but do a bit of research before your best friend sends it right back to you with a big "HOAX" sign attached to it.

The HOAX Sites

Snopes.com began in 1995 and is operated by Barbara and David P. Mikkelson. They have collected a huge amount of information about all sorts of folklore, urban legends, hoaxes, rumors, and old wives' tales. They have meticulously categorized the information and post links in the sidebar to the most popular of the latest stories circulating the Internet. Check to see if your e-mail topic is there.

The U.S. Department of Energy operates Hoaxbusters.com as part of the CIAC (the computer incident advisory capability). This website also categorizes information about the latest e-mail chain letters and stories circulating. The DOE advises everyone to refrain from perpetuating the spread of these chain letters. If an e-mail is being sent to you so you can send it along to "everyone you know," it is most likely a chain letter, and although the information may be true and valuable, in most instances it is a hoax, urban legend, or old wives' tale. The information can be checked at their website.

Financial Precautions

At some point, most elderly people will panic to some degree about living on a fixed income or the fact that their life savings are slowly dwindling. The reality of the fact that they are no longer earning an income and building up this account begins to set in and frightens them. This makes them vulnerable to any number of get-rich schemes and scams.

Many financial institutions have specialists who oversee and help manage accounts for their customers. These accounts may require a significant balance, or the service may be available to all bank customers. If a significant balance is not required, an account can be set up that requires two signatures on all checks; one of them has to be yours or another family member, not just both of your parents.

It is also advisable to consider having an account in which only a small balance is maintained. This would be the account from which household bills are paid and purchases made. The majority of funds are kept in a separate account and transferred as needed. This way, if a checkbook is stolen or debit card purchases are made from nonsecure transactions, only a small amount of money is at risk.

QUESTION?

How do you protect them from these scams?
Some people are naturally much more vulnerable to being swindled than others, but don't count anyone out. One way to help protect your loved ones from being scammed is to have parameters set on their financial accounts so withdrawals over a certain amount need approval. This can be an approval from the bank manger or other financial officer, or by a designated family member. This approval can be cumbersome in times of true need, but it can mean the difference between holding onto and throwing away a lifetime of savings.

Should your parents be persuaded to make donations or invest money, they can't write checks for huge amounts of their savings. It makes it easier for them to honestly tell someone they don't have immediate access to that amount of money, and it serves to remind them they can't spend or invest large amounts of money without approval. If someone is trying to swindle them, they may think twice before having to justify their sale to a financial advisor.

If your parents or in-laws have a caregiver who may be tempted to spend their funds, this also helps control the amount of money that could be misused. Credit cards with lower fixed limits can also be helpful to prohibit extravagant expenses by your loved ones as well as any others who might exploit them.

This may be a very sensitive issue to approach with your parents, but reminding them these funds are not limitless and must be protected, as well as giving them the control to choose who gives approval, may help ease the situation. If there is any question of mental stability or dementia, access to funds must be controlled.

Keeping Up to Date on the Newest Scams

Staying one step ahead of your children has undoubtedly presented a number of challenges. Similarly, staying ahead of those who wish to prey on the elderly is a big job.

For many people, as they age, they become more gregarious and trusting; they want to help everyone and leave behind a legacy of caring and thoughtfulness. That's fine, as long as it doesn't involve being victimized.

FACT

Developing an eye and ear for the latest scams can require some effort, but once you begin, you'll find many sources of valuable information. In fact, you may suddenly become overwhelmed by the number of scams to watch out for.

The nightly news often has a segment devoted to some new scheme to make money or that preys on some element of society, and watch for notices at the senior center. Your local and even throwaway newspapers usually have a story about someone in the community being victimized recently or door-to-door schemes being reported. Larger schemes such as financial scams are usually well covered in business magazines and on national news programs. Sometimes, even those chain-letter e-mails may alert you to something you need to consider.

Remind your parents and in-laws to stop and think carefully before making promises and spending large sums of money. Encourage them not to open the door to strangers and screen phone calls if necessary to avoid telephone scams. Remind them if it seems too good to be true, it is. Sign them up for the Do Not Call Registry so they will be alert to the fact that any unsolicited phone calls could be a possible scam.

CHAPTER 13

Medications and Treatments

Medications and treatments are just another of the many issues you will eventually face in the course of caring for your elderly parents or in-laws. Remember that the goal is to keep them as independent as possible for as long as possible. Medication and treatments can present a challenge, but they are not a roadblock. In fact, managing medications can be something they can do for themselves easier than many other self-care or household tasks. Again, remember that the more you expect them to do for themselves the less likely they will be to rely on you.

How to Set Up and Monitor a Med Box

Medication boxes come in many sizes and varieties and are available from most pharmacies. Sometimes you can acquire them for free from pharmaceutical manufacturers or other health-care vendors. You may be able to get one from your PCP.

They are plastic boxes with dividers to delineate the different days of the week. Each section has a snap-down lid to hold in the medications and keep them dry. Some have sections for A.M. and P.M. doses for each day; some have four sections named breakfast, lunch, dinner, and bedtime. Some have seven daily sets of compartments, and some may have enough to cover a month at a time.

You could also use four different seven-day boxes and use materials such as nail polish, acrylic paints, or markers to label them for four weeks of the month. If your parent has medication times that don't jive with the ones on the boxes, you can use some masking or adhesive tape to make changes and mark the appropriate times. You could also use a combination of different boxes to meet various needs. If, for example, one medication is prescribed every six hours and all others are either morning, bedtime, or with meals, you could use one med box with four compartments each day to set up the every-six-hours medication and another for all of the other times.

Small paper cups can be labeled and utilized in the same manner as a med box, but cups don't protect the medications from spilling or from the elements the way the snap-down lids do.

Whatever your choice, make sure to label them clearly and use color codes if need be; make sure your parent understands your setup. Place all of the medications to be taken at the same time together in each compartment. Be sure to keep all medications and med boxes out of the reach of small children and anyone who is confused or disoriented. Med boxes are not childproof!

For example, Mom takes a heart medication, blood-pressure medication, and thyroid medication each morning. The heart medication is a small white pill, the blood-pressure medication is a large white pill, and the thyroid is a small pink pill. One of each of these is put into the A.M. section of the A.M./P.M. med box. In the notebook under A.M., there are three pictures—one of each of the A.M. medications with the name and dose on the index card in the picture. At dinnertime, Mom takes a blood thinner. This is a small blue pill. In the notebook is a picture of the blood thinner with the name and dose on the index card.

If Mom dropped the med box, she could look at the pictures and determine which pills go back into which compartments. This could buy you a little time before you'd need to go by and make sure they are all back in place. If you have an identical notebook, you could review it with her more comfortably over the phone.

A good way to help you and your parents ensure they are getting the correct medications, or in case they drop the med box or otherwise mix up the pills, is to take a photograph of each medication. In the photograph, use an index card to write the name and dose of the medicine on each. Then using a small notebook, group the medications together by time or day of the week.

Over the phone, you can check in and have your parents or in-laws tell you which compartment they opened today and how many are left unopened. When you visit periodically to refill the med box, you can see whether all medications have been taken to date and whether any are still in their compartments. This will help you get an idea of whether or not this system works. You might need to enlist the help of a neighbor or someone else to check more frequently to see that medications are being taken.

You may have to experiment with different med boxes to find one that works well for your situation. In the event that you don't have or can't use a med box, you can utilize the pill bottles themselves. A color-coded system could be used to tell which pills to take when. Make sure to color the lid as well as the bottle so they don't put the wrong lid on a bottle and get them all mixed up. You should write the medication's name on the lid as well.

Other systems include placing the morning medications in a certain location, such as next to the coffee pot, and the evening medications somewhere else, such as on the bedside table. Have them turn the bottle upside down when they've taken the medication and then turn it right-side up when they go to bed.

Daily Reminders

A series of daily routines can be set up to remind your parents to take their medications. It's not a good idea to store medications in the bathroom due to the moisture buildup, but getting in the habit of taking medications when brushing your teeth is a good habit to instill.

Turning the bottle one way or another can be a reminder and ensure whether they've taken a dose or not. Setting the pills out with morning or other meal dishes is a good reminder as well.

FACT

Double checks can be done by making tick marks on the calendar, first when you set the pills out, then making an X out of it when the pills have been taken. This is also a good way of keeping track of what day it is and any other appointments or events that take place that day. It helps older people maintain their memory when they frequently make note of the day and date.

You, or even a family member who lives some distance away, can make daily phone calls to remind Dad to take his pills and have him do it while he's on the phone with you. This can also be a good double-check system. If you spoke, then the medication must have been taken. Two heads are better than one if there is doubt.

Daily phone calls or even an e-mail—as long as you receive a response back—can be used to ensure other treatments or procedures are accomplished. Again, utilizing other family members to help share in the responsibility can be very helpful. If Mom is supposed to change her pain patch every three days and your sister can make that phone call, it can relieve you of one more responsibility. It gets your sister involved and helps keep Mom independent.

Some pharmacies now color-code prescription bottles or caps so each individual's medications can be easily distinguished (unless your parent is colorblind). For example, Mom's pills all have red caps and Dad's pills all have blue caps.

You should also request nonchildproof caps; childproof caps can be very difficult for older persons to open, and consequently they often leave the caps off or loose, which may interfere with the effectiveness or shelf life of the medication. If small children are in the home, these medications should be secured in a locked room or cabinet.

Use One Pharmacy

The pharmacist is a major player on the health-care team. By using one pharmacy, you maintain the integrity of the continuity of care. The pharmacy has complete records of all of the prescription medications being taken and a list of all allergies. The pharmacist is expected to review these records each time a new medication is prescribed or one is refilled.

In the event that you must use a different pharmacy, it would be helpful to provide it with a list of allergies and other medications your parent or in-law is taking. The pharmacist is expected to provide counsel when a new medication is dispensed. This would be a good time to hand him the list of other medications to ensure there aren't contraindications.

The pharmacist reviews the prescription for accuracy and compares this prescription to the other medications in the patient's profile. Although you may see the technician check to see that a medication is in stock when you submit a new prescription, a lot more is involved than just typing and slapping on the label. By utilizing one pharmacy, you increase the probability that duplications and contraindications are caught and questioned before a medication is dispensed.

Mail-order pharmacies can provide cost savings, and many of the new Medicare Part D plans encourage or require the use of mail-order pharmacies and ninety-day supplies of medications. These pharmacies have the same responsibilities to oversee your medication profile. When using a mail-order pharmacy, it is a good idea to use a partner retail pharmacy whenever possible for any new prescriptions that can't wait for mail-order delivery.

Mail-order prescriptions can be managed by phone or over the Internet, and many accounts can be set up to provide e-mail refill reminders. With mail-order prescriptions, refills need to be ordered in advance to allow for postal delivery. Remember to consider postal holidays, weekends, and peak mailing periods, such as during the month of December, that can cause delays.

Many of these pharmacies can arrange to provide emergency supplies of medications from a local retail pharmacy in the event a package is lost or the medication gets damaged, or even for times when you need a supply earlier because of travel plans. Don't hesitate to call the mail-order pharmacy should any of these situations arise. Again, managing mail-order prescriptions could be a task that is delegated to another family member.

The pharmacist can also be a good resource if you have questions about medications and their actions or reactions. If you need assistance with an over-the-counter medication, the pharmacist should be able to assist you as well. If he has a list of all of the medications your parent or in-law takes, he can provide a more informed suggestion or answer.

If your elders are having difficulty swallowing a medication, the pharmacist can offer alternatives. Sometimes a medication can be crushed and given in a small spoonful of applesauce, peanut butter, or Jell-O; other times, a medication should not be crushed or broken. Ask the pharmacist before you do this. Sometimes there is a liquid alternative, or a compounding pharmacy may be able to formulate a suppository form. Liquid medications can be flavored to make them less offensive. Make your pharmacist your new best friend if your parents or in-laws have medication issues.

Transportation Issues for Appointments and Treatments

Mom has a chronic wound, Dad has to get dialysis three times a week, and you have a full-time job. Your great-aunt lives with your parents and she has to get chemotherapy daily for the next few weeks. Your children have baseball practice or games at least three times a week. Your parents should not be driving, and especially not after a medical treatment. Yikes! What are you going to do?

FACT

Wound-care treatment centers and chemotherapy centers may also have arrangements with transportation sources or can provide you with resources to contact. The local chapter of the American Cancer Society may run volunteer transportation services.

Organization is the key to success in this situation. There are many possible solutions, if even on a temporary or part-time basis. Most communities run a Dial-a-Ride-type program that offers door-to-door transportation within your community to medical facilities, shopping, and senior centers. Your local senior center or area on aging agency will have information on transportation services. Sometimes the transportation can be set up in advance and other times it has to be done on a per-ride situation. The cost is about $1–$3 each way, and the van may be picking up several riders at a time. Call early to ensure you get to the appointment on time.

Medical transportation services can be arranged for those who need a wheelchair or assistance getting into and out of a specific medical office or treatment center. Most treatment centers can provide you with a list of all possible sources of transportation.

Dialysis centers often have their own transportation issues covered either through volunteers or specific arrangements with systems such as Dial-a-Ride. Dialysis centers have medical social workers on staff to assist patients and families with issues surrounding dialysis. Ask to speak with the social worker and get referrals for community resources to assist you. Taxis and bus services should be considered, as well as hiring a private driver. A neighbor, friend, or even a local college student may be willing to take on the responsibility for a set fee. Your local senior center may also have a list of volunteers willing to help with transportation or those willing to drive for nominal fees.

Caregiver Training

When it comes time to hire a caregiver or to train a family member to assist in the basic care of your parents or in-laws, whether or not they have professional nursing or other caregiver training, you will need to devote some time and attention to training them to care for your elders.

If your parents or in-laws have an agenda of their own regarding their care, you may have all of the best intentions and plans and still fail. Accepting the fact that they need some assistance may be the furthest thing from their minds despite the fact that they are no longer capable of living alone or without some sort of daily assistance. Getting them to accept help may be next to impossible; their agenda may be to live with you or only have you provide care for them. To these ends, they may sabotage all of your best efforts.

QUESTION?

How do you make the best of this situation?
First, you need to pay close attention to the things you learned from your parents in Chapter 2 about their wishes, current habits, and how they feel about losing their independence. Add to this a list of likes and dislikes and top it off with pet peeves.

They may not even consciously realize they have an agenda or are resistant to accepting help. Even if they are willing to accept help, they may have some very different ideas about the type of help they want or are willing to accept. It is important to discuss this openly and as honestly as possible. It may be that you will have to introduce a caregiver in very small steps. Most people, however needy they may be, don't want a stranger in their home. Aside from fears that they may be taken advantage of or have things stolen, there is also the natural social grace of feeling they must entertain the person. If they are having difficulty taking care of themselves, they certainly don't feel up to entertaining someone else. Home health-care nurses and other home-health professionals meet this form of resistance on a regular basis; it becomes an issue of convincing the patient that this is a professional visit to assist with the patient's care because she isn't feeling her best.

Any caregiver is going to need specific training in how to care for your parents or in-laws. If the caregivers come from an agency, there will be restrictions on what they can and cannot do according to their scope of practice. To dispense medications, for instance, you have to hire an LPN or RN if using an agency. If you are hiring privately, you can train anyone in how to dispense medications specifically to your loved ones. If the medications are complicated or require some form of judgment such as how much pain medication to dispense at one time, you may want to hire someone with nursing experience.

Similarly, caregivers from an agency cannot perform any form of wound care or similar procedures unless they are an LPN or RN. However, again, hiring privately allows you or the home-health nurse to instruct the new caregiver in how to perform the procedure.

You should also demonstrate and have the caregiver demonstrate back any specific care instructions you provide. If your parent needs assistance in transferring in and out of the bed, bathtub, or shower, or on and off the toilet, you should demonstrate and have them show you how she will do this. Make sure you have been instructed in proper body mechanics and that the caregiver understands these principles as well. A back injury is preventable, and you don't need a disabled caregiver!

Discuss your expectations openly and all instructions for care. Ask questions to ensure the caregiver understands the expectations the time schedule, and pay. Leave written instructions in a notebook for reinforcement and reference. You might use a notebook for communication purposes— for you to leave new information or instructions and for the caregiver to leave you notes as well. Explain the way your parents expects things to be done and what times they want such things as meals and bathing. Is there a certain way to do the laundry? Do towels get folded into quarters or thirds? Are there specific recipes your parents like? What about TV programs they watch without interruptions?

Have a backup plan. Anticipate problems and be prepared for what to do if and when the caregiver doesn't show up or needs a day off without any warning. Try to cover all of the special needs and wants and pet peeves to avoid issues. Make sure the caregiver gets the best chance possible.

CHAPTER 14

In Case of Emergency

Emergencies come in all shapes and sizes. They can be large-scale natural disasters such as earthquakes, fires, floods, tornadoes, and hurricanes or a smaller-scale situation such as a heat wave, sever cold snap, or power outage. They can also be personal emergencies such as a fall, a heart attack, or a stroke. The one thing these all have in common is that they don't give much, if any, warning, and they can all play havoc with daily routines and schedules.

Making and Maintaining an Emergency Kit

Emergencies, at the very least, are always an inconvenience. Being prepared for the most common types of emergencies in your area can go a long way in easing the effects of the emergency. There are many factors to consider in making preparations for emergencies.

FACT

In the aftermath of Hurricane Katrina, thousands of people suffered and some died needlessly because of the lack of access to medical records. Too many people didn't have their medications with them and did not know the names or doses of their medications. Too many didn't even know their medical conditions or history and precious time was lost performing tests and assessments before treatments could begin.

You can go overboard and become completely neurotic trying to anticipate all of the kinds of emergencies and natural disasters that might affect your parents or in-laws, but it is important to help them be prepared with at least the very basics to ride out an emergency for a few days if necessary.

Food, water, and at least a three-day supply of all medications are basic life-sustaining items. These need to be kept in a watertight container such as a five-gallon bucket with a lid in an easily accessible area of the home. All items must be rotated periodically to ensure they have not expired or spoiled. A smaller version of this emergency kit should be kept in the car if they still drive.

In addition, there should be a list of medications along with prescriptions numbers and pharmacy information. A brief medical history and contact information for all health-care practitioners as well as contact information for family members should also be listed. These items can be laminated and should be stored in a clear-plastic zip-lock bag. The bag should be taped to the lid of the bucket or other watertight container.

The emergency bucket should also contain a basic first-aid kit with, at the least:

- Bottle of nonprescription pain reliever such as aspirin, ibuprofen, or Tylenol
- Bottle of water
- Several sizes of bandages
- Antibiotic ointment
- Gauze pads and tape
- Gloves

These items should be rotated to ensure freshness as well, and don't get in the habit of using this kit without replenishing it immediately.

Food should include easy-to-open cans or packages of nonperishable items such as tuna, fruits, and vegetables. These can be eaten out of the container; they don't require cooking. Again, they should be rotated periodically to prevent spoilage. Take into consideration special dietary needs, but remember in an emergency supplies will be limited and sugar or salt may not be the worst enemy. Water is essential and there should be a three-day supply per person. Don't forget water and some pet food for any animals they have.

Emergency blankets such as the small foil type found in camping stores should be in the kit. There should be at least one for each person. These were designed for use in space, and although they are quite thin, they will hold in body temperature and keep you warm.

The kit should include a small radio and extra batteries as well as at least one flashlight and extra batteries. Again, batteries don't keep forever; they should be rotated periodically and not borrowed without being replaced immediately. Test these items periodically to make sure they are in good working order.

A knit cap for each person would be advisable, as body heat is lost through the top of the head, and covering it will help to keep a person warm. Gloves would be another good addition if there is room.

Access to Medical Information

Progress is being made toward standardizing and implementing electronic medical records, but presently there is no system in place to ensure access to your medical records or history. One of the biggest blocks to establishing this type of system is ensuring that privacy is maintained.

Again, Hurricane Katrina clearly illustrated the ramifications of not having immediate access to medical and pharmacy records and the need for electronic storage. Several hospitals were severely damaged by the storm and remain closed today. Typically, paper medical records are stored in the basement, where the worst of the flooding took place, and many of these records were lost.

ALERT!

In addition to keeping an up-to-date, brief medical history in an emergency kit, it is advisable to keep medical records for all family members in an off-site place such as a safe deposit box, or send copies to out-of-town relatives to store. Medical record information can be kept updated on a computer and stored on CDs. It can also be saved and e-mailed to you at a designated address accessible from any computer.

This information should include all contact information for health-care practitioners, medications, and prescription information, as well as information such as diagnoses, medical tests and results, medication history, allergies, surgeries, and injuries such as broken bones. All entries should include dates. This should be updated periodically and again e-mailed and or a new CD written. (See Appendix C for suggested formats.)

You can request copies of the results from medical tests from your health-care practitioner and scan them so you can include them in your own electronic records and place the physical copies in a file in the safe deposit box or with your designated out-of-town relatives.

There are a few companies, and more will no doubt be created, that provide services or software for setting up your own electronic medical records. Some offer you the option of storing the information by uploading it to them over the Internet or sending a CD to them.

Some insurance companies offer you an option of entering information on their websites in your own personal portals. They may also add information to this file as information is obtained through medical expenditures such as lab work, medications, and hospitalizations. There are advantages and disadvantages to storing info on such websites. Questions about privacy arise, such as whether this information is then available to the employer who pays for a portion of the medical insurance; pre-existing illnesses may be disclosed or misinterpreted. The U.S. Congress is still debating issues of electronic medical records and standards for formatting as well as privacy issues.

Power Outages and Oxygen or Other Care Issues

Aside from major natural disasters, storms, excessive heat, and physical interference such as a car hitting a power pole can cause power dips and outages. These can be lengthy, and are always sudden and usually unexpected. At the very least they are an inconvenient annoyance. For some they can present life-threatening circumstances. For instance, some oxygen systems are dependent on electrical power to generate the oxygen.

FACT

Backup generators are required for anyone on a ventilator. It is essential that all persons involved in the care of anyone on a ventilator be trained in how to switch the system over. The generator needs to be appropriately housed in an accessible area. In the event of a storm or other predictable event that could cause a power outage, preparations should be made to get to the generator quickly.

Ventilators require electrical power or a generator backup to continue functioning. Those who are totally dependent on a ventilator can be in serious trouble in a power outage. Ventilators are devices that assist a person to breathe or actually breathe for the person by forcing air in and out of the lungs mechanically. Typically, a person who is paralyzed from the neck or chest down requires some form of ventilator assistance.

Generators run on gasoline or other fossil fuel and cannot be placed inside the house due to exhaust fumes. In preparing for the event of power outages due to storms, placement and access should be an important consideration.

Anyone using oxygen that requires electricity to make it should have a backup tank of oxygen in case of a power outage. Again, anyone involved in the care of this person should know how to use the oxygen equipment and switch over to a tank. Oxygen is dangerous, but when handled correctly it can be safe to use.

Oxygen should not be used near an open flame. In other words, while cooking over a gas stove, the oxygen should be turned off and the tubing removed from the person. Obviously, there should be no smoking by anyone in a house where oxygen is in use. Many times these rules are ignored. It should be noted that it's not just the person using the oxygen who is in danger; anyone inside that home at the time of the misuse is in danger of being injured by an explosion or fire. And anyone or any building nearby is in danger as well. This can be particularly dangerous to other residents in an apartment building. Oxygen must be used carefully and responsibly.

Other Power Considerations

Power outages can affect many other aspects of care, such as electric beds. Most of these have a crank system for emergency use. Many low air-loss mattresses or other air-mattress toppers use an electrical pump for continuous airflow. In the event of a power outage, there are procedures to follow to shut off the pumps and keep the mattresses inflated. Some have built-in battery backup systems. All caregivers should know how to perform these procedures. Routine, surprise emergency drills should be implemented, especially when care is being provided to someone dependent on electrical systems for life support, such as a ventilator.

Notify Utility Companies

It is also imperative to notify utility companies when such medical devices are in use. The utility company may offer a discounted rate for the electricity due to medical needs. They will also keep the residence on a priority list to restore power first. Should the outage be due to a brown-out or flex-power situation because of an overload of the entire grid from excessive usage, the utility company may be able to keep power on at that residence. This type of grid overload is most often due to times of extreme heat or cold, which causes a continuous use of excessive power to run air-conditioning or heating systems.

Suction equipment, IV pumps, and a number of other medical devices that can be used in a home setting may require electricity. Most have battery backup systems, but once again, all caregivers should be familiar with this switching procedure and any associated safety procedures.

Similarly, if the house is heated with gas, in times of extreme cold, if the utility company is aware of medical needs, they will list this residence as a high priority for consumption and restore any loss of access as soon as possible. Discount rates for gas usage may also be considered due to special needs.

Disaster Planning and Communication Issues

In addition to an emergency kit, medical records access, and considerations for power outages, disaster planning can include other factors as well. Your parents and in-laws probably don't move quickly; they may need an assistive device such as a cane or walker. They may not hear well or see well either and may need assistive devices such as glasses, dentures, and hearing aids.

In the event that they need to evacuate or move to another area of the house quickly, these factors may need to be considered:

- Are all of these items (glasses, hearing aids, canes, walkers) nearby and easily accessible?
- Do they need assistance from someone to get up out of bed or a chair? Or to walk with them?
- Will they hear you if you have to call out for them to get up?

Again, these may be things to consider for a monthly surprise emergency drill.

Additionally, other items to consider include where important papers are stored. Are they easily accessible? Should they be stored somewhere else or at least copies made and stored offsite? What personal items such as photographs or other mementoes should be grabbed in an evacuation? Are there pets to assist with? Do they have carriers?

Communication Issues

Lines of communication need to be considered well in advance of any emergency. Phone lines can go down completely or quickly become jammed in the event of an emergency. Internet service may or may not be disrupted. It may be impossible to call out, but calls can come in. Sometimes you can call out of the area, but not to a neighbor across the street. There may be no time to make any calls until hours later.

It is important for all families to designate an out-of-town relative to call in case of any emergency or disaster. In case you get separated or cannot contact friends and relatives nearby, there is someone that everyone will contact and eventually you'll find out where the others have gone.

If your parents or in-laws are in a facility, it's important for that facility to have the same emergency out-of-state contact person. In the event they have to evacuate the facility, having this information ensures someone will be notified eventually as to the whereabouts or status of your loved ones.

Hopefully you will never be faced with an emergency or natural-disaster situation, but being prepared will help keep everyone calmer and focused on what to do. The aftereffects will be minimized if you have planned for the most important issues.

Evacuation Issues for the Disabled

Under normal circumstances, someone with moderate to severe disabilities can function and even live alone with periodic outside assistance. But what happens in the event of an emergency?

People who functioned quite well on a day-to-day basis from a wheelchair suddenly found themselves challenged and even trapped in such disasters as Hurricane Katrina and the World Trade Center on 9/11. Emergency responders prioritized finding and helping the disabled. In many instances they were successful, but in many they were not.

What happens if there was a fire or other emergency in your neighborhood? How would emergency responders know that your mother-in-law is alone in the house in her wheelchair and unable to get out on her own?

In many communities, the fire and police departments encourage residents to let them know where people who would need extra assistance in an emergency live. Some may use a small decal or other indicator to place in a front window of the house or other designated area and another in the window of the bedroom of the disabled person. The decals are subtle and depict several circumstances such as babies, disabled, hard of hearing, and other situations, so no one would know just by looking at it there is someone in a wheelchair living there.

ALERT!

In the event of an emergency situation, don't assume your loved ones will hear an evacuation notice or that they have gotten out of their home. Pay attention to news broadcasts and contact emergency workers to check on a relative if there has been an evacuation in their neighborhood.

Sometimes the fire department makes automated phone calls along with using a bullhorn to announce an evacuation order. They don't always knock on all the doors, or even wait for a response—they need to move through a neighborhood quickly. It may be late or even in the middle of the night that an evacuation takes place. Would your mother hear or pay attention to a loudspeaker? Would she decipher an automated phone call?

If emergency workers are aware of those who may need extra assistance in an evacuation, they will provide safe assistance out. Usually an evacuation order is issued long before there is imminent danger, but don't wait for hours to find out that your mother and her dog are still sitting in the house (oblivious to the evacuation) and can't get out on their own, and the fire department isn't going to let you in to get them.

CHAPTER 15

Are You Too Far Away?

Becoming the caregiver for your parents or in-laws presents a whole set of unique challenges. When you try to do this from a distance, you also add a whole new dimension to the situation. That isn't to say it makes it impossible, it just makes it more challenging and interesting. It requires more creativity, organization, and flexibility.

15

Can This Work from a Distance?

Although this may not be the ideal situation now, there are probably many reasons how and why you find yourself a significant distance from your aging parents or in-laws. Careers, education, and family commitments take children in different directions from their parents. At retirement, your parents may have moved away from you. Now years later, you are facing the situation of becoming a caregiver from a distance.

This is not impossible, but it does require commitment, organization, patience, and a great deal of creativity. For one thing, it isn't easy to assess a situation from a distance. Can you get a true reading on what is actually happening to your father? Is he becoming confused and forgetful, or do his neighbors actually dislike him enough to taunt him and steal his mail and newspapers?

You may need to visit to get a real handle on the situation. However, this may be just the first of many such situations, and you will need to learn how to determine which of the battles needs your attention and which you can let slide. You can't go running there each time there is a problem, and yet you need to be able to prevent a crisis. Sometimes a sibling or even your spouse or children may be able to be more objective and assist with these issues.

Keeping in mind that your parents probably don't want to leave their home and move closer to you, and they may be better off to remain in their own home as long as possible, you are going to have to set some plans in motion to make that happen.

FACT

The same arrangements you would make for them if they lived nearby can be made for your parents from a distance—it's just going to take a little more organization and effort on your part. Finding resources and managing the situation from a different time zone will take some thought and planning.

Perhaps you can begin this process best by visiting your parents and getting a firsthand view of the big picture. You can also begin to gather information, resources, and contacts to help you in the future as they demand more care and assistance.

In the past, you may have visited your parents and paid little attention to their neighbors or their community as a whole. This time you need to explore and scope out the town. If you can't afford time off from work, perhaps a long weekend will work. Have a set plan for the things you need to visit or at least see where they are in relation to your parents' home. Take a tour of the city and find these places.

Some of the places you need to see include their PCP's office, dentist's office, and offices of other members of their health-care team, plus the local hospital, senior center, pharmacy, bank, and grocery stores, as well as their favorite places to shop and eat.

Think about their daily life and activities: Who cuts their hair? Where do they buy gas? How do they get their car repaired? Where's the local movie theater, golf course, bowling alley? Do they have a gardener or a handyman? Who shovels the snow? Where do they get their mail? How is the trash handled? Try to meet some of their friends and especially any neighbors who could keep an eye on things for you if you need them.

Gather business cards and make a list of addresses, phone numbers, and e-mail addresses for all of these people and places. Put them all into a separate address book or database of information about your parents for future reference. Pick up a copy of the local phone book from the phone company, and get copies of local newspapers. Take these items home with you.

As you tour the city, you may want to take pictures of the offices and locations of your parents' favorite hangouts. Having a visual reference can sometimes help you discern fact versus confusion from a distance. It can also help you later if you have to get a neighbor or friend to find a place for you. If you can tell them it's a three-story brick building next to a gas station or across the street from a certain park, they may be more willing to assist you than if you send them on a task to find someplace they've never been before.

Make Some Observations

While you're visiting your parents, stand back and objectively watch how they function. Are they still able to drive safely? Can your father see well at night? Does your mother need someone to remind her to take her medications? Do they leave the stove on? Is there adequate food in the pantry and refrigerator, and is it appropriate for any special dietary needs they have? Check for home-safety factors such as throw rugs, clutter, and grab bars. When they pay for things are they mindful of their purse or wallet as well as money and credit cards? Can they figure out the tip and total at a restaurant easily?

This may be a difficult process for you; it's not easy to observe and admit that your parents are getting older and are no longer as strong, capable, and confident as they once were. Recognizing their strengths and weaknesses now, however, can help keep them as safe and independent as possible. Accentuate the positive, but don't get lost in denial.

When and How to Move Your Parents Closer

It's certainly one thing if your parents or in-laws live within a few hours' driving time—you can take a long weekend each month and attend to matters to assist them in remaining in their own home. However, if they live across the country or even in another country this may make things much more difficult. At some point, you will probably have to consider moving them closer to you, or you and your family closer to them.

This too won't be an easy task, and there are many considerations to take into account. Moving them away from friends and familiar surroundings can exacerbate or even initiate issues such as dementia and depression. While there may be no other alternatives, you need to be aware of this fact and prepared to deal with it.

Change can bring about changes in other conditions as well. Blood pressure can become unstable for a while. Blood sugar can be either raised or lowered by stress. Pain management and coping mechanisms can also be affected.

If the risks of leaving them in their own home outweigh the risks of change, then you may have no choice. Be mindful of the fact that your parents should always be informed and involved in these decisions. Giving them the opportunity to express their concerns and to provide input will help them cope with and accept the changes.

ALERT!

New surroundings can cause confusion. Your parents could experience greater or even a sudden difficulty with balance and gait. They get used to a place and know where the furniture is. They depend on it to hang onto or to maneuver with confidence and are even able to avoid stubbing toes in the dark. Move them to a new place and they might have issues or even fall.

Help Them Stay in Touch and Make Choices

Providing ways to help them keep in touch with the friends and neighbors they leave behind will also help them adjust. Webcams and e-mail can help them stay in touch on a regular basis. VoIP (voice over Internet Protocol) phone systems, also known as Internet phones, provide local and long-distance phone service for one low monthly rate. Cell phones usually include a free or low-cost long-distance calling option as well.

Allowing them to make choices or have input in the options for new living arrangements will also help them adjust to the move. If you are moving them into your home and they feel this is a burden, assure them they will have responsibilities and ways to help you that will help ease that burden and guilt.

One of the most important factors in moving your parents closer to you is changing their health-care team. This is something you may want to begin to do long before you actually make the move, especially if your parents have any severe or chronic medical problems. Seek a referral from their present PCP if possible. You might also request a recommendation from your own PCP. Contact the new office to arrange for a visit to establish care soon after they arrive. Moving may cause an exacerbation of these issues and you may find an urgent need for medical care. If you are prepared, this will be a much easier transition.

Enlisting Neighbors and Friends

Long before you move your parents or in-laws, you may need someone close by to look in on them or alert you if they notice anything unusual or in case of an emergency. If you made contact with your parents' neighbors during a visit, you will have established a rapport. Be sure to let them know you don't expect them to assume any major responsibilities for your parents; you just need someone to alert you to possible problems.

As with your siblings, you may want to put in writing what you want them to report to you. This could be in the form of a letter after you return home from your visit.

Dear Mrs. Jones,

Thank you for being such a good friend and neighbor to my parents. I don't expect you to ever have to assume any responsibility for them; it's just comforting to know that someone can alert me if there are problems I would otherwise be unaware of. We realize they are getting older and will need some additional care, which we will provide.

I would appreciate it if you could please let me know, of course, if there is any emergency, but also if you notice anything unusual such as newspapers left on the driveway or mail not being picked up.

Mom makes a trip to the grocery store almost every day. If she can ever assist you by picking up something, please feel free to ask her.

Thanks so much. My number again is xxx-xxx-xxxx. Please call me collect. My e-mail address is: me@me.com

Always be sure to say please and thank you, and as appropriate send holiday wishes. If there is ever any expense incurred by the neighbors, reimburse it immediately. If the neighbor has had to become involved frequently, a thank-you gift such as a fruit basket or flowers would be a nice gesture. Remember, this person is helping you keep an eye on things; reassure her that you are taking steps to avoid these issues.

Friends Helping Friends

Often in large retirement communities, friends band together to help take care of each other. They may be lifelong friends who all moved to the same community upon retirement or they may have become friends after they moved in.

They are all acutely aware of the fact that their families live a distance away and that, unfortunately, some have less loyal families they can depend on in their old age.

These friends take care of each other as much as they can. One or two may do the grocery shopping; others make sure their friends get to medical appointments. Some help each other out with other tasks such as bill paying or collecting reimbursements from health-insurance policies. Their strong bond of friendship also serves as self-preservation; they don't want their group of friends separated so they do what they can to help each other stay in their homes.

They may have an alert system worked out whereby the residents open their drapes or blinds in the front window first thing when they get up; they close them at sundown. If someone notices this pattern is off, he'll investigate.

In these situations or other instances your parents may have close friends nearby who could alert you to possible problems or situations where you need to step in and offer assistance, or take charge and possibly move your parent closer to you.

It is a good idea to have the contact information for at least a few of your parents' best friends. This helps to enlarge their circle of support and to improve your abilities to know and understand what is happening in your parents' lives. Friends can provide a good basis for understanding and recognizing changes in mental status or physical condition. Make it a point to meet your parents' friends when you visit your parents.

How and When to Contact the Physician

If possible, during a visit to your parents you should go with them to see their PCP. Introduce yourself and let her know you are involved and interested in the care of your aging parents and welcome her contacting you with any concerns about your parents.

If this is not possible, you should send a letter to the physician introducing yourself and providing emergency contact information for you and your siblings. If you have already begun to divide the care of your parents or in-laws—dividing responsibilities for financial matters or direct care—you can include this information and encourage the PCP to contact you with any questions or concerns.

Be mindful of HIPAA regulations and privacy issues, but encourage the physician to obtain any necessary written permission from your parents to communicate with you as needed.

Inquire if the PCP welcomes or uses e-mail. Also find out if you can arrange a telephone conference with her to introduce yourself and address your concerns. There is probably going to be a fee associated with this, as there would be for an in-person appointment. Offer to pay for this up front, especially if you meet with any resistance from the reception staff.

You should also obtain the name of the PCP's nurse or back office contact. Ask if there is a preferred time of day for you to call or to expect a call to be returned by the PCP. Most physicians return these kinds of calls after office hours have ended for the day, which is usually after 5:00 P.M.; some make them even later, depending on their family or personal life. They may have obligations to children and will make nonemergency calls after 8:00 P.M. local time. Find out whether the PCP has a specific day off during the week and which days, if any, he work's shorter hours. Understand that none of this is set in stone, but it can help alleviate frustrations and feelings of being ignored, especially if you forget and call on a Wednesday (her day off) and don't hear back from her.

When you call, it's always a good idea to ask if the physician is working and when you might expect to hear back. This way, if he is in, but perhaps very backed up with an overbooked schedule of patients, you might not hear back until after 6:00 or 7:00 P.M., and then you won't become anxious when he hasn't called by his usual 5:00 P.M.

If possible, provide a cell phone number where he can call you back, so that in the event you aren't at a specific landline number, he isn't wasting time trying to return your call. Physicians are very busy and they rightfully get upset if you waste their time.

Be Prepared When Contacting Physicians

Be prepared with a list of concerns or questions and get right to the point. Again, they are busy and don't have time for a lot of unnecessary conversation. For example, if you suspect your mother is suffering from depression, be prepared to provide a list of symptoms and back them up with examples. If your father is having some issues with urinary incontinence, the physician may ask you about his intake of fluids and any symptoms of urinary infection such as blood in the urine, burning, or fever. Try to be prepared, and if possible, you might have your parent available on another phone line to consult. You can also provide the physician with as much information as you can, get a list of his questions, and arrange for a time to call him back with answers.

ALERT!

If, for example, you're calling about an issue and hope to get a medication prescribed for your parent, you should be prepared with the phone number for the pharmacy, a list of any allergies your parent has, and know what other medications (including dose) he is taking at the present time.

One thing you definitely need to understand is that antibiotics are not effective for viruses such as colds and flu. This is true even if they are experiencing fever and have a productive cough with green mucous. The physician won't prescribe antibiotics over the telephone; you will need to arrange for your parent to be seen, or at the very least have a chest X-ray. Antibiotics have been overprescribed in the past, and now there is a serious immunity issue with certain bacteria. Therefore, physicians are often overly cautious in prescribing them.

Finding Community Resources from a Distance

Locate the documents you collected when you visited your parents. This collection should include business cards, newspapers, and a phone book. These will be important components of your community resources list and research sources. Keep them in an easy-to-access area, but protect them—you may need them frequently.

In fact, in order to keep yourself efficient and organized in the care of your parents, you will need to keep the most frequently used numbers in your Rolodex at work and in personal organizers such as Day Timers, cell phones, or PDAs. This is true whether your parents live far away or in your own home.

FACT

One of the best ways to determine the needs and appropriate community resources for your parents is to arrange for a home-health care evaluation. If neither of your parents has a known need for a nurse, one or the other should be able to qualify for a physical therapy home-safety evaluation. Ask the physician to request a medical social-work visit for assistance with community resources as well.

If your parents don't need or qualify for any home-health nursing or therapy evaluations, you can request and pay for a medical social-work visit from a home-health agency to evaluate for community resources and assist with short-term and long-range planning for your parents. The physician will still need to call in an order for this, but it won't be reimbursable by Medicare. The cost should be in the range of $100–$150. Ask the social worker to contact you after he has made the evaluation.

Other Sources of Information

The newspapers and phone book you collected on your visit to your parents' home can come in handy to locate such sources as private caregivers; house cleaning, gardening and other household services; transportation services; government offices; assisted-living facilities; and nursing homes. The sources you can find in these publications can also help you locate other services and assistance you may need. Search through the list of business cards you collected from your tour of your parents' community and you may find a wealth of other services as well.

On the Internet, you can perform a search for the community and then access yellow and white page-type listings, as well as listings for general business headings, health care, shopping, and food services.

Community resources themselves are usually great sources of information for other community resources, so don't forget to ask one source what it may know or recommend for another resource. See Chapter 19 for more information about community resources.

The Geriatric Case Manager

A geriatric case manager can be your best friend, whether your parents live with you, a few miles away, or across the country. These are professionals, usually registered nurses or medical social workers, trained in geriatrics and managing the care of the elderly.

They make periodic visits as needed to assess the home situation and arrange for or recommend resources to meet the current needs of your parents. They coordinate with the PCP and family members to supervise and evaluate the effectiveness of these resources.

Health insurance and Medicare do not usually reimburse this service. The cost of an evaluation is usually about $200–$350 and ongoing costs range from about $200–$1,000 per month, depending upon the needs.

The National Association of Professional Geriatric Care Managers can provide referrals from their member list. They can be reached at 602-881-8008. Their website is *www.caremanager.org*. Some public health departments, senior centers, or local area on aging agencies offer free or low-cost geriatric case-management services on a short-term basis.

The Discharge Planner

If your parent is hospitalized, the case manager or discharge planner can and should become your best friend. This person's primary job is to get your parent discharged either back home or to an appropriate level of care with the equipment and assistance needed to keep your parent safe and help him recover quickly. They can help arrange for home-health care, provide you with other resources, and advocate for your parent to receive appropriate care while still in the hospital.

If you have issues or concerns while your parent is hospitalized, speak to the physician first. Usually, she can help get issues resolved. If not, there are other patient advocates as well. You can speak to the nurse manger on the floor if you are concerned about the level or quality of care. Above the nurse manager is the director of nursing for the facility.

If you don't receive any satisfaction, find out if the hospital is accredited. Most likely this will be through JCAHO, the Joint Commission on Accreditation of Healthcare Organizations. JCAHO will take your complaint seriously and investigate the situation. This may not happen while your parent is still in the hospital, but they can advise you on what other steps to take at the time. Sometimes just mentioning to the hospital staff or directors that you plan to call JCAHO can help get a response and action. (JCAHO's website is *http://jointcommission.org.*)

CHAPTER 16

End-of-Life Issues

Facing the fact that you and your spouse will not always have your parents with you can be a very painful experience. The thought of losing the people who gave you life and have been there for you all this time is often too emotional to imagine, much less discuss with your parents. However, it may be time to do so.

How to Prepare for the End

Believe it or not, sometimes it is easier to face the impending death of your parents if they have a terminal illness. You at least have a timetable before you. Knowing that your loved one has only a small amount of time left gives you the opportunity to ensure things are in order and provides an opening for discussion should you choose to take it. It also leaves you time to talk about things you may have put off intentionally or to get answers to questions you always thought you'd have time to discuss someday.

When a parent dies suddenly, there may be a lot of things left undone and unsaid, and guilt and regrets left to live with. If your parents are healthy and fairly independent, it is easy to avoid the subject of dying altogether. You may spend years anticipating and fearing the moment when you will walk in and find them gone.

Denial is quite a comfortable state. As Scarlett O'Hara might say, "I'll think about that tomorrow." Unfortunately, death is part of life, and sometimes things cannot be avoided or put off. Stepping outside that level of comfort can be very difficult and traumatic. Take it one day at a time if you have the luxury, but move forward.

If your parents haven't already prepared and signed wills, advance Directives, DPOA, and a health-care proxy, then they should get them done now. If they have done this, you need to locate these documents and be sure all medical personnel have copies of all those pertaining to health care.

You should also have them complete an Emergency Profile (See Appendix C) with the most current information, including contact information, medication profile, allergies, medical- and life-insurance policies, health-care team members, their attorney, their accountant or financial advisor, location of all important documents, and any special notes regarding their care and aftercare.

Don't be afraid to show your emotions and cry together—death is not a happy time. Your parents may be as uncertain or as uncomfortable as you are about how to talk about their death. Simply taking the plunge can release a lot of tension and apprehension. In some instances, just releasing this tension can help make the experience a lot less traumatic for all of you.

Do your parents have fears about dying? Perhaps they fear having a lot of pain, or difficulty breathing, or not being able to communicate. Perhaps they don't want to be alone. Maybe they want to do or see something or someone one last time. By talking about these things, they can gain some control over the situation and make this a more peaceful event.

What Is Hospice?

In the event that your parent or in-law is diagnosed with a terminal illness (typically less than six months to live), hospice services can assist with general care as well as spiritual and bereavement aspects. Hospice will help provide comfort and support throughout the end-of-life care to help provide quality and dignity to the dying person's life.

Hospice is a word derived from the Latin term *hospitium*, meaning "guesthouse." Originally, this hospitium, or guesthouse, was a specific shelter designed for the sick and weary travelers who were returning from religious pilgrimages. Today, hospice is more of a concept than an actual place.

FACT

Hospice care as it is known today began in Britain in the 1960s, when Dr. Cicely Saunders established St. Christopher's Hospice near London. The health-care team developed care-giving and pain-management techniques that formed the foundation for hospice care today.

In 1974, the first hospice in the U.S. was founded in New Haven, Connecticut. Today, there are over 3,200 hospice programs in the U.S. and 80 percent of hospice care is provided in the patient's home, a family member's home, or in nursing homes. Only a small number of in-house hospices exist.

Hospice care does not hasten death, nor does it prolong life. The goal of hospice care is to provide an improved quality of life in the patient's last days by addressing all of the symptoms presented by the terminal disease. The emphasis is on maintaining dignity while controlling pain and discomfort.

Attempts at curative treatments are not a part of hospice care. Hospice care begins when these treatments are no longer effective and the patient is ready to stop this aspect of treatment and move into the hospice mode.

Hospice helps the patient and his or her family and friends deal with the emotional, spiritual, and social impact of the terminal disease. Hospice care offer's a variety of bereavement and counseling services before and after the patient's death.

The Hospice Team

The hospice team consists of physician(s), nurses, nursing or home-health aides, a medical social worker, chaplain or clergy, and usually a team of volunteers. They work together with the patient, family, friends, and personal clergy or spiritual advisors to form and carry out a plan of care.

Medicare, Medicaid, and most private insurances cover the cost of hospice care. Some insurance plans have limited or very specific hospice benefits, but most home-health and hospice agencies will work with patients and families within these constraints to provide end-of-life care.

How to Set Up Hospice Care

A referral to hospice has to come from a physician who is willing to manage the care under hospice. Sometimes a hospice agency may have a physician on staff that will assume this responsibility or will work with the patient's physician to direct hospice care, but the initial referral has to come from the patient's physician. This may be the PCP or it can be an oncologist, cardiologist, or other specialist treating the terminal diagnosis.

The patient has to have a terminal diagnosis and usually less than six months to live. Sometimes, an expected lifespan of less than one year is appropriate. Even if the patient outlives this six months, she can still remain on hospice care.

In far too many instances, hospice care isn't initiated until the last few days, or sometimes hours, before death occurs. This doesn't always provide the best experience for the patient or his family, as sometimes maximum symptom control can't be achieved and the patient has to suffer more than necessary. Counseling and bereavement services may be compromised as well.

It is often best to explore the hospice option when the terminal diagnosis is first made. The choice to pursue curative treatment may indeed be made at this time, but the connection to hospice is also made and can be optioned when the patient is ready.

Once the referral has been made, the patient or designated family member will be contacted within twenty-four hours to arrange an evaluation visit. At that time, a registered nurse or medical social worker will explore the hospice option with the patient, primary caregiver, and family members. Appropriate documentation will be signed and a plan of care specific to the needs of the patient will be made, and subsequently reviewed and approved, by the hospice team.

QUESTION?

What happens if my father, who has a terminal illness, falls and breaks a hip? Can he have surgery to repair it or does he just have to live with it until he dies?
If the patient sustains an injury or other illness not related to the terminal diagnosis, it can be treated as if he wasn't on hospice. If he chooses not to treat it, only palliative care will be provided, as determined by the patient and the hospice team.

As the patient's condition worsens from her terminal disease, the team will work together to provide symptom control to keep her comfortable. Upon death, a member of the hospice team will pronounce the patient gone, notify the hospice team including the physician, and the preappointed mortuary will pick up the body.

There are no resuscitative measures taken; however, should the patient change his mind, hospice care can be revoked or stopped at any time and reinstated again if he decides to resume hospice care. This is not common practice, but the option is always there.

A Clear Understanding of Wishes

End-of-life wishes should be discussed and necessary written documents signed long before the need arises, or before your parents fall victim to some form of dementia. However, this doesn't always happen. Cultural issues and rituals can dictate decisions, and well-meaning family members can jump in and make decisions by proxy that your parent never wanted. These can lead to regrets, guilt, and family feuds.

Hospice can help you explore these decisions with your parents. After-care (including grief counseling for up to one year after the death) and burial issues are part of the hospice plan and have to be included in their documentation. But what happens if your parent dies suddenly or never develops a terminal illness to qualify for hospice?

At the very least, you should make an effort to encourage your parents to speak with an attorney and sign appropriate paperwork to protect their financial assets for the surviving spouse. This will get them on the path, and usually the attorney will discuss advance directives, DPOA, and a health-care proxy. You need to get copies of the paperwork and give it to the PCP and local hospital.

If you or your parent is hospitalized, the question of whether there is an advanced directive and health-care proxy on file will arise. The hospital is obligated to provide you with information and directions on how to obtain necessary forms. This could easily prompt a discussion if you are unable to initiate one. Most hospitals have medical social workers on staff. Ask to speak to one—they may be able to assist you with this process. If your parent is receiving home-health care, ask to have a social worker visit to assist you with these decisions.

It is imperative to understand whether your parent wants any or all heroic measures taken; if she wants to be kept alive on a ventilator to assist or breathe for her; if she wishes to have a feeding tube placed; and under what circumstances she would or would not want these measures taken.

Aftercare, such as burial versus cremation, may seem obvious to you, but do you really know for sure whether your parent wants to be buried? Do you know what he'd like done with his ashes? And do you know how strongly your sister feels about the matter? If your parents haven't made legal documents addressing this issue and haven't discussed it openly with you and your siblings, you could find yourself in a big fight in the middle of a hospital room or corridor.

If you are the primary caregiver for your parents or in-laws, you need to get this information from them—if not in a legal document, then in writing and witnessed would be the next best choice. Documents are available online and can be downloaded for free. If you don't have this option, use a tape recorder or video camera to record the conversation. State the date and time or show a current newspaper to validate the date. Be sure to make their wishes known to other family members so there are no surprises and a discussion can take place before anything happens.

These decisions must be made while your parents or in-laws are mentally competent. If there is any early dementia developing, then it is imperative to get them done now or you may have to go to court to be appointed the decision maker. This can become a very complicated situation, especially if you and your surviving parent and siblings have basic differences of opinion.

Myths of Pain

There can be three very misunderstood elements in regards to end-of-life care. Controlling pain and other symptoms are essential to a death with dignity and quality of life to the end. There are many myths surrounding pain and symptom control, and there are issues of controversy about the need for continued hydration and nutrition to the very end.

Dying is not necessarily painful, and not all terminal diseases produce pain. But pain can be controlled and in many instances reduced to a level of tolerance that allows for normal activity without sedating effects.

FACT

Palliative care involves keeping the patient's pain and other levels of discomfort under control, allowing him to have as much quality of life as possible. The term palliative comes from the Latin word *palliare*, meaning "to cloak." When there is no hope of cure, the goal is to reduce suffering. It does not mean sedating the patient for the duration.

One of the most common myths about pain medication is that it has to be sedating to work. When people experience severe or chronic pain, it often interferes with sleep. It may take some strong medications to control this pain, such as opiod analgesics like morphine. Initially theses medications will indeed induce sedation that can last about twenty-four hours. This sedation allows the person to catch up on lost sleep.

Once this has happened, the sedative effects wear off. The patient can then function with mental clarity. Any continuing sedation is usually due to other medications that may have been prescribed for anxiety or depression.

Many fear that once morphine is prescribed the end is near. Effective pain management for severe and chronic pain involves quickly controlling the symptoms, and this often requires using "the big guns." Once pain control is achieved, the dose can actually be reduced without the pain returning. Pain that is only partially controlled or controlled on a part-time basis usually increases in severity; therefore, getting the pain under control quickly involves using stronger medications and routine administration. Experimenting with milder medications can actually induce more severe pain and prolong suffering.

The Truth about Addiction

Another common issue is addiction. With an end-of-life situation, addiction is probably the least of anyone's concerns, but physicians, patients, friends, and family alike can make a huge issue out of this. In fact, there is no empirically based evidence of addiction from morphine if it is prescribed in an appropriate dose to control the pain.

Additionally, when used for severe pain or chronic pain, the withdrawal is mild once there is no longer a need for an opiod analgesic such as morphine. In fact, the dose is usually titrated down as the pain becomes controlled, which produces no withdrawal effect.

One of the most important aspects of pain management is to take the pain medication routinely until the pain is controlled at a tolerable level. That means taking the medication as directed, such as every four or six hours around the clock. Waiting until the pain returns or becomes intense again before taking the medication does not help gain control over the pain. It can take forty-five minutes to an hour before the medication takes hold, and if the pain is intense, this suffering can be unnecessary. This can slow or prevent pain control.

Achieving Pain Management

Taking the medication routinely for several doses allows the body to relax and better cope with the pain. This is especially true for severe or chronic pain that interferes with activities of daily living such as sleep habits, appetite, activity, and mental status. Morphine, for instance, can provide a sense of comfort along with pain relief. It makes it easier to breathe, relax, sleep, eat, or move with greater ease.

Another myth about pain is that it builds character, and taking pain medication shows a weakness. Before pain-management techniques were discovered, sucking it up and being strong and stoic may have had some merit. Without the ability to control pain, fooling oneself into thinking suffering was noble may have made it less powerful and more tolerable, but today there is no need for anyone to suffer needlessly from pain and there is never a need to die a horrible, painful death.

The Pain Scale

Pain is typically measured on a comfort scale of zero to ten, with zero being no pain and ten being the worst pain imaginable. Using this scale, practitioners can prescribe pain medication and titrate it up or down according to the effectiveness. Achieving zero pain is not always the goal, especially if dealing with an underlying disease process that causes severe pain. In some instances, achieving a comfort level between zero to three is realistic. Controlling the pain to allow for ease of movement and improved sleep and eating habits provides an improved quality of life and a death with dignity.

In addition to analgesics, other modalities such as radiation, chemotherapy, antidepressants, and antianxiety medications can help achieve symptom control as well as pain control.

Dealing with Death

One of the greatest fears most people express is that of dying alone. Hospice hopes to allow families and dying patients to put those fears to rest. Most hospice care takes place in the home, which allows many freedoms from rules and restrictions on visitors and hours of visitation. However, some hospice is provided in facilities such as skilled nursing homes. In these instances, there is often a lot of bending of the rules, especially in the last hours.

In some instances, hospices have their own in-house facilities, but these are rare. Most of these facilities are run by specialty groups for AIDS patients. The need for these homes grew mostly out of ignorance, family members' fears of working with AIDS patients, and homophobic responses. Many AIDS patients were left alone to die, so support organizations formed in-house hospices to provide them a place to die with love and dignity.

Facilities such as assisted living and skilled nursing homes can provide hospice under waivers from the Department of Health Services. Sometimes the hospice care is provided in these settings and sometimes a patient is placed for a short term to give the caregivers some respite. Sometimes the patient actually requests to be placed near the time of death rather than to die at home.

There are many signs and symptoms of impending death (See Chapter 17) that will provide patients and caregivers the clues necessary to ensure the likelihood of being together at the moment of death. However, it should be noted that in many cases patients tend to take the opportunity to slip away quietly when family members leave the room, even momentarily.

The last sense to go is hearing, and patients are comforted by knowing their family is with them. Gentle voices and soft touches seem to soothe them during their last hours. However, many times they can hang on too long if there is too much loving stimulus or they have some unfinished business. When they are ready, they often will wait for family members to leave to go to the bathroom or to get a snack or cup of coffee.

There should be no feelings of guilt. It's never easy to face the final good-bye, but a death with dignity and without pain or suffering was achieved; the ultimate goal was reached, and you as a caregiver did your very best to make that happen. They knew you were present in spirit.

What Do You Do Now?

If you haven't already done so with your parent, you'll need to make arrangements for a funeral or other service. If friends are available to help carry out these plans and notify family and friends of the ceremony, by all means ask them to help.

After that, there are a number of other affairs to oversee. You will need to order at least a dozen copies of the death certificate to accomplish many of these. These can be obtained from the funeral director or from the county clerks office. You will need to:

- Take a copy of the death certificate to the Social Security office and apply for death benefits. This is about $250. Apply for death benefits from any life-insurance policies and retirement plans.
- Take a copy of the death certificate and your parent's will to the local county government office of probate to file for probate. If you have joint tenancy on property, or your other parent is still alive and has joint tenancy and the estate is valued at less than $600,000, you may not need to go through probate—discuss this with your

attorney. You will need to change the names on the deed(s) at the local county registrar's office.

- Notify creditors of your parent's death and settle debts. Make sure to pay any taxes due on the estate until it is closed.
- If your other parent is still alive, assist with making all beneficiary changes on wills, insurance policies, investments, and any joint accounts. Discuss how and when to dispose of personal belongings and property.

Don't make changes without consulting your surviving parent. Thinking that you are making things easier for the surviving spouse by quickly getting rid of all reminders of your deceased parent may be the worst thing possible. Even though they may present painful reminders, there may be some great comfort derived from holding on to some personal items and being able to sit in a loved one's favorite chair.

CHAPTER 17

Death, Dying, and Grief

Understanding the dying process and what to expect can help ease your fears and give you the opportunity to help your parent die at home, or in a nursing facility, if he so chooses. In addition to being a sad time and one everyone would rather not have to face, there is a mysterious air about death that frightens most people. Death and dying has been studied for years, and many of the findings can help prepare caregivers to handle the situation with grace.

Dying Trajectories

The concept of dying trajectories, or patterns of death, was first suggested in 1965 by Barney Glaser and Anselm Strauss. Although each death is unique, these two researchers found patterns of dying associated with different types of illnesses. These patterns have helped physicians and end-of-life health-care teams have a better understanding of what is likely to happen and when to provide support as well as palliative and spiritual care for the dying and their loved ones.

When the health-care team as well as patients and families have a better understanding of what is likely to occur and how quickly the decline will take place, they are better able to cope with the unknown. They are also better prepared to accept and deal with the physical and financial burdens as well as the emotional roller coaster associated with the dying process. There are four basic trajectories of dying.

Sudden Death

The trajectory for sudden death from accidents, violence, and sudden severe illness such as a heart attack or stroke is characterized by a rapid downward slant. The patient as well as the family is not prepared for death, and there has usually been no time for goodbyes. There may be many regrets and a lot of guilt associated with this sudden, unexpected loss. Bereavement needs are intense and often health-care systems are caught off-guard and ill-prepared to support those in need. With no need for prolonged connection with the health-care team, these families are left to find their own support and assistance through the grieving and healing process.

Cancer Deaths

The cancer death trajectory is probably the most predictable and familiar. In fact, the study of dying trajectories began by looking at cancer deaths. Their dying trajectory is a series of descending plateaus. However, once the treatment phase is no longer effective and the cancer becomes advanced, there is usually a steady decline, which may take weeks to months to progress toward death. As death approaches, the decline becomes rapid.

This rapid decline sometimes comes as a surprise, but when recognized and used effectively, it gives patients and families time to say their goodbyes and get things in order. In fact, once patients take to their beds, this process usually takes a matter of weeks.

Chronic Illness

This trajectory is a series of peaks and valleys that can even give the impression of near recovery due to alternating phases of remission and relapse. This continues until the pattern becomes more of an alternation between acute illness and brief relapses, but a chronic decline in overall health status.

This is commonly seen in patients with CHF (congestive heart failure), COPD (chronic obstructive pulmonary disease) including emphysema, and those living with the long-term effects of stroke or other chronically debilitating diseases. They bounce in and out of hospitals or nursing homes and may be on and off antibiotics or other periodic treatments. They have a crisis and then go into remission.

There is always the hope that one more round of treatment may do the trick, and yet one more round could be the beginning of the end. This is an uncertain trajectory, and unless or until the patient and family has had enough and takes measure to stop aggressive forms of treatment, the pattern is likely to continue for a year or two.

In fact, physicians are often reluctant to acknowledge this as being a trajectory of dying. However, if they were asked whether they would be surprised if this patient died sometime in the next two years, they would probably say no.

When your parent or in-law has dealt with a long-term chronic illness, it may be necessary to question the physician about whether she would be surprised if your parent died in the next year or two. If the answer is no, then some serious consideration of hospice care or other end-of-life care decisions should be undertaken at this point.

The Long Steady Decline

For patients who have had major health issues such as massive strokes, multiple or massive heart attacks or other catastrophic events, life threatening infection, or a surgical event that went terribly wrong, a long, steady decline in health status is the fourth dying trajectory. Despite acute, intense care including many life-prolonging efforts, there is no improvement. Everything possible has been done, and still no positive response is elicited.

At some point, either the patient dies despite all of the best efforts or decisions need to be made whether or not to continue these efforts. How many tubes do you insert? How long do you rely on a ventilator to breathe? When do you discontinue life-support measures?

Stages of Dying

Fear of the unknown makes death and dying a mysterious and sometimes frightening event. Being afraid of death often causes patients or families to forgo hospice care, fearing they could not be there to support their loved one through this process.

Understanding the common symptoms and how to deal with them can help alleviate these fears. The hospice team holds many a hand through this process and helps patients die with dignity in their own home surrounded by those they love.

FACT

The truth is that food and fluids can become painful and even harmful to the dying patient. As the body shuts down, nourishment is no longer necessary. Digestion is slowed and a feeling of bloating and fullness can create pain and nausea. Difficulty swallowing can cause food or fluids to enter the lungs instead of the stomach and cause a form of pneumonia.

The dying person usually experiences a feeling of detachment from his physical world. He loses interest and prefers to sleep more. Talking is not important and he begins to let go. There is a loss of appetite. At first, he may still agree to take small bites of soft foods or liquids and then will begin to refuse any food. This is often difficult for caregivers to accept; food is commonly associated with comfort and lack of food with starving and hunger pains.

The mouth can become very dry. To help with this, the caregiver can wet the lips and mouth with a few drops of water from an eyedropper or a straw, or place a few ice chips inside the cheek or feed with a spoon. A sponge-tipped applicator can be dipped in water and placed in the mouth inside the cheek used to swab out the mouth. Sometimes these come in a lemon flavor. Some patients like this and others do not. Body language and facial expressions will give you an indication if there is a preference or not. Lip balm can help protect and moisturize the lips. Good mouth hygiene can help as well. Use a small dab of toothpaste on a damp cloth or sponge-tipped applicator and wipe the teeth on both sides. Gently wipe the tongue, but be careful of the gag reflex.

Bowel and Bladder Function

In the early stages of active dying, it is important to prevent constipation and fecal impaction. Sometimes laxatives or suppositories are needed to counteract the effects of immobility, pain medication, and a decreased fluid intake. If the bowels have been active, it is normal for bowel activity to decrease after there has been no intake for a few days.

Urine will become much more concentrated and tea colored. Urinary incontinence is quite common, and diapering or having a urinary catheter inserted will help keep the patient from soiling bed linens.

Hallucinations and Visions

The patient may hallucinate or have visions. It is quite normal for them to "see" and have conversations with friends and relatives who have preceded them in death. Sit quietly and let them be comforted and reassured by these visions.

If they are disturbed or frightened by their visions, they may actually be having bad dreams and may need to have medications adjusted to correct this.

Terminal Agitation

At some point, they may experience what is referred to as "terminal delirium" or "terminal agitation." This is characterized by a sudden confusion, restlessness, or agitation. This is usually due to normal factors associated with dying such as a reduction in oxygen to the brain, pain medications, metabolic changes, and dehydration. This is not a painful experience for the patient, but it can be distressing to caregivers and loved ones. It often happens late at night when everyone is exhausted and has no patience for this newfound energy.

Patients become fidgety; they pick and pull at things. They might pull out catheters and other tubes, and sometimes they climb over bedrails to get out of bed. They suddenly have seemingly twice your physical strength. Safety can be an issue; don't try to fight with them, but gently coax them back into bed.

This usually happens at a time when they are very close to death. It can be exacerbated if they have some unfinished business to attend to. If you can figure out what this unfinished business is and help them find a sense of security and closure, they will relax. This is often very difficult to achieve, as they are not usually coherent. There are several things you can do:

- Speak in a soft, gentle voice and use a gentle touch.
- Identify yourself and be patient. He may not recognize you and may think you are someone else.
- If medication was prescribed for restlessness, now is the time to give it.
- Go along with the cues he's giving you and offer support. Try to help him settle unfinished business.
- Light massage and soft music may help to calm him down.

Relax and try to be patient. You aren't going to get sleep right now, but you will later. You are probably exhausted; if someone else is available to help you or to take turns, ask them to do so. This agitated state may last a few minutes to several hours. It may become a nightly event for a few days until she feels she has settled her business.

Changes in Breathing

As death nears, changes in breathing patterns will occur. It may become quick and shallow or very slow and labored. There may be some gurgling sounds as well. This is often referred to as a "death rattle." There may be a pool of secretions the patient can no longer cough up. If they are pooling in the mouth you can gently wipe out the mouth with a soft, moist cloth or sponge-tipped swab and turn the head so they can drain out.

Another pattern of breathing that may happen is called Cheyne-Stokes breathing. This is characterized by periods of no breathing for about thirty to forty-five seconds followed by a few deeper yet rapid respirations. This breathing pattern is due to a decrease in oxygen and a build up of carbon dioxide and other wastes in the body. It is not painful or uncomfortable, but can be disturbing to witness.

Don't panic. Raise the head of the bed slightly or place another pillow under his head to help his breathing. Speak softly and use a gentle touch to reassure him. Notify the physician or hospice nurse of this change in breathing. Remember that mouth breathing can make the mouth dry. Moisten the lips and mouth for comfort.

Skin Temperature and Color

In the last stages of dying, blood and oxygen are more concentrated in the vital organs and less in the extremities. You'll find evidence of this in the fact that the arms and legs may be cool or even cold to touch, and yet the abdomen is still warm. The nose may be ice cold and the lips may take on a bluish tint.

You may also begin to notice small little blue-purplish blotches on the legs, arms, and backside. This mottling is due to blood collecting in dependent areas. As death nears, the skin may become yellowish and take on a waxen appearance.

Keep your parent as comfortable as possible. If she is kicking the covers off, she may be too hot. You can help cool her by wiping her with a cool, damp washcloth. A fan to circulate air can also be comforting. If she's cold, add another blanket. Don't use electric blankets or heating pads, as these can cause burns.

When Death Comes

The last of the senses to go is hearing. In your parent's last hours, you may want to sit with her and read softly or enjoy some soft, quiet music. Talk to her and let her know it's okay to let go. Gently stroke her face or hold her hand; gentle touch is comforting.

She will probably lie quietly and may even appear to stare off into space. Her eyes may look like they are glassed over and she won't respond to your movements. She might even have short periods of lucidity. She may also have periods of restlessness. Some of this may actually just be muscle reflexes.

There are some unpleasant events surrounding death you should be prepared for. Sometimes there is a loss of bowel and bladder control at the moment of death. Muscles may twitch and she may even try to sit up or stand, but this is most likely a muscle response and not an intentional movement.

Sometimes patients yawn or make an audible yell or groan. This isn't a cry or indication of pain; it is just the last big expiration of air passing over her voice box. Her eyes can open and the jaw may drop open as well. Don't be frightened, these are all just normal reflexes as the body dies. You can gently close her jaw and pull her eyelids down.

In some instances, if the doctors have said death is imminent and yet she continues to hang on for days, it may be you are providing too much loving stimulus and causing her to fight to stay alive. Although it's hard to let go, if there is no hope for quality life, then it's time to let her go. You may have to each say a last goodbye and stroke her face or kiss her softly and then leave the room for a little while to let her peacefully slip away.

There is no rush to call anyone when death has occurred. Sit with her for a while; share a quiet moment of closure. Let other family members know and allow them to come and say goodbye if they wish. Then call the hospice nurse and physician. After she has been officially pronounced dead by the nurse, physician, or medical examiner (depending on your state and circumstances), you can contact the mortuary. If it's the middle of the night, they may not come until the morning.

The hospice nurse will notify the equipment companies to come and pick up the bed and rented equipment as appropriate with your schedule. The nurse will dispose of unused medications and instruct you in disposing of other items.

Stages of Grief

Elisabeth Kübler-Ross defined the five stages of grief in her 1969 book, *On Death and Dying*. They are denial, anger, bargaining, depression, and acceptance. She originally applied these to any loss such as the loss of a job, finances, or marriage.

Other researchers studying the process of loss and grief have recognized these stages as well as the fact that they do not have to be experienced in any specific order but are all part of the grieving process. You may vacillate in and out of some stages before completing this part of the process.

Grief begins at the moment a loss is recognized, and often that is with the terminal diagnosis, long before death actually happens.

- **Denial.** Shock and disbelief that this is happening. Numbness and even a sense of isolation that takes over you and only for brief periods of time do you remember that your parent is dying or has died.
- **Anger.** Why me? You may even find yourself angry at your parent for leaving you or at yourself for wishing it would all end when you were so tired and exhausted you didn't think you could continue for another day.
- **Bargaining.** This is usually about making a compromise with God or other deity. Just let Mom live long enough to see her great grandson born and you'll never skip church again or your dad asks God to let him live a while longer and he'll promise to quit smoking.
- **Depression.** Becoming so sad that things just don't matter anymore. Feelings of hopelessness, sorrow, and despair overwhelm you.

- **Acceptance.** Coming to terms with reality. Death is part of life and cannot be avoided. It is okay to die. Or a feeling of calmness and peace that your loved one is no longer suffering and is at rest or peace, having gone on to a better place.

These stages can come in any order and can be intertwined. Each person will experience grief in her own way and in her own time. Some people will move through the grieving process quickly and others take much more time. Some will effectively remain in denial for a long time and put off their grieving. Sometimes, the person who feels he must remain strong for everyone else will delay his grieving for years. This is not necessarily healthy.

Dealing with Your Grief and Helping the Surviving Spouse

You cannot hurry through grief; you have to let it happen and grow from it. Long after the funeral is over and extended family and friends have gone home and back to their lives, you may be hit by a whole new wave of grief, or just begin to experience it.

ALERT!

If your parent has been ill and suffering for a long time, you may not even feel sorrow, you may actually feel a sense of relief and peace. There is no need to feel guilty that you are relieved. You may have actually completed your grieving process long ago. This can be especially true for family members of Alzheimer's patients. The loss of memory was such a tremendous loss that your grieving was done over the loss of your parent as you knew her.

Each death is unique and so is each person's grieving process. Friends and family may urge you to let it all out, to cry and to express your anger and other emotions, but until you are ready, you won't.

Sometimes the surviving spouse may not experience grief after the death because she grieved long ago as well. If your mom has taken care of your dad for many years while he suffered from a chronic illness, she may have grieved for the loss of her husband years ago. She may have experienced a disassociation from him and will express it in terms of that man wasn't her husband, he was just a man she was taking care of. Her husband was lost to her many years ago when he became so disabled.

You might even see your surviving parent emerge with a whole new personality. The role of dutiful wife has ended. This new life as a single woman may give her the freedom to express herself in ways she has kept hidden away for years. Or she may become totally dependent on you and your family and seemingly unable to function on her own.

The first instinct may be to move your surviving parent into your home or an assisted-living situation, but be cautious. Giving up a home she shared with this newly deceased spouse can prove to be too difficult.

While you might think it too sad to remain in a place full of so many memories, it can be comforting and reassuring to the surviving spouse. Sometimes immersing oneself in all of the memories helps facilitate the grieving process and at the same time present some comfort in knowing the person is always present in those memories.

The most important thing you need to do for yourself and for your surviving parent is to take care of your health issues. Grief can make you susceptible to illness, hormonal imbalances, and disrupt sleep and eating patterns. Chronic headaches, irritability, and general fatigue can plague you.

Focus your efforts on normalizing routines and don't take on any extra responsibilities. Maximize the nutrition in the foods you eat, and even if you are unable to sleep, rest and relaxation is essential. Try to distract yourself for a little while with television, playing a board game, reading, or going to the movies. Take a break from active grieving to let your body recover. Drink plenty of liquids if you have been crying. Tears are healing, but you can become dehydrated.

As time goes by, the pain and grieving will lessen. It's normal to forget that your father is gone and pick up the phone to call him. It's normal to want to talk to your dad about how his favorite team just won an important game. Birthdays, anniversaries, and holidays will be especially hard. Plan something to keep you and your parent busy that day. You might even include a special moment of silence or a time for sharing memories. If possible, end on a note of laughter about a funny memory or something that has happened lately that your late father would find funny. Remember that grief is an ongoing process and you will always miss the people you have lost.

CHAPTER 18

Caregiver Issues

Care-giving responsibilities can creep up slowly and with some advanced warning, but in many instances, a crisis suddenly raises the level of the situation to one demanding immediate attention. If you aren't careful, you will spread yourself too thin and quickly burn yourself out. Care giving can sometimes be a thankless job, and caregivers must remember they need time and caring as well.

How to Handle Caring for Your Parents and Your Children

Yesterday you were happily pursuing your career, enjoying being a mother and wife, and content to know that your parents and in-laws were safe in their own little worlds of retirement and spoiling their grandchildren. This morning you were rudely awakened by a frantic phone call from your father clear across the country. Your mother apparently had a stroke this morning, and when she tried to get out of bed, she fell and broke her hip. The paramedics have just left and he's on his way to the hospital.

Welcome to the sandwich generation. You just returned from two wonderful relaxing weeks in Hawaii, and now you have to call your boss and tell her you're heading to Florida to take care of your dad and help make arrangements for your mother's future care. She's not happy, but you have no choice.

Hopefully, your situation can transition easily in a crisis. This is not always the case. Suppose your children are all younger or not so reliable. Maybe your spouse isn't so quick to jump in and help you out. Your siblings are completely disinterested and refuse to help in any way. And your boss threatens to fire you for taking more time off. These can all be real circumstances, and indeed, perhaps more the norm.

ALERT!

Remember, the average caregiver is a forty-six-year-old female who is married and works full time, earning $35,000 per year. She has children under the age of twenty-one and most likely both of her parents as well as her in-laws are alive and over the age of seventy.

For your own self-preservation, it would be best for you to be prepared for a crisis to interrupt your life. How do you do that?

Prepare in Advance

Talk to your children and let them know that their grandparents are aging and the time is going to come when they will need some help from all of you. It could happen suddenly and everyone is going to have to pitch in and help out. Discuss with your spouse how you might have to respond to such a crisis with your parents or his. Consider what types of arrangements you might have to make for your children and how your spouse may have to help out.

Rehearsing in your imagination how you would respond to such a situation and all of the things you would need to arrange will help you be prepared and less stressed should you actually have to face such a crisis. Think of it as a fire drill: The key to success will be how well organized you are and how easily you can delegate.

When You Are Truly Sandwiched

Once ensconced in a sandwich situation, you will need to be organized and work efficiently. You will need to make efforts to find and spend quality time with your children as well as your spouse. It is normal to put your own family first and try to minimize the time you need to spend with your parents or in-laws. Sometimes that won't be possible, as your parents' needs outweigh your family for the moment. Whenever possible, you may need to combine the time.

Take your children along when you have to help out at your parents' house. They can help with chores or keep the grandparents entertained and lift their spirits. Your spouse may be a big help in doing the grocery shopping, handyman projects, or other heavy household chores. Or he may be just the person to help entertain your father while you get some chores done or business taken care of for your mother. Enjoy your time together and thank your spouse and children for helping you.

Burnout

Burnout is the result of constantly giving and giving without replenishing yourself. Your parents need you, your in-laws need you, your spouse pouts if he doesn't get some attention, and your children begin to act out to make you pay attention to them. You find yourself physically as well as emotionally exhausted. If your house caught fire, you would probably just sit there. What about you? When does it get to be your turn?

Caregivers are at risk for depression, and depression is often the root of burnout. Feeling guilty because you can't give each of your responsibilities the amount of time and attention you think you should can make you feel overwhelmed and stressed. This only adds to the situation and leads to depression and burnout.

FACT

Other symptoms of burnout include anger, depression, anxiety, irritability, feelings of detachment, and numbness. You may neglect your own appearance and health issues. You don't sleep well; you don't eat well. You hate and even resent your responsibilities. You may turn to substances such as alcohol or tobacco. You may have withdrawn from your usual activities. Work and personal relationships are strained.

You have to learn to set limits and stick to them. You have to accept the fact that you don't have superpowers—you can only do so much. Prioritize, decide which things are more important, and direct your best efforts in this direction. Face the fact that you can't do this alone and that you need to find some help. Asking for help is not a weakness; it is, in fact, a strength and necessity. You also have to realize you must put yourself first sometimes and take time to replenish yourself or you will not be able to continue, and then you won't be able to help anybody.

Try to get your parent into an adult day-care setting or arrange for some respite and spend the time for yourself. Make a list of all of the tasks you have to accomplish each day and determine whom you can delegate some of them to. You may need to hire someone to assist you with some of these tasks or chores.

When you take care of yourself, you will have more to give. Don't feel guilty about needing some time and attention for yourself; this is a basic necessity and should not be ignored or postponed. This is an ongoing process—the more you need to give, the more you will need to replenish yourself.

Care giving is a thankless job. Although your parents may indeed tell you constantly how much they love and appreciate all that you do for them, in the end they will die. Despite all of your efforts, you cannot prevent this from happening and it's something that will haunt you throughout the experience. You will have to learn to reap your own satisfaction and reward by knowing you have done your best to make life easier and provide for them. It will not be perfect, and things will not always go as you plan. All you can do is give it your best shot and accept the fact that you cannot be all things to all people at the same time!

Elder Abuse

There are a number of ways that elders can be abused, including physically, emotionally, verbally, and financially. Two of the most obvious causes are when a caregiver is unfit from the beginning and when even the best of caregivers becomes completely overwhelmed or burned out.

The aging process is not always kind, and sometimes it may seem as though your father is a two-year-old having a temper tantrum, or your mother has reverted to a toddler as she wets her pants, seemingly on purpose, just as you are leaving for her doctor's appointment. These scenarios can be stressful enough, but when you are faced with the fact that your parents are no longer the people you have always known, you can easily become emotionally overwhelmed.

Try making a phone call, and suddenly your parents and your children all want your attention at once and are all acting out to get your attention. Everyone is pulling you in a different direction at the same time. At some point, you will probably snap. If your parent is suffering from dementia and you cannot reason with her at all, this just compounds the problem. Long before things get to the boiling or snapping point it's time to take a break. Unfortunately, that doesn't always happen.

So you snap and yell at everyone, or concentrate your venting on one person. You have never raised your voice to your father before, but the last straw just broke your back. As you really get started yelling at your dad, in walks your sister, and suddenly she's accusing you of abuse. From there things escalate into a huge family disagreement and all of your efforts in caring for dad for years are being subjected to unwarranted criticism by all of your siblings. These are the same siblings who have never raised a finger to help out but can certainly find all kinds of fault with your care giving now.

It's important to recognize your limits and get help long before you reach them or exceed them. That's easier said than done, but when you have crossed the line, it's essential. Yelling at your dad may have cleared the air for both of you, but you don't want to keep getting to that point— that will be elder abuse. Recognizing there is a problem and dealing with it is not abuse.

Alzheimer's patients especially can become combative. Other dementias can cause a perfectly calm, sweet, little old lady to suddenly attack you with a chair she has lifted over her head because it's now sundown and she has become confused for the evening. The abuse is not always unprovoked; it can be a knee-jerk reaction to an event. Nonetheless, it has to be addressed and dealt with.

FACT

Not all care-giving situations are created equal; therefore, you need to be sure anyone caring for you mother with Alzheimer's has had proper training. That includes you. Contact your local Alzheimer's Association about caregiver classes and tips for caregivers.

Other elder-abuse issues can involve neglect. Caregivers don't feed their patients or not enough. They don't clean them and don't change diapers when they are soiled. They don't turn bedbound patients frequently enough and they get bedsores. Neglect is often a worse kind of abuse than even physical or verbal abuse. Sometimes the neglect is not blatant and it takes some investigating to find it, but if you have hired caregivers for your parents, be sure they are giving the care needed. If they live far away, ask a neighbor to drop in unexpectedly and see how things look or set up a hidden camera.

Stealing from your parents or milking them for "gratuities" and "gifts" is a form of abuse as well. That's why it is best to oversee the financial matters with any hired caregivers. You pay them, and if your parents want to give them a gift or gratuity, you give it to them with their paycheck. Put the valuables away so there is no temptation.

Anyone taking advantage of the elderly through schemes and scams can be charged with elder abuse in addition to the fraud. E-mail scams, unauthorized door-to-door solicitors, and mail fraud can be elder abuse when they have stolen identity or money from the elderly.

ALERT!

If your parent is in a nursing home or assisted-living facility, any abusive caregivers need to be reported to the administration. The long-term-care ombudsman oversees these facilities. Contact your local county area on aging office for more information.

If you suspect abuse or neglect, contact the area agency on aging through your county government office and make a report. They will investigate this for you.

Resolving Family Disputes and Conflicts

Keeping family members involved and informed can be a significant task, but it can help prevent a lot of conflicts, resentments, and hurt feelings. Even so, you may not be able to avoid these. There will be siblings who refuse to help out and tell you this up front. There will be those who promise to help and then flake every time. There will be those who resent you taking charge and criticize every move you make but are unwilling to do anything. There will also be the spouses who prevent the most likely helpers from becoming involved.

You may find that everyone works well together and your parents are content and well cared for. A few years after the fact, your sister starts criticizing or blaming you for not letting her help when she wanted to, or not listening to her suggestions or needs. You may not ever understand where this came from or why she harbored these feelings for so long.

Family meetings with or without an outsider to referee can help discuss and resolve issues, or they can turn into shouting matches and have no value at all. You have to set and agree on ground rules, then you have to follow them. Oftentimes, having a referee can help you all be a little more objective and less likely to slip into old roles or become emotionally swayed by actions or problems.

FACT

Old family rivalries and differences won't necessarily get put aside because your mother is ill and needs your help. You might be able to make an effort to consciously get along for the time being, but even the best-laid plans may fail.

Everyone should have a turn to speak and to be heard. Sometimes you will also have to take turns at trying some of the suggestions you may know will fail, if for no other reason than to illustrate why they won't work. Sometimes you have to resort to rock-paper-scissors or drawing names or ideas from a hat. And sometimes you just have to be adults and agree to disagree.

Don't forget the obvious choice: to let your parents step in and decide for themselves what they need and want from each of you or to make you all hug and be nice to each other.

Try to keep care-giving issues less complicated by not pulling in aunts, uncles, cousins, and other extended family members unless they are directly involved with the care. Siblings will have enough baggage to bring to the table. Spouses and grandchildren may only complicate the situation as well, but again, if they are directly involved they should be included in the meetings and discussions. You need to keep all family informed of events and decisions.

Stay focused on the fact that you need to provide care for your parents within the realistic realms of their wishes and in their best interests.

This isn't about you, and it isn't about your siblings, spouses, or children. It is about your parents.

Caregiver Support Groups

There are a number of caregiver support groups. Often, they are associated with the fundraising/awareness organizations for a specific disease such as MS, Alzheimer's, and Parkinson's. They offer caregivers the opportunity to commiserate and share problems, to vent, and to share ideas for improving or making care giving easier for people who suffer from these diseases.

These groups provide information and education about the disease, treatments, prognosis, and research. This information may be of benefit to help educate your siblings and other family members who may have preconceived notions about cures and unrealistic goals for your parents.

There are a number of nonspecific support groups associated with aging in general. These can be associated with AARP, your local senior center, or area agency on aging. Your local hospital may run a support group for caregivers. Hospices offer bereavement and support groups for caregivers and family members involved with patients who have been diagnosed as terminal.

Fraternal organizations such as the Elks, Moose, or Eagles lodges may also have some support groups or offer assistance to longtime members. Sometimes they can help with making phone calls or home visits to shut-in members and provide even a few minutes of respite for the caregiver to take an uninterrupted shower, bubble bath, or just sit outside alone.

The Veteran's Administration can also offer many services including medical care and long-term-care options to those who served in the armed forces. However, your parent has to register with the local VA in order to be eligible to receive these benefits. You will have to locate honorary discharge papers in order to complete this process.

Many support groups also have Internet sites that may include such options as chat rooms, forums, and bulletin-board services for those seeking help to post a message or question. Sometimes it can be helpful just to read through the postings and realize you are not alone, or that there are others who have worse situations than you.

You may also find a collection of helpful suggestions from how to deal with family conflicts to how to make or use an adaptive device so your father can perform some of his own grooming and dressing tasks.

In some instances, venting or sharing your experiences can be cathartic and provide sufficient relief. Other times you may receive responses from others with messages of support or suggestions and ideas to help you deal with a particular issue. You may find you have suggestions to contribute as well, which can bolster your self-esteem and help you find a renewed faith and interest in your efforts.

Make a phone call, send a letter of request for assistance and information, or send an e-mail. Ask for information about support-group meetings, respite services, and how to get involved. Ask for help for yourself, your parents, and for your family members.

Respite services can range from a companion or sitter to stay with your parent for a few hours for a one-time event or periodically, such as weekly or monthly, to temporary placement in a facility. Respite care can include placing your parent in a board-and-care home or nursing home short term. This may be necessary if, for example, you become ill, wish to take a family vacation, or need to travel for work.

Long-term-care policies and hospice programs usually offer respite arrangements. Some of the nonprofit support groups such as those associated with Alzheimer's, MS, Parkinson's, and cancer may offer respite services in your area. Contact local chapters for more information.

How to Care for Yourself

You can't continue to help anyone if you don't have the energy to do it. If you have let yourself burn out, you need to rest and replenish before you can provide care again. If you don't, you can become physically ill. You can wear down your immune system and become susceptible to colds and flu, any chronic illness you may have become exacerbated by the stress, and you may see new health issues emerge.

In addition to seeking respite care or temporary placement, some things that can help prevent or relieve burnout include scheduling time for you:

- Have a regular date night with your spouse.
- Plan for a thirty-minute soak in the tub with bubbles, candles, and maybe a glass of wine.
- If you're stuck in the house with your parent, set aside a time each day for a personal phone call with your spouse, children, or a good friend.
- Be sure to eat regular meals and nutritious foods. Resist the urge for fast food or sweets.
- Get plenty of rest. If you have to get up frequently at night to attend to your parent, schedule a power nap in the afternoon. The goal is at least seven hours of sleep every day.
- Schedule exercise into your day. If that means dancing while vacuuming or doing the dishes, running up and down the stairs, or just taking five minutes for some stretching, at least you are doing something for yourself.
- Join a support group or participate online.
- Spend time with friends. Go out with them or invite them in. Share some food and good time together.

Something else that can be helpful is writing a daily diary. Share your most intimate thoughts, fears, and experiences about this time in your life. Expressing your feelings can help you find a new perspective and release pent-up emotions. The diary can also become a source of comfort to you sometime in the future when you want or need to remember specifics about this time in your life and the care you provided for your parents. You probably won't remember as much as you think you will, and having a written remembrance can help ease your guilt or revisit special moments during the last days, weeks, or years of your parents' lives.

Another place you may turn is to your faith. Your pastor, priest, rabbi, or other spiritual leader may be able to visit with you alone or with you and your parents and help bring some perspective and guidance to the situation. He may also provide you with some welcome encouragement for your efforts or suggestions for other assistance. Going to church or synagogue may provide you with some well-needed respite and time to reflect.

One of the most important things you can do for yourself is to laugh every day. Laughter is cathartic; it will help you release other emotions and stressors. It can help your whole system find balance. Laughter is healing and can renew your spirit and revitalize your energy.

Make an effort to find something funny. Read the daily comics or find a light-hearted comedy to read or movie to watch. Try to see the humor in the day's events. Laugh about your mistakes or mishaps. Laughter is contagious; tell a joke and make your parents laugh. Talk about old times and family outings that got ridiculous. Laugh together and enjoy your memories.

Lastly, don't overlook or avoid your own health issues. Take care of your body. See your own physician as needed. If you have health issues of your own such as high blood pressure, elevated cholesterol levels, diabetes, or arthritis, follow your regimens carefully. Take your medications as directed, eat right, have a mammogram, get a flu shot. If you are depressed, can't sleep, or have other issues, ask about some medication to get you over the hump. You might be deficient in a few vitamins or minerals from the stress and need a good multivitamin. You are an integral part of the solution; don't become part of the problem.

CHAPTER 19

Using Resources

In your experience and efforts to care for your parents and in-laws, community resources will become an everyday term in your vocabulary. They will be your lifeline and your best friend throughout this period in your life as well as your own future. Community resources will be the difference between winning in this battle and failing. Like anything else, there are good and bad resources. Some resources will be right there on the surface and easy to find; others you will have to dig for.

What Are Community Resources?

On July 14, 1965, President Lyndon B. Johnson signed the Older Americans Act. This act established the Administration on Aging and authorized grants to the states to establish agencies on aging to research, plan, and set up services for the aging population. In 2000, the Older Americans Act Amendments of 2000 was signed into law, reauthorizing the act and adding a very special amendment known as the National Family Caregiver Support Program.

FACT

The Older Americans Act was updated again in 2006 and addressed such issues as greater flexibility to states to create programs specific to the needs of their citizens; a greater focus on mental health; an emphasis on planning for the growing number of aging Americans; and enhanced coordination of efforts to protect elders from abuse, exploitation, and neglect.

All of these programs were set up to help provide such basics as nutrition and health promotion as well as disease prevention for the elderly. It also established the long-term-care ombudsman program to oversee standards of care in nursing homes and other long-term-care facilities.

The Caregiver Support Program has established grants to state agencies on aging to develop programs to educate, assist, counsel, and provide respite and support to family caregivers who provide the majority of care to the elders in this country. Under this act, there is also a special provision for the grandparents who are the caregivers to their grandchildren when the parents are not able to care for their children.

Community services are more abundant and accessible in larger cities, but even in rural areas there are services available to the elderly. Among these are transportation services, nutrition services such as Meals-on-Wheels, adult day-care centers, and senior centers.

Your local area agency on aging also supports health fairs, flu-shot clinics, and other health-screening services. It may also provide information and referral services, telephone reassurance programs, respite care, friendly visitor or companion programs, and homemaker chore services.

Area agencies on aging can be known by myriad other names such as senior concerns, center for elder affairs, eldercare center, bureau on aging, and so on. You can locate your state and local offices by calling the Elder Locator at 800-677-1116. Their website is *www.eldercare.gov/Eldercare/Public/Home.asp.*

How to Find and Use Community Resources

The first place to start is with your AAA, known in this instance as the Area Agency on Aging, and not the automobile club. (To avoid confusion, they have changed this to AAoA, but there may still be some references using AAA.) You can locate your local agency by calling the Eldercare Locator or you can look in the white pages of your phone book under "Government Offices." The website address is *www.aoa.gov.* Many services are free or available at low cost or on sliding-scale costs according to the ability to pay.

Request information and pamphlets or other publications on as many different services as you can think of for your parent. Then get a file box and organize the literature you receive as you get it. File the information under categories of need such as health care, transportation, respite care, housing options, meals/nutrition, day-care services, long-term care, support groups, legal services, senior centers.

Get organized and stay organized. You may never need this information, but you may encounter someone who does, or if you do need it, it might be an emergency and you don't want to be rummaging through junk drawers, old purses, or your briefcase. If you don't have time or energy to organize things, ask a friend to help you. Friends are always looking for ways to be helpful to friends in crisis. Put one to work.

Keep a small notebook in your purse and one by the phone so information is not lost on scraps of paper, napkins, backs of business cards, and other extraneous sources. If possible, date your notes and be sure to get names.

Use your phone book or the one you brought home from your parents' house. Use sticky notes or flags to highlight pages as you find them and highlighter pens to note the numbers you need. Some of the terms you may want to search under include "elder," "senior," and "aging." You also want to look for "nurses," "home health," "medical supplies," and "hospitals." There may also be a section (sometimes it's green) that gives you alternative names or words to search under in the phone book.

Find your local United Way and explore what services it offers. Churches and synagogues can be good sources as well. Catholic Charities and Jewish Family Services can provide resources and information even if you don't belong to their religious affiliates. Visit the local senior center and your local library. Usually, they have racks full of brochures, pamphlets, and even bulletin boards that can provide a wealth of information and contacts.

Don't overlook your employer and your spouse's employer. Find out about family leave options. Under the Family and Medical Leave Act (FMLA), if your employer has more than fifty employees and you have logged greater than 1,250 hours of employment in the past twelve months, you are eligible for up to twelve weeks of leave to care for a family member. This time can be used in a flexible manner such as in a single block or applied to part-time hours. Some states have their own family medical leave programs as well. Also, inquire if your employer offers any support or counseling services for employees who are caring for aging parents. And investigate your health-insurance plan for alternative care such as stress-reduction programs.

Consider the specific needs your parents have and try to anticipate future needs. Make a list of those things and begin your search for community resources with this list. When you contact the AAoA or other sources, request information specific to these needs first.

Hiring Extra Help

In addition to hiring caregivers, you may need to consider a few other options to help your parents remain in their own home for as long as possible. At the top of this list could be a geriatric care manager to assess and manage your parents' care. This can be especially important if you and your siblings live far away, simply cannot participate at this time, are overwhelmed, or cannot agree on what is needed.

FACT

A geriatric care or case manager is usually a registered nurse or medical social worker specifically trained in geriatrics and how to manage the care of elders. These case managers can mange as much or as little of the situation as you need and pay them to do. If your parents are completely resistant to outside help, a case manager can be the ideal person to step in and mediate.

Geriatric case managers usually manage a caseload of twenty to thirty patients at a time and have about an hour each week to devote to overseeing the care of your parents. In many instances, once a case is established, this can be adequate time. However, if your parents are especially difficult or needy, you may need someone who has a lighter caseload. Make sure the case manager is familiar with your parents' community or a lot of time can be wasted trying to set up care, and the cost of that time is going to be billed to you or your parents.

Case managers usually cost $200–$350 for an evaluation and monthly fees can range $200–$1,000. This is an out-of-pocket expense and not covered by insurance or Medicare, but it may be some of the best money you spend. You can find a geriatric care manager from the National Association of Professional Geriatric Care Managers. Their phone number is 602-881-8008 and their website is *www.caremanager.org.*

Hiring Other Workers

Other sources of help you may consider hiring to assist your parents include a driver or chauffeur, a cook, or a general housekeeper. You might look for a local college student willing to trade some time driving, cooking, and or cleaning for your parents in exchange for room and board. Or perhaps with some flexibility for school hours, this person might be willing to do any of these jobs for a specific salary.

In some areas, private chefs can be hired. This could be an option if your parents are otherwise still able to take care of themselves but can't or shouldn't be cooking any longer. There are also several gourmet-type meal services available. Some areas have gourmet meals for delivery daily or weekly, and there are some who send out frozen meals weekly or monthly. These include kosher meals as well as many other dietary restrictions. Search online for "frozen gourmet meals."

If your parents are in need of part-time services such as driving, cooking, or cleaning, you might consider whether several of their friends or neighbors would like to share the services. That way, you would be able to hire one or two people on a full-time basis. Each day the person works for a different family. This can help reduce costs and also help in the event your parents are hospitalized or will be otherwise unavailable for a week or so; the person still has a job and a space is reserved for your parents upon their return.

Always ask for references, and if possible, get a background check on the person. Pay by check, and do not allow your parents to give cash or other gratuities. If need be, you can include a cash gratuity with the person's paycheck. Remember, by hiring privately you are responsible for paying Social Security, taxes, and worker's compensation insurance. Discuss this with a professional accountant or payroll expert if you don't understand how to do this. You don't want to be liable for illegal practices or paying for someone's injury on the job.

Another word of caution is to use common sense about valuables. Anytime you have someone working in your home or your parents' home, put the valuables away. Again, if you hire privately, the person doesn't come with bonding insurance.

Understanding Medicare

Three months before turning sixty-five, all American citizens should sign up for Medicare whether or not they plan to use the insurance at that time. Medicare taxes are deducted from payroll, and all citizens are entitled. Some employers or unions may have optioned for a Medicare Advantage or HMO program; that is the plan available to employees. If a person has never worked, she can buy into Medicare. Check with the Social Security office in your city or county for specifics and how your parents can apply.

FACT

Basic Medicare offers two parts: Part A and Part B. Part A is the hospital insurance and Part B is the medical insurance, which includes such things as doctor visits, therapy, home-health care, and any covered medical supplies. This is a fee-for-service plan, and any physician or medical supplier who accepts Medicare and is accepting new patients can be seen.

If a Medigap or supplemental policy is selected, this policy may pay all or a portion of deductibles and coinsurance fees. These policies are purchased from private insurance companies such as Blue Cross. Usually, the insured pays the deductibles and coinsurances and then sends the appropriate forms to the Medigap company, who will reimburse. This requires good record-keeping skills.

In most instances, if a person has worked forty quarters or more, he will not have a premium for Medicare Part A. If he has worked thirty to thirty-nine quarters, the premium in 2007 was $226 per month. If he worked less than thirty quarters, the premium was $410 per month. In 2007, the premium for Medicare Part B was $93.50 per month and can be deducted from a Social Security check. If a person's income was greater than $80,000 (single) or $160,000 (married), the premium may be as much as $161.40 per month depending on income.

The Prescription Plan

Medicare Part D is the prescription-drug plan. There are a number of choices available to each beneficiary, and your mom can have a different plan from your dad. They have varying deductibles and copays depending on ability to pay.

Basically, the patient pays $25 for a prescription and Medicare pays the remaining amount to the pharmacy. When the patient and Medicare combined have paid out $2,250, Medicare stops paying and the patient is responsible to pay for the entire cost of all drugs until he has paid out $3,600. This is affectionately known as the Donut Hole. Once the patient has paid out the $3,600, Medicare will kick in again and pay 95 percent of the cost of the medications for the rest of the year. On January 1, the slate is cleared and the process begins again.

The key is to find a pharmacy with low costs for prescription drugs to keep from reaching the Donut Hole. While in the Donut Hole, patients pay the Medicare-negotiated costs for their drugs, but these may still be prohibitive on fixed incomes. Using generic drugs and ordering larger amounts such as ninety-day supplies from mail-order pharmacies can help keep costs down and avoid or delay reaching the Donut Hole.

Medicare Advantage Plans and HMOs

The Balanced Budget Act of 1997 split the Medicare program into multiple-delivery systems by creating Medicare Part C, which was also known as Medicare+Choice. The Medicare Modernization Act of 2003 changed the name to Medicare Advantage. This delivery system broadened its horizon to provide Medicare coverage under new plans. These include HMOs (health maintenance organizations), PPOs (preferred provider organizations), and new mechanisms known as medical savings plans (MSAs).

One of the most well-known HMO plans is Kaiser Medicare. Others include Secure Horizon's and plans run by insurance plans such as Blue Shield, Aetna, and Blue Cross.

In 2006, PPO plans began to appear, many primarily geared for specific beneficiaries such as those in nursing homes and others who have Medicare and Medicaid.

All of these plans must provide beneficiaries with the same level of coverage that is available to traditional Medicare beneficiaries. They may also include other options and may (or may not) charge an additional premium for those options. These options can include dental care, vision, and hearing, including hearing aids. Most also encompass the Part D prescription-drug plan; therefore, no additional Part D choice would be necessary. Deductibles and coinsurance charges can be less than those paid under traditional Medicare, and premiums can be reduced.

Choices are not as open as with the traditional plan. You must live within a service area of the Advantage Plan. A PCP is chosen from a network of physicians and all care is managed by the PCP. Second opinions, procedures, treatments, and visits to specialists must be preauthorized by the PCP.

Open Enrollment

Each year, open enrollment begins November 15 and continues through December 31. This is the only time of the year when changes can be made to Medicare plans. On January 1, choices made are locked in until the following November 15, when open enrollment begins again. In past years, this enrollment period was longer, and several years ago, plans could be switched on the first of each month if desired.

Part D prescription plans can only be changed during open enrollment as well. All Medicare plans and Part D options for the next year are available for comparison on the Medicare website: *www.medicare.gov*. These should be studied carefully each year and a plan chosen that best meets your parents' medical needs. The plans can be different for each spouse.

Understanding Medicaid

Medicaid is a program for people with a low income and limited assets. It also assists when other assets and programs have been exhausted, such as medical insurance that has reached the maximum allowable expenditures. Medicaid is most often sought by seniors needing nursing-home care that is not skilled or when their stay has exceeded the 100 days. Medicaid is a combined program of federal and state aid. Each state runs a Medicaid program, and eligibility varies from state to state. It is usually run by the welfare department in each state but is not part of the welfare programs. In California, Medicaid is known as MediCal.

Contact your AAoA office for information on Medicaid eligibility in your state. They will refer you to your local Medicaid office to make an application. If your parent or in-law is in the hospital, ask to speak with a case manager or discharge planner, who can assist you with the application process.

ALERT!

Financial guidelines to qualify for Medicaid change from year to year, but generally you are allowed to own a home and a car of reasonable value, a burial plot, and a prepaid funeral plan, and have a minimal amount of savings or cash for emergencies. Most states will carefully scrutinize financial records for the past thirty-six months for transactions of gifts of money and assets.

Discuss your parents' options with an attorney who specializes in eldercare issues and Medicaid laws. There are ways to protect assets for heirs, such as an irrevocable trust. The issue may not be about protecting an inheritance for their children but in protecting the assets for the surviving spouse. Your parents may actually qualify for Medicaid long before they think they will. It is advisable to investigate Medicaid long before a need arises so any necessary spend-down or transfer of assets can be made before they affect qualification. Consult a qualified attorney.

Many times a widow can become eligible for Medicaid because her income is significantly reduced by the loss of her husband's Social Security. Sometimes pensions are also greatly reduced upon the death of the retiree or don't have survivor benefits. Usually anyone receiving SSI benefits is eligible for Medicaid.

For those who qualify, Medicaid serves as the supplemental plan to cover deductibles and coinsurance. It can also cover medication coinsurance and assist with the Donut Hole gap in Part D coverage.

Most often, Medicaid is sought to help cover the costs of a nursing home after Medicare benefits run out. Legislators have been trying to eliminate Medicare and Medicaid coverage for nursing-home care in recent years, which has increased the interest in long-term-care policies. Consequently, Medicaid coverage varies by state and can vary by facility. Talk to the administrator of the nursing homes you are considering for specific up-to-date information. Many nursing homes, if they even have Medicaid beds, only have a few and they may have long waiting lists to get into one. Others have made some creative arrangements to accommodate more Medicaid beds.

Long-Term-Care Insurance

Long-term-care insurance is something you and your parents need to consider. Medicare pays about 2 percent of nursing-home costs nationwide; private insurance covers about 1 percent. Nursing-home care can cost $50,000 a year or more. One out of five people who enter a nursing home spend five years there; half of the people who enter nursing homes spend one year in it. Custodial care at home is not covered by Medicare or insurance.

FACT

Most people depend on Medicaid to be there for them if they need nursing-home care, but the government is trying to cut back on how much Medicaid will pay for long-term care. As the elder population continues to grow, the burden on the Medicaid system is going to increase. The baby-boom generation has just begun to reach retirement and tax an already overburdened system.

Long-term-care insurance offers some measure of relief. However, it is expensive. Like any other insurance, the costs will go down as more and more people buy into these policies and share the risk. Currently, the cost ranges from about $3,000 to $8,000 per year and depends on several issues, such as:

- The kinds of benefits you choose such as nursing-home coverage, in-home care, and lifetime limits

- The length of the waiting period before the policy kicks in
- Inflation protection
- Restrictions such as requiring a hospital stay prior to nursing-home care
- The amount of daily coverage
- A waiver of premium while the policy is being used
- Fixed premiums
- Coverage for dementia
- Current age and health status

A long-term-care policy will not cover all expenses, but it can help greatly reduce the out-of-pocket expenditures. Using home-health and private-duty care services as opposed to nursing-home care will also reduce the costs for care, but this may not always be a viable option.

CHAPTER 20

Finding and Conveying Information

Staying in touch with family and conveying information about your aging parents can be time consuming and challenging. One of the best ways to keep everyone up to date with the same information is to use written sources. This way you may have the best chance at keeping everyone on the same page; however, you must beware that written words can be misinterpreted. The Internet is a vast source of information, and you can easily provide links for family members through a family newsletter, blog, or website.

Staying Connected

Making a dozen phone calls can be an overwhelming chore and take you the better part of a day to accomplish. Yet conveying information about a family member and perhaps a crisis or new development can be very important. Helping your parents keep in touch with family members and friends can also help ease your burden as caregiver. It can keep them occupied and not dependent on you as their sole source of daily contact.

Teaching your parents how to use technology can be a challenge. There are simpler systems for e-mail that don't require computers, and this may be a good alternative for your parents. Some hook up to the television set and this could be a great option, especially for those who need larger print or for viewing photos.

Teach your children to e-mail their grandparents, and how to scan or photograph school projects and art projects to attach to the e-mails to share with them. Encourage your siblings and nieces and nephews to keep in touch with grandparents this way as well.

There are many ways to cut costs on long-distance calling, including using cell phones, VoIP phone systems (voice over Internet Protocol phones) from your cable TV/Internet company, and specialized rates from traditional phone companies. Beware of the small print and contractual agreements. Also, understand that if the power or cable service is out, you won't have phone service from VoIP phones.

For emergencies, your parents should have a cell phone as a backup. This could be a pay-as-you-use phone so you aren't paying monthly service fees for a phone that isn't used regularly. You could also add a line to your cell phone service for a nominal monthly fee and make this the backup line for your parents. Make sure they keep the phone charged and know how to use it.

Text messaging on cell phones is another new techno challenge, but once you understand it, it can be a timesaver as well. For instance, if Dad is being taken to the hospital and you need to notify your spouse, three children, and four siblings, you could type in one message and select several recipients for it to be sent to at one time. This lets them all know about the incident at once and that you will call your spouse once you know more and he'll be the designated contact person. You can also use your cell phone to send the message as an e-mail to those who may not have or not know how to use text messaging.

How to Search the Internet

There are simple ways to find the information you need on the Internet. You probably have your favorite home page set up on your computer. This is the first page that comes up when you access the Internet. Some of the most popular home pages include Aol.com, MSN.com, Yahoo.com, and Google.com. Each of these have a search engine incorporated into their front page and will conduct a search when you type in the terms you want to search for.

FACT

Webmasters build in a list of keywords or search terms for their site as they develop it. This is how they help people find their site and drive traffic to the website. Search engines periodically search the web to find and catalog the websites so when someone is looking for information the search engine can find it for them.

Consequently, there are also some very elaborate ways to search for information on the Internet. If you are a professional researcher, you may want to use these more elaborate methods. However, for general purposes, it doesn't have to be a complicated process.

Say, for example, you need to find a nursing home for your mom. You want to find one in or near your home in San Diego. Using Google.com, you would type in the words "nursing homes" and you would get a little over 3 million websites listed to search through. If you type in "nursing homes San Diego," you'll get back about 450,000. If you make the search just a little more specific and type "nursing homes in San Diego," you'll get 280,000.

Following the link, which is in blue lettering, there will be a short description of the website to help you decide if it's worth your time to view the page. Click on the blue link and it will bring up that website. Click your back button and you'll return to your search results.

Another example would be to search for information about Alzheimer's. For just the one word, "Alzheimer's," you'll get about 3,460,000 results. But say you want to know about medications for Alzheimer's and you don't want to sift through all of these sites. Type in "medications for Alzheimer's" and you'll get 1,430,000 results. The most relevant sites will be listed first, with their descriptions under the link. Want to narrow the search to the newest medications? Type in "newest medications for Alzheimer's" and you'll have 229,000 results.

If you are coming up with a lot of results that don't meet your criteria, try putting the search terms into quotation marks. This makes the search more specific, but sometimes this can make your search too specific and you won't get any responses. Experiment and try reversing your terms or use a thesaurus to improve your terms.

If you want to know what something is, you can type in "What is ___?" If you don't get an answer, try a different search engine. They all use slightly different processes to find and catalog information.

How to Set Up a Blog

Blogs, or weblogs, are journals, diaries, or newsletters that are updated periodically. They are for posting personal opinion and information for general reading by the public. They can be private and even require a subscription or password. They are updated in chronological order.

Many business websites use a blog to tease or advertise the basic content of their site as it is updated or changed. The blog provides a link to the whole story or article. Where the article may present information, the blog might be used to give the author's editorial opinion about the information.

Personal blogs have become quite popular to help families keep in touch. A young mother may use the blog as a daily diary of life with her children. She might post pictures and write stories about them. She can also post her children's artwork and an anecdote about it. It helps her let friends and families know what's happening in their lives when she doesn't have time to call or write. A blog can be updated at 2:00 A.M. when she has time to work quietly and reflect on the day.

Personal blogs can be used for any purpose. They have, however, been known to get employees in trouble for venting about their employer publicly, so there are some common-sense issues to consider. Even a private site can be hacked into or the text printed out.

A blog could be a perfect way to keep your family informed about your parents or in-laws. It can help encourage communication from extended family, and photos can help tell a story far better sometimes than words. While it can be a time-consuming process, you can use a blog to communicate with many people at one time and save yourself dozens of phone calls or letters. It can be updated at anytime of the day or night.

You can set up your blog at a variety of sites. Some of the more well known are Blogger.com and WordPress.com. You simply register for free and sign in. Then, using their software and website, you set up your blog and begin writing and uploading pictures from your computer. These sites have great information and help or support sites. The hardest part may be in deciding what to write.

Use the opportunity to record and reflect on your experiences. Use it to help you find some humor and to laugh about the day's challenges. A blog can help make a situation real to those who are not so involved. Use the opportunity to let them know how much time and effort you put into the care-giving process. Write about a typical day and all of the things you have done. Of course, be careful not to say anything that would hurt or offend your parents.

How to Use E-mail and Distribution Lists

Saying the exact same thing to each person over and over can be frustrating, tiring, and even boring, but to keep everyone on the same page, they all have to hear the same thing. Office memos came about for the same reason. Keeping all employees on the same page is a difficult challenge, but to prevent rumors and avoid leaving someone out, mass communication has been a tremendous help.

ALERT!

A telephone tree can be a great thing, too, when you need to quickly spread the word throughout a family, but we all know from playing the game telephone how information can get twisted, turned, and completely messed up. Someone adds their opinion and pretty soon that opinion has been passed along as fact.

If a situation like this has gotten out of control, or it is complicated and family members who don't understand medical issues will potentially get it all mixed up, a written document can be quite handy. For those who don't have e-mail, you can print out your messages and mail them.

By using e-mail, everyone will get the same information straight from the horse's mouth. Again, you can write and send it at anytime of the day or night convenient to you. You can write it one time and send it to a whole group of people all at once using a distribution list, as opposed to adding in each recipient individually each time.

If you don't know how to set up a distribution list, click on the help menu of your e-mail software. Most have some way of making distribution lists. This might also be known as setting up a group and using the group contact name in your "To:" selection.

For instance, in Outlook 2003, you would click on the menu "File" then select "New." To the right you'll see "Distribution List." Click on it and in the new box that opens you'll give the list a name and then click on "Select Members." This will bring up a list of your contacts and you double-click on the names you want to add. Click "OK" when you have all the people you want in this list, and then "Save and Close" from the next menu.

When you want to send e-mail to this list, click on the "To" in your new e-mail and double-click on the group name in your contacts list. If you want to hide recipients' names or e-mail addresses, add the distribution list to the "BCC" box instead of the "To" box. Then click "OK" and your distribution list will be added to the box. If you have used the BCC, you'll only see the title of your distribution list's name.

FACT

You will be asked to give this list of contacts a name. Using different titles that make sense to you will help you remember who the members of each list are. You might want to title the list that includes your family members by the last name of your parents, and title another list that includes your spouse's family members using his last name.

How to Set Up a Family Website

To some extent, blogs have replaced personal websites, but the personal website still has its place and uses. In fact, some of the free website hosts also include blogs and photo albums as part of their website package.

The advantage of a website over a blog is visual space. This may not necessarily be in the space behind the scenes to upload and hold all of the things you want it to; it simply means a spatial representation on the screen. And along with this, the ability to visually organize the space so it is easier to find things such as photo albums, blogs, links to useful information or other websites, how to subscribe to mailing lists, and how to contact the webmaster to send information, photos, and links to be included on the site.

Sometimes a blog archives this information or you have to scroll forever to get to the information you want. A website offers more options for organizing and accessing information easier. This is probably even more important for an older person trying to find something on a computer screen.

You don't have to have knowledge of html or how to build a website to get a simple site up and running in a short period of time. There are a number of long-standing, free hosting sites offering web-building tools built into their sites. Some have tools that are easier to use than others, but since these sites are free, you can try out a few and see what works well for you. Some of them also let you use your own web-building tools such as Adobe's Dreamweaver and Microsoft's Front Page if you prefer.

Most of these free web tools are WYSWIG, which simply means "What You See Is What You Get." As you type in text and upload photos, the tool builder shows you what your page will look like when it's complete. Others toggle from the building tool to a preview screen. It's a matter of personal preference as to which one will work best for you. Most of the free sites also offer upgrades to a monthly fee for more space and better tools. It's best to start out with the free stuff and see how you like doing this first.

Some of the sites you may want to investigate for setting up a free website include:

- *www.bravenet.com*
- *www.tripod.lycos.com*
- *http://geocities.yahoo.com*
- *www.angelfire.lycos.com*
- *www.zoomshare.com*

Most of these sites have been around for a number of years and have great support staff to help you with problems as well as comprehensive FAQs (frequently asked questions) and quality web tools. A family website can be something that grows with your family and helps keep you all close, even if your family is spread out all over the country.

Even though you might run a small website, you can include links to sites all over the web. For instance, perhaps your niece took some cute videos of her baby boy and uploaded them to YouTube, or your brother uploaded video of himself and his wife zip lining in Hawaii. You may be able to place a direct link to YouTube so people can view the video from your site or just a link leading to where the video has been uploaded on YouTube itself.

Again, setting up and managing family blogs or websites might even be a project for your teenage or college-aged children to do. You feed them the information you want posted and they can set up the pages, upload the photos, and keep the site up to date.

It does afford you the opportunity to post bulletins and information, photos, and links to websites for more information about your parent's disease process, treatment options, and prognosis. This can be helpful when you don't have a lot of time and patience for explaining things to high-maintenance relatives and friends.

What Information Is Available to You Online

The Internet is an ever-growing compilation of information. Remember, it was termed the "Information Highway" a few years back. There is a lot of misinformation available, too, but if you stick to reputable sites, you can find good, honest information and assistance.

There are a lot of how-to sites as well as vast numbers of articles about how to do something. Become familiar with the larger search engines such as Google, Yahoo, and Ask.com. Type in your question or a few keywords to describe what you need assistance with and you'll probably find far more information than you ever thought possible.

You can also access medical journals. Some give you free access to past issues, some let you read abstracts, and some let you purchase an individual article for a fee.

WebMD is a huge site full of valuable information for consumers and health-care professionals alike. Healthline.com is a good search engine for health-related information. You can access insurance companies and Medicare (Medicare.gov) for provider information such as doctors and dentists, information about the quality of providers such as physicians and home-health agencies, as well as benefits, coinsurance, and deductibles met.

You can search for disease entities for information about the disease, treatments, prognosis, and research as well as to find support groups or discussion forums. You can also access information about medical devices, how to purchase them, how they work, and how to clean them.

You can find a wealth of information for caregivers, from tips to emotional and spiritual support. You can also find providers such as lawyers, accountants, doctors, nurses, nursing homes, home-health agencies, clinics, hospitals, and laboratories and you can access forms such as a simple DNR (do not resuscitate), health-care proxy, advance directives, and living wills. Make sure they are legal in your area and have been appropriately signed and witnessed. The Internet is available 24/7. When you have the time and energy to research your needs, it is there. Learn to use it effectively.

CHAPTER 21

Plan Now for Your Own Future

As you help your aging parents and in-laws with such items as legal issues, Medicare and insurance processes, medical care, and housing, do what you can and need to for your own personal situation. Now that you have had an opportunity to see first hand how this process can affect the lives of so many people, plan now to make your own situation better for yourself, your spouse, and your children. Learn from the process and try to improve where you can. The goal is to make your last years as easy as possible for yourself and your family.

Organize Your Information and Your Files

Gather all of your information in one place. You may also want to make copies of documents and put them off site somewhere safe. Keep copies of your childrens' information, and if they are old enough, encourage them to start and maintain their own files. These documents should include:

- Social Security numbers and copies of the actual cards
- Life-insurance policies—don't forget any policy your employer has for you
- Pension, IRA, and 401(k) portfolios
- Other financial portfolio documents
- A list of all bank account numbers including checking, savings, and any other accounts
- A photocopy of the front and back of all credit cards, and contact information
- Birth certificates
- Vaccination records
- Passports
- Marriage licenses, driver's licenses, divorce papers
- House papers including deed and insurance
- Military paperwork
- A copy of the last three years' tax documents including property taxes
- Pink slips or loan information for all vehicles
- Wills, trusts, and advance directives
- Contact information for your legal, financial, and other advisors
- Up-to-date medical information including a list of contacts, prescriptions, allergies, and medical conditions

Organize the information in files according to like information such as identification, insurance, financial, and medical. Set periodic dates to review the files and make sure they are up to date. If anything changes in between, be sure to add the new information to your files.

You can scan all of the documents and keep copies on your computer, but this should be password protected and not in plain sight on your computer directory. You can also burn a CD with copies of the information to save on making several sets of paper copies.

ALERT!

This information is all very sensitive and could be used to steal your identity, therefore it must be protected. A safe deposit box may be a good place to keep copies, but in the event of a death or emergency, it may not be the most accessible place to have it. A safe or strong box in your home would be ideal, but the whereabouts should be protected.

Your lawyer should have a copy or know where the files are stored. Your children should know where to find the files and how to contact your attorney. You may even want to let your parents and siblings have a copy or know where to access your files in the event of an emergency, especially if your children are younger.

Appoint a Health-Care Proxy and Write Your Advance Directives

Even though you are probably at far less risk of needing to make end-of-life decisions at this point, it is always a good idea to make your wishes known and to put them into writing. As you age, you may change your mind for any number of reasons such as a new disease process or changes in technology that are unknown today.

Organ donation is not necessarily an issue for your parents, as due to their advanced age, most of their organs would not be accepted. However, their corneas may be of use, and in some instances, they may be able to donate their body or organs to a medical school. Organ donation is a subject to give plenty of consideration to. In the event of your untimely death, you could save the life of someone else. You can designate which organs can be donated if you have concerns about having all of your organs harvested.

Even if you are just having some minor surgery today, the hospital will ask you about advance directives. If something were to go awry during surgery, who would make decisions for your care? In most instances, one would assume it would be your spouse, but what if your adult children disagree, or your parents? Suddenly, the doctor and hospital can be caught in the middle, and without written instructions from you, they will do whatever causes the least possibility of legal disputes. Protect yourself and your loved ones by assigning a health-care proxy and completing your advance directives.

QUESTION?

Do you want anyone to have to make those decisions for you? What if you were hit by a car or injured at work and unable to speak for yourself?
Think about your wishes and consider organ donation if you were to die. Put your choices in writing. You can always change your mind and have new documents drawn up. They don't have to be drawn up by a lawyer; you can find forms online that are recognized by your state. They just have to be witnessed, and sometimes notarized.

Talk with Your Children

Your children may be as reluctant as your parents are to discuss your plans for long-term care and end-of-life issues, but if you can even just begin to open the lines of communication about these issues, you'll make it easier down the line.

Use opportunities as they arise with your parents and in-laws to discuss uncomfortable subjects. For example, if your father's Alzheimer's has progressed to a point where he no longer knows who you are, he may still recognize your mother most of the time but gets very confused when you come around. Perhaps he thinks you are your mother. This can happen especially if you look a lot like she did at your age. His mind isn't capable of understanding how your mother is now two people.

When you aren't there, he still knows her, but he is very difficult and often disagreeable. He hasn't become combative or dangerous, but he wears your mother out. Take the opportunity to discuss with your children how you feel about the fact that you may soon have to place your father in a nursing home for everyone's best interest. Perhaps you have guilt about this or your own fears of being in a nursing home without familiar surroundings.

You should also discuss what you would want your family to do if this happens to you. Perhaps you wouldn't want your husband to have to care for you for so long before placing you in a nursing home. Maybe your mother is exhausted and her own health is being jeopardized, but she's stubborn and wants to keep your father at home with her.

Perhaps you would want your children to be more persuasive with your husband if this happens to you, or maybe you are certain he would be less inclined to care for you and you don't want anyone to feel guilty or to place blame.

These are not easy times, and the subject of caring for anyone who is growing old or becoming incapacitated is not a pleasant topic of conversation, but think of how things could be better for your situation if you had had the opportunity to share your thoughts with your father before he got to this point.

Another point to make with your children is to get them to understand they all share in the responsibilities for your family. They need to be there for each other; no one should have to do it alone, and they all need to be involved. Perhaps they will all be better prepared to partake in whatever care is needed and not overburden any of their siblings.

Long-Term-Care Policies and Financial Planning

It may be too late to consider a long-term-care policy for your parents, but it is the right time to consider one for yourself and your spouse. The younger you are and the healthier you are when you buy into the policy, the better the rate you will get.

As more and more people begin to buy these policies, the rates will go down, but don't wait for that to happen unless you have the finances to pay for custodial care and five years in a nursing home.

Advance planning is required if you have many assets, property, and money you want to protect and be able to pass on to your children. Otherwise, as you have probably seen with your parents, these assets will be used to help pay for your care.

FACT

A long-term-care policy will not cover all expenses, but it should be sufficient to pay enough to make the expenses affordable for your parents or you and your siblings to pay for. One of the most important factors to look for in a policy is an inflation factor. Today's dollars will not cover costs in tomorrow's financial world.

If you have significant assets, you may need to discuss the best way to protect them with an attorney or financial planner. How much is reasonable to keep you and your spouse comfortable as you age, and how much do you want to pass on to your children?

Perhaps it would be advisable to begin to make gifts now or in the next few years so that your children can make their own investments or so you are able to enjoy watching them using or spending these funds to buy their own homes.

Spending down to become eligible for Medicaid or gifting assets or money to your children to reduce taxes needs to be done over a period of time and well in advance of your application for Medicaid or for other purposes such as inheritance taxes. Learn from your experiences with your parents and in-laws. For example, entering into joint tenancy with your children on your home should be done so they aren't penalized with taxes.

A living trust may be what your financial advisor suggests, but timing can be critical to avoid excessive taxes for your heirs. This may be something to do now rather than waiting even a few years.

Just as you began to plan for your retirement years ago with IRAs and 401(k)s, now is the time to begin to plan for your old age. Consult with an attorney or financial planner to set up a plan that benefits you as well as your heirs.

Maintain Your Own Health Status

It is always in your best interest to do whatever it takes to maintain or improve your own health status. Whenever you are involved in a situation of responsibility, it is also important to ensure you remain part of the solution and don't become part of the problem. Therefore, as a caregiver, it is even more important for you to take care of yourself.

Even first responders are taught to evaluate a situation before they jump right in. If it isn't safe for them to help, they have to stand back and do what they can to make the situation safe or give their best efforts without becoming part of the emergency. This may seem awkward, but it is necessary to provide for the best possible outcomes.

The flight attendant tells you to put your oxygen mask on first and then assist your children with theirs; if you can't breathe you aren't going to be much help for your children. In SCUBA diving, if your partner's oxygen is cut off for some reason, you need to take several breaths first and then share your mask.

To be effective at care giving, you have to take care of you. You have to:

- Set limits and learn to ask for help.
- Find a support group.
- Learn when it's time to take a break, and do it.
- Nurture your own life and keep up with your hobbies.
- Take care of your relationships with your spouse and your children.
- Laugh every chance you get.
- Enjoy the fact that you are helping make the last years for your parents comfortable and manageable.

- Learn all you can about the situation to make your job easier.
- Avoid addictive habits with tobacco and alcohol.
- Accept the fact that you may need to place your parent(s) in a nursing home.

You need to forgive yourself. You will find times you are angry and resentful. If you have had a bad relationship with your parents, this will be even harder. Understand that some of your anger and resentment is focused on the situation and not directed at your parent. However, if dementia is involved, you may find you have little patience and a short temper that is directed at your parent.

This is all normal. An underlying factor is grieving for the loss of your parent as you knew her, as well as for the loss of your life as you knew it. Being thrust into a situation you aren't prepared for and don't want to face is difficult. Having little control over events is not a happy circumstance. Much like having to give up a vacation because your children have all come down with chicken pox, your life is going to be put on hold frequently while you take care of your parents.

Some of the most important things you can do include eating right, getting plenty of sleep, and taking a break. A multivitamin will help keep your immune system strong. Get regular exercise, and keep up to date with your medical and dental checkups.

Feeling Normal Again

Your role as caregiver for your parent or in-law will end with the death of that person. Perhaps it continues or will one day resume as you have to care for surviving parents, but for now it has come to a close. Be patient with yourself and allow yourself to feel.

You will suddenly find yourself with a lot more time on your hands and perhaps even a sense of feeling lost and not knowing what to do with yourself. This may or may not be the time to consider returning to work or starting a new job. Too many changes within a short time after the death of a close relative can play havoc with your immune system, but if this has been a long process, a positive change could be good for you. This will be a personal choice after some careful consideration of the risks and benefits. However, do take sufficient time to heal and replenish yourself. Make some minor changes such as a new routine—get back into life by trying something new or pursuing a hobby or talent. You might even begin by volunteering.

FACT

You will have to deal with your grief. Don't force it; grief cannot be rushed. You have to allow yourself to experience it and go through all of the stages. You will most likely also begin to experience some grief for the loss of your role as caregiver. Although you may welcome this change, you will grieve for the change along with the loss of your parent.

Consider grief counseling or a bereavement group. If your parent had hospice care, this option should have been presented to you. You may have declined it and need to consider revisiting this choice. Or you may need to seek some individual professional counseling. Even one or two sessions can point you in the direction of understanding your feelings and moving through the grief process.

Don't beat yourself up. Stop playing the "what if," "if only," and "I should have" games. Take pride in the fact that you made a difference in your elder's life. The fact is that if you hadn't done what you did, his life would have been very different and most likely not as he wanted at all.

Put a moratorium on making major changes in regards to your parents' home or belongings. If you don't have to sell the house or clean out her belongings, wait about six months. You'll have a better perspective on things by then and will have given yourself some time to heal and separate from the fresh emotions of the situation and make plans for the future.

While deeply involved in the emotions of your parent's death, you might think that getting rid of everything or even rearranging the furniture and giving away clothing will help you and your loved ones heal and move on. However, after a few months, having a personal item of clothing or some trinket you may have dismissed earlier would now be of great comfort to you. Acting hastily can be cause for remorse and regret. Give yourself some time and make decisions with careful thought.

Your journal may also be a great source of encouragement and comfort in the future in remembering this time with your parent. You may have spent a tremendous amount of time together, and if you have recorded special moments and memories, they can serve to comfort you in moments of loneliness and help keep your loved one alive in your heart.

If you have used a journal to help you through this process, continue to record your thoughts and feelings. This will help you with closure and at some point in the future will remind you of this special time in your life. If you will face another round of care giving, the journal may be very helpful to avoid pitfalls and remember how you got through some of your darkest and most difficult moments.

With time and patience, you will begin to feel normal again. Your experience will have no doubt changed you, but you will begin to move back into a routine and feel alive again. Be proud of what you did. As you will have learned all too well, not everyone can do what you did nor do it with as much love, compassion, and devotion.

APPENDIX A

Glossary

activities of daily living (adls)

Routine activities including eating, dressing, grooming, bathing, toileting, sleeping, bed mobility, transferring, and ambulating.

adult day care

A group setting that provides care and supervision to older or disabled adults and offers a structured program of activities and meals. Hours of operation are usually weekdays from 8:00 a.m.–6:00 p.m. Some may offer weekend or extended hours and some offer transportation to and from the client's home.

advanced directive

A legal document that provides information in advance about the expressed wishes for medical treatment and intervention, health care, end-of-life issues, and appoints a spokesperson to make health-care decisions in the event that the author is unable to make these decisions. A living will, durable power of attorney for health care, and a health-care proxy are all examples of advance directives.

Alzheimer's disease

First discovered in 1906 by German physician Dr. Alois Alzheimer, Alzheimer's disease is a progressive presenile dementia that can begin in the forties or fifties. It affects the part of the brain that controls language, memory, and thought. As it progresses, these processes can be lost. There is no known cause or cure.

ambulation

The action of walking.

assisted living

A group residence for adults in which the adults live independently in separate apartments or dwellings but share services such as meals, laundry, housekeeping, limited transportation and group activities, and can pay for additional assistance with bathing, dressing, grooming, ambulation, and medication supervision. There is staff available twenty-four hours in case of urgent need. No skilled care is provided.

board-and-care home

A shared residential setting for seniors or the disabled that provides twenty-four-hour supervision and assisted living. Often these are large single-family homes in which each resident has his own bedroom or may share a bedroom. A staff is available twenty-four hours to provide assistance with ADLs. Congregate meals are provided.

burnout

A condition that results from chronic stress caused by a job or other set of responsibilities. Caregivers can burn out from the stress of care-giving responsibilities. It is a state of physical and emotional exhaustion, and can include physical illness.

care manager

A care manager or case manager is a professional social worker or registered nurse trained to assist in evaluating, coordinating, and managing the care of seniors or others in need of health-care or assisted-living issues. Geriatric care or case managers specialize in managing care for seniors.

caregiver

A person who assumes responsibility for and provides care to another person.

commode

A bedside commode is a chair with a seat that lifts up to reveal a toilet seat with a detachable bucket underneath. It is placed at or near the bedside for toileting when the patient can't get to the bathroom. The bucket can be removed and the urine or feces dumped into the toilet for disposal. With the bucket removed, the commode can also be placed over a toilet to provide a raised toilet seat for those who need a higher seat, such as after hip surgery.

competency

The ability to understand information, make informed decisions, and legally act on your own behalf.

custodial care

Custodial care is not skilled and therefore not medically necessary. It involves assisting with ADLs and supervision to prevent personal harm or injury. Custodial care is not covered by insurance, Medicare, or Medicaid.

decubitus

A pressure sore also known as a bedsore, which is a breakdown of the skin caused by friction or pressure from sitting or lying in one position and diminishing the blood flow to the area. Areas of the body where the skin is thin or over bony spots are more prone to breakdown.

dementia

An irreversible progressive decline in mental function characterized by deficits in memory, impaired judgment or reasoning, and loss of cognitive abilities such as social or intellectual processes.

durable medical equipment (DME)

Used for assisting or treating an illness, injury, or condition, and maintaining safety. Examples of DME include a hospital bed, walker, cane, commode, bath bench, suction machines, colostomy supplies, catheter supplies, and wound care supplies.

durable power of attorney (DPOA)

A legal document that appoints another person to manage your affairs in the event you are unable or unavailable to do so. The specific responsibilities are outlined in the document and the power is limited to those responsibilities. To appoint a DPOA for health care, the specific responsibilities would be to make health-care decisions for you if you are unable to do so, based on your written wishes. Unless otherwise specified, the only decisions covered by this would be for health care.

gait

The pattern or manner of walking. An unsteady gait may be due to pain or decreased strength and can be seen as a limp or staggering.

homebound

Being confined to the home, rarely able to leave, and then only with great difficulty and usually for medical appointments. The reason for being homebound can be physical or mental. This can also be a temporary situation such as during the recovery from surgery or major illness or injury. However, just because a person no longer drives does not necessarily mean she is homebound. A person must be homebound to meet criteria to receive home-health care.

incontinence

The loss of self-control over the bladder or bowel and having involuntary discharge of urine or feces.

JCAHO

An acronym for the Joint Commission on Accreditation of Health Care Organizations. Hospitals, home-health agencies, and DME companies often seek accreditation from JCAHO to ensure they meet quality-care standards.

levels of care

The stages or degrees of care provided by residential facilities such as independent and assisted-living services.

living will

A legal document and one form of advance directive in which instructions and wishes regarding medical care and treatment are specified in advance so they can be carried out in the event the person is not able to communicate or make decisions. Some states limit how specific the instructions can be.

long-term-care facility

A facility that provides skilled and custodial care to seniors or others who are unable to care for themselves due to disabilities, illness, injury, age, and health conditions.

long-term-care insurance

A private insurance policy designed to provide benefits to cover some of the costs of custodial care in such settings as nursing homes, adult day cares, at-home care, and assisted-living facilities.

medically necessary

A term used to designate the fact that prescribed medical care and services, medications, supplies, DME, X-rays, and laboratory tests are essential to the diagnosis and treatment of an illness, disease, or injury.

Medicare certified

If a facility, practitioner or provider, or health-care agency is Medicare certified, it meets the federal regulations and is approved to provide care and be reimbursed under Medicare for services rendered.

ombudsman

Someone who investigates complaints and helps mediate disagreements and grievances between patients and facilities or providers. They play an active role in overseeing the quality of patient care in skilled nursing facilities and nursing homes.

personal care

Includes assistance with ADLs such as bathing, grooming, dressing, toileting, and eating.

primary care practitioner (PCP)

The PCP can be a physician, D.O. (osteopath), or ND (naturopath) who oversees and coordinates the care of patients with other health-care providers such as physicians, hospitals, and home-health agencies. The NP (nurse practitioner) or PA (physician assistant) working with a physician can also act as a PCP to coordinate care.

respite care

Care that is provided by another in relief of the primary caregiver in order to provide the caregiver a break for such purposes as to replenish herself or to meet other obligations.

skilled care

Medically necessary care provided by a nurse, therapist (physical, occupational, or speech), or other licensed health-care provider. The care requires the skills and education of that provider.

Additional Resources

Books

Cohen, Donna and Carl Eisdorfer. *Seven Steps to Effective Parent Care.* (New York: G. P. Putnam's Sons, 1993).

Connor, Jim. *When Roles Reverse: A Guide to Parenting Your Parents.* (Charlottesville, VA: Hampton Roads Publishing Co., 2006).

Delahanty, Hugh, Ginzler, Elinor and Mary Pipher. *Caring for Your Aging Parents: The Complete AARP Guide.* (New York: Sterling Publishing, 2005).

Hallenbeck, James L. *Palliative Care Perspectives.* (USA: Oxford University Press, 2003).

Jacobs, Barry. *The Emotional Survival Guide for Caregivers: Looking after Yourself and Your Family While Helping an Aging Parent.* (New York: Guilford Press, 2006).

Morris, Virginia. *How to Care for Aging Parents.* (New York: Workman Publishing, 1996).

Rhodes, Linda Colvin. *The Complete Idiot's Guide to Caring for Aging Parents.* (Indianapolis, IN: Alpha Books, 2001).

Rubenson, Ellen F. *When Aging Parents Can't Live Alone: A Practical Family Guide.* (Los Angeles, CA: Lowell House, 2000).

Sember, Brette. *The Complete Legal Guide to Senior Care* (Legal Survival Guide). (Naperville, IL: Sourcebooks, Inc., 2003)

Sember, Brette. *Seniors' Rights, 2E; Your Legal Guide to Living Life to the Fullest.* (Naperville, IL: Sphinx Publishing, an imprint of Sourcebooks, Inc., 2006).

Van Booven, Valerie. *Aging Answers: Secrets to Successful Long-term Care Planning,* Caregiving, and Crisis Management. (St. Louis, MO: LTC Expert Publications, LLC, 2003).

Williams, Gene B., Kay, Patie and David Williams. *The Baby Boomers Guide to Caring for Your Aging Parent.* (Lanham, MD: Taylor Trade Publishing, an imprint of The Rowman & Littlefield Publishing Group, Inc., 2005).

Websites

Websites come and go. Most of those listed here are government websites. Unfortunately, government websites URLs do change from time to time. If you cannot find one of the websites by the URL given here, you may have to perform an Internet search to find the new URL. Go ahead and mark up this book to keep your copy up to date. Add an "Aging Parents" folder to your Bookmarks or Favorites on your browser and bookmark the sites you find most useful.

AARP

Formerly known as the American Association of Retired People, AARP is a nonprofit organization that advocates for healthy living, wellness, and fitness for those fifty and over. Join the organization and enjoy a variety of benefits and information on a long list of topics for those over fifty. They publish a magazine, newspaper, and have a large website.
www.aarp.org

About.com

About.com has over 600 sites, several of which are devoted specifically to seniors including Senior Health, Senior Living, and Senior Travel.

www.about.com
http://seniorhealth.about.com
http://seniorliving.about.com
http://seniortravel.about.com

Centers for Medicare & Medicaid Services (CMS)

This comprehensive site is part of the Department of Health and Human Services. It provides information and links to Medicare and Medicaid as well as other health-care related sites. It contains extensive information about Medicare and Medicaid systems for providers as well as consumers.
www.cms.hhs.gov

Eldercare Locator

This site has information about your local area agency on aging. Their phone number is 800-677-1116. There is a lot of information and links online as well.

www.eldercare.gov

HelpGuide.org

A nonprofit organization with a large amount of information and links to resources about all aspects of eldercare.

www.helpguide.org

Hospice Foundation of America

An informative site all about hospice, death and dying, grief and loss, and end-of-life issues, how to locate a hospice, and links to hospice organizations and resources.

www.hospicefoundation.org

Housecalls-Online

This is a website from the author Kathy Quan. It contains information for home-health care professionals and consumers of home-health care. Also has a list of forms for consumers to assist caregivers in evaluating and caring for their aging parents. (See Consumers link.)

http://housecalls-online.com

Housing for Seniors from Housing and Urban Development (HUD)

This site has information about low-income housing.

www.hud.gov

Medicare.gov

A site for Medicare beneficiaries and consumers with the most up-to-date information about premiums, coverage, Medicare plans, brochures, and a formulary for the prescription plan.

www.medicare.gov

National Institutes of Health

The NIH has links to the National Institutes of Aging, Cancer, and Mental Health. Medical information is available from Medline and numerous links for information about clinical trials and prescription-drug information.

www.nih.gov

(NIA) www.nia.nih.gov

Nursing Home Solutions

Information from a commercial site about long-term planning, using the Medicaid system, and asset/estate protection. Request a free video. Review the information with your legal and financial advisors.

http://nhscare.com

Social Security Administration

Informative site answers your questions about Social Security benefits, survivor's benefits, disability insurance, supplemental income, and retirement and death benefits.

www.ssa.gov

USA.gov

A huge source for information. Select the "Seniors" tab to find a long list of resources about such subjects as aging, dying, legal issues, health care, housing, money, taxes, and travel.

www.usa.gov

Veteran's Administration

Information for eligibility, benefits, contact information, and medical services for veterans. Veterans must register with the VA to be eligible.

www.va.gov

Forms and Tips to Help Organize Care

Organization is an essential key to successful care giving and surviving the sandwich effect. You will find that checklists, tips, and forms can help you organize your thoughts, plans, and information. They will help you prioritize and set in motion plans and achieve goals.

A Few Tips

As you begin to make plans for hiring help or even assuming the role yourself, you need to take inventory and observe your parents' habits and activities. Don't make assumptions based on how things were when you were growing up in their home. Some things may never change, yet some things may surprise you.

For example, what things are routine? Does your mother have a specific menu she follows every week such as pot roast every Sunday, meat loaf on Monday, and baked chicken on Tuesday? Do you have those recipes, and do you know her secret ingredients or the specific techniques she uses? If she was unable to cook, could someone come close to duplicating this for her and or your dad? If you hire a caregiver who only cooks with an ethnic flair or very spicy foods and your parents are used to bland, you could find trouble brewing quickly.

❑ Take the time to write out favorite recipes and cooking instructions.

❑ Go through the pantry and make a shopping list of the specific staples they use.

❑ Do they use specific, brand-name items only? Will a store brand be okay?

❑ Put away heirlooms, antiques, and other items your parents are nervous about others using. Replace them if they are items used frequently.

❑ Are the appliances and cooking utensils in good condition? Replace any that are outdated, worn out, or dangerous.

❑ Make a list of foods they like.

❑ Make a list of foods they don't like or need to avoid.

❑ Are they particular about how things are washed, such as not putting certain dishes in the dishwasher?

❑ Is there a specific way they like the table set?

❑ Are meals at specific times such as dinner exactly at 5:30 P.M.?

Think of any other issues with meals, cooking, shopping, and the kitchen in general that should be spelled out and discussed with a potential caregiver. This will help improve the probability of your parents actually accepting help in the home.

Beyond the kitchen, think about other specifics of household chores and activities that could help the caregiver get off on the right foot. For instance, consider making the bed. Is there a special way your parents want the bed made? Are the sheets ironed and starched? Are the corners mitered? Is the top sheet tucked under or not? Do they use a bedspread everyday or do they turn the covers back a certain way?

Think about general household chores and whether your parents have particular ways of completing them. If you can't think of anything specific, consider whether they have any pet peeves and add them to your list of things to discuss with potential hired help.

The more helpful hints you can give to a hired caregiver, the less likely your parents will find problems and sabotage your efforts.

What Do Your Parents Need Help With?

In determining what kind of help you need to hire or provide for your parents, begin to make a list of the things they are having trouble doing for themselves. Consider their basics ADLs and related activities:

- Dressing
- Bathing
- Grooming
- Toileting
- Walking/transferring
- Eating
- Cooking
- Medications (administration or just supervision?)
- Shopping
- Driving/transportation
- Paying bills
- General supervision
- Laundry
- Housekeeping
- Gardening, shoveling snow, pool/spa upkeep
- Handyman chores

As you list each of these categories, consider how much assistance they need now and may need in the future and how many you could combine to minimize the number of hired helpers you need. These may also be items you can delegate to family members.

In hiring help, you should have a list of duties you expect the person to perform. When interviewing, be sure you ask the potential caregiver about her experience and whether she feels confident she can perform these duties specifically for your parent. This is important, for example, if your father is a large man who requires maximum assistance in transferring to and from a wheelchair. Can a small woman handle these physical demands? What kind of training has she had? Has she had successful experience doing this? Is your mother extremely picky and prone to be outspoken? How would the potential caregiver respond to her? Role play, and ask for references from other patients she has cared for and call them.

Checklist of Home-Safety Issues

Home safety is an issue for everyone, not just your parents and in-laws. You probably childproofed your home when your children began to walk, and again as you may have begun to have grandchildren around. Issues for adults are similar and in some ways even more complex, depending upon a variety of circumstances such as physical disabilities and mental conditions such as dementia and Alzheimer's. This list includes most of the basics:

❐ Install grab bars in the bathroom.
❐ Install handrails on stairways and possibly in hallways.
❐ Remove throw rugs.
❐ Check for electrical cords in pathways. Don't overuse extension cords and outlets.
❐ Oxygen tubing can create a tripping hazard.
❐ Clear out clutter, especially excess furniture and piles of magazines and newspapers.
❐ Turn down the temperature on the hot water heater to 120°F.
❐ Label hot-water faucets in large red letters.
❐ Post emergency numbers next to each phone in the house.

❐ NO SMOKING in a house where oxygen is used, whether it's turned off or not.

❐ Don't cook while using oxygen.

For dementia, consider some of these issues:

❐ Place locks on outside doors in high or low locations so they aren't easily found.

❐ Consider removing bathroom and bedroom door locks so they can't get locked inside.

❐ Use locks or childproof latches on cabinets with hazardous materials such as solvents, paint, cleaners, liquor, matches, knives, and scissors. Lock away tools and garden equipment.

❐ Take away cigarettes and cigars and only allow smoking if supervised.

❐ Make sure they have identification on them at all times.

Tips for Avoiding Incontinence

Losing bowel or bladder control can be a sign there is something wrong such as an infection, a prolapsed uterus, or enlarged prostate gland. These should be ruled out or treated by a physician. There are medications that can help regain control as well as using many different forms of diapers or incontinence supplies. Additionally, some of these tips can help reduce the possibility of accidents:

• Schedule frequent visits to the bathroom, whether or not there is an urge to go. These can be every hour while awake, and slowly you can begin to lengthen the time between visits. Go first thing on waking up and last thing before going to bed.

• Have a clear path to the bathroom.

• Consider having a bedside commode in the bedroom if the bathroom is far away or it takes a long time to get out of the bed.

• Use Kegel exercises to improve muscle tone. To learn to do this, practice starting and stopping the flow of urine while urinating. Then without urinating, practice squeezing those muscles about twenty-five times in a row. Do this a few times a day. No one will know.

- Eliminate or reduce intake of caffeine, sodas, tea, and alcohol. These can irritate the bladder.
- Stop drinking liquids three hours before going to bed, but be sure to drink adequate amounts during the day.
- Take diuretics early in the morning so they'll stop causing frequent urination by mid- to late afternoon.
- Try to establish a normal bowel habit at the same time every day and sit long enough to empty the bowel. Don't allow interruptions.
- Use the bathroom before leaving home and find out where toilets are available when you arrive at your destination.
- Use diapers or incontinence pads when going out and have some wet wipes and a change of clothes with you.

Organize the Paperwork

Make yourself master contact lists and keep a copy by your home phone, your parents' home phone, at work, and perhaps even one in your car. Program the most important numbers into your phones. Give copies to your siblings. Be sure to take precautions to protect this sensitive information! Some of the most important information you will need to have at your fingertips includes:

- ❐ Your parents' full names and dates of birth
- ❐ Social Security numbers
- ❐ Medicare, Medicaid, and other insurance numbers (have a copy of the cards)
- ❐ Physician names, addresses, phone numbers (PCP, specialists, vision, hearing, and dental)
- ❐ Pharmacy name, address, phone number
- ❐ Hospital name, address, phone number
- ❐ Name and phone numbers for neighbor(s) and friends who live nearby
- ❐ Find out where your parents have their legal papers and get copies of them.

You should also have a medical history or vital emergency information form available to reference such things as medical conditions, medications, and allergies.

Complete and keep with emergency kits. Update if any changes are made.

VITAL EMERGENCY INFORMATION FORM

Name

Address

City	State	Zip

Phone	Cell Phone

HEALTH-CARE TEAM

Primary Care Physician

Name

Address

City	State	Zip

Phone

SPECIALIST

Name

Address

City	State	Zip

Phone

SPECIALIST

Name

Address

City	State	Zip

Phone

SPECIALIST

Name

Address

City	State	Zip

Phone

SPECIALIST

Name

Address

City   State   Zip

Phone

DENTIST

Name

Address

City   State   Zip

Phone

PHARMACY (LOCAL)

Name   Phone

Address

City   State   Zip

PHARMACY (MAIL ORDER)

Name   Phone

Address

City   State   Zip

Web Address   E-mail

Date of Birth

INSURANCE

Medicare Number

HMO or Medicare Advantage Name

Other Insurance   Policy #

Phone

ALLERGIES (ESPECIALLY MEDICATIONS)

HEALTH-CARE PROXY CONTACT INFORMATION

Name		
Phone	Cell Phone	
Address		
City	State	Zip
Advance Directives?	Yes	No
Who has a copy?		

MAJOR MEDICAL PROBLEMS (CHRONIC OR ACUTE DISEASES)

Medical Problem	How Long?
Medical Problem	How Long?
Medical Problem	How Long?
Medical Problem	How Long?
Medical Problem	How Long?
Medical Problem	How Long?
Medical Problem	How Long?
Medical Problem	How Long?
Medical Problem	How Long?

CURRENT MEDICATIONS

Name	Dose	Frequency
Name	Dose	Frequency
Name	Dose	Frequency
Name	Dose	Frequency
Name	Dose	Frequency
Name	Dose	Frequency
Name	Dose	Frequency
Name	Dose	Frequency
Name	Dose	Frequency
Name	Dose	Frequency

PRIOR SURGERIES

Surgery	Date
Surgery	Date
Surgery	Date
Surgery	Date
Surgery	Date
Surgery	Date
Surgery	Date
Surgery	Date

LIFESTYLE INFORMATION

Smoke:	Yes	No	Quit?	When	Cigarettes	Cigars
Drink	Yes	No	Daily	Socially		

RELIGION

Religious Beliefs

Clergy	Name	Phone
Address		
City	State	Zip

NEXT OF KIN

Name	Relationship
Phone	Cell Phone
Address	
City	State	Zip

Today's Date

Give a copy of the vital emergency information form as well as the health-care proxy to your next of kin. Place a copy in a container inside your refrigerator and mark the container "In Case of Emergency"—EMTs and paramedics are trained to look in the refrigerator for such documents. If you have a DNR, put it with these papers.

Make Doctor Visits and Calls Count

When visiting your parents' health-care practitioner or calling him with concerns or questions, be prepared so you get all of your questions answered and understand what he said. Write your questions down and take the paper and a pen with you. Some of the questions you may have about new medications or treatments include:

- What is the name of the medication or treatment?
- What is the purpose of this medication or treatment?
- How will it affect them?
- How soon should you expect to see some results?
- How often to take the medication? (Routinely or as needed?)
- How long will this medication or treatment be taken? Is there a refill ordered?
- What are the side effects to look for and report?
- Are there foods, medications (including OTC meds), or activities to avoid while taking this?
- What do you do if they forget to take it?
- If they get sick with a cold or flu, should they continue to take it?
- How much does it cost? If you or your parents can't afford it, speak up and ask about an alternative.

Always have a list of current medications including dose and frequency (such as 25 mg. twice a day), as well as any OTC (over the counter) medications such as aspirin, benedryl, Imodium, or laxatives that are taken frequently. Tell the doctor if your parent stops taking something. Know about food and medicine allergies and medical conditions including any severe reactions to medications or treatments in the past. Express concerns if a medication is too expensive.

Keep a list of medications such as this one:

MEDICATIONS

Medication Name		
Dose(mg)	Frequency	Prescribing Dr.
Medication Name		
Dose(mg)	Frequency	Prescribing Dr.
Medication Name		
Dose(mg)	Frequency	Prescribing Dr.
Medication Name		
Dose(mg)	Frequency	Prescribing Dr.
Medication Name		
Dose(mg)	Frequency	Prescribing Dr.
Medication Name		
Dose(mg)	Frequency	Prescribing Dr.

OTC MEDICATIONS

Medication Name	
How Often	Why Taking
Medication Name	
How Often	Why Taking
Medication Name	
How Often	Why Taking
Medication Name	
How Often	Why Taking

Hiring a Caregiver

Here are some suggested questions to ask potential caregivers and some to pose to their references. You will need to add specifics to tailor these to your situation. You may also find it helpful to describe a typical situation the applicant would encounter with your parents and see how she would respond. Then ask the references how they think the applicant would have responded.

For the Applicant

- Do you have experience caring for elderly people?
- Do you have any formal training in care giving?
- When did you receive this training? Are you certified or licensed?
- What was your last care-giving experience like?
- What did you like most about it?
- What did you like least about it?
- How many times did you call in sick?
- What hours are you available to work for my parent?
- Can you work weekends? Nights?
- Are you currently working at another job?
- Do you consider yourself dependable?
- Do you have your own car? Is it in good working condition?
- Do you smoke?
- Do you have a copy of a recent police background check on yourself?
- Are you comfortable with me calling your references?

Questions for the References

- How would you describe the applicant?
- Would you recommend this person as a caregiver?
- How many times did she call in sick or was otherwise unable work?
- Is this person able to handle difficult situations?
- What were the applicant's strong points?
- What were the applicant's weak points?

- Did you have any difficulties with this applicant? If so, what?
- Is this applicant dependable? Honest? Trustworthy? Hardworking? Flexible? Punctual?
- How would you rate the applicant's care-giving skills? Excellent? Good? Fair? Unsatisfactory?
- Would you hire this person again?

Gathering the Information from Your Parents

In the event that your parent becomes incapacitated or dies, you will need to know where to find documents and how to obtain information in order to assume responsibility for your parent or to settle the estate. Before that happens, go over this list with your parent and see if he has any additions to this list. He may not want to give you this information right now, but make a plan to gather the information and place it in a specified location so it can be found when needed.

☐ Names, addresses, phone numbers, and account numbers for all financial institutions such as checking accounts, savings accounts, and long-term investments such as money market accounts and CDs. Also IRA, KEOUGH, SEP, and 401(k) account information

☐ Contact information for accountants and financial advisors, lawyers, insurance agents, real estate agents

☐ Contact information for all health-care providers

☐ Copies of the wills, codicils, letters of instruction, DPOAs, health-care proxies, living wills, advance directives, trusts, and any other estate paperwork

☐ Location of and keys, pass codes, and combinations to safe deposit boxes, post office boxes, and safes

☐ Insurance policies including life, health, disability, homeowner's, automobile, mortgage, accidental death, and credit card policies

☐ Copies of Social Security cards, Medicare cards, Medicaid cards, Medigap insurance cards, other insurance cards, driver's licenses, or other ID cards. Location of the originals if not kept in a purse or wallet.

☐ A complete list of all assets and copies of the deeds or titles (houses, boats, vehicles)

- ❏ Copies of any rental agreements, business contracts, partnership agreements
- ❏ Computer passwords
- ❏ A complete list of valuables, including jewelry and antiques, along with any written appraisals of personal property
- ❏ Location of any hidden valuables
- ❏ Copies of state and federal income taxes for the past three to five years
- ❏ Receipts of property taxes for the last two to three years
- ❏ A list of all routine household bills including mortgages, utilities, insurance premiums
- ❏ A list of debts including mortgage, loans, credit cards, outstanding medical bills, other liabilities
- ❏ A list of any personal loans owed to your parents by family, friends, or business associates

When you complete this list with your parents, gather the same information for yourself and let your adult children or your siblings know the whereabouts in case anything should happen to you.

Other forms such as medication-administration records and symptom diaries can be downloaded from Housecalls-Online.com, a site maintained and written for home-health care professionals by Kathy Quan. The website is: *http://housecalls-online.com.*

Index

A

Abdominal distention, 72
Acceptance, 202
Accidents, as cause of death, 11, 26
Activities of daily living (ADLs)
  ability to perform, 61
  adult day care and, 129
  cooking, 63–65
  defined, 250
  exercise and mobility, 65–67
  hygiene, 62–63
  sleeping habits, 67–69
Adaptive devices, 81
Addiction, 188–89
Administration on Aging, 218
Adult day care, 129–30, 250
Adult-education classes, 70
Adult Protective Services, 27
Advance directives, 17, 97–100, 182, 186, 241–42, 250
Advertising gimmicks, 140
African Americans, 8, 9
Aftercare, 187
Agencies on Aging, 218–19
Aging
  arthritis and, 80–81
  cognitive issues and, 91–92
  digestive disorders and, 81–84
  effects on body of, 75
  hearing loss and, 78–80
  incontinence and, 84–86
  mobility issues and, 87–88
  osteoporosis and, 80

  process, 21
  skin and, 86–87
  statistics on, 2–3
  vision problems and, 76–78
Aging parents
  caring for, long distance, 3
  communicating with, 14–15, 39, 40
  decision making by, 6, 7, 23–24, 46–48
  discussing mortality with, 18, 182–83
  levels of care for, 113–23
  moving closer to you, 172–73
  observing, 172
  present habits of, 19–20
  refusal by, to accept help, 156–57
  relationship with, 6–7, 42–44
  resistance from, 44–45
  respect for, 6
  time spent caring for, 5
  understanding perspective of, 13–24
  wishes of, 16–18, 39, 46, xii
  Aging population, 1, 2
AIDS patients, 190
Alcohol, 67, 82, 89
Alzheimer's disease, 72, 91–92, 250
Alzheimer's patients, 210
Ambulation, 250
American Association of Retired Persons (AARP), 8, 10

Anger, 201
Antacids, 82
Antibiotics, 177
Antihistamines, 68
Apathy, 71
Appetite, 82, 88
Area Agency on Aging (AAoA), 130, 219
Arthritis, 65, 76, 80–81, 88
Asian Americans, 8, 9
Assisting-living facilities, 120–21, 137, 250
Audiologists, 79

B

Baby boomers, 2, 4–6
Baby-bust generation, 4
Backup generators, 163–64
Balance, 87, 88
Balance issues, 90
Bandages, 87, 90
Bank accounts, 145–46
Bargaining, 201
Bathing, 62–63
Bathroom safety, 28
Bathtub seats, 28, 62, 133, 134–35
Bedside commode, 133, 135, 251
Bedsores, 62, 84, 87, 90, 251
Bedtime rituals, 69
Bill paying, 7, 37
Bladder control, 66–67

THE EVERYTHING SERIES!

BUSINESS & PERSONAL FINANCE

Everything® Accounting Book
Everything® Budgeting Book, 2nd Ed.
Everything® Business Planning Book
Everything® Coaching and Mentoring Book, 2nd Ed.
Everything® Fundraising Book
Everything® Get Out of Debt Book
Everything® Grant Writing Book, 2nd Ed.
Everything® Guide to Buying Foreclosures
Everything® Guide to Fundraising, $15.95
Everything® Guide to Mortgages
Everything® Guide to Personal Finance for Single Mothers
Everything® Home-Based Business Book, 2nd Ed.
Everything® Homebuying Book, 3rd Ed., $15.95
Everything® Homeselling Book, 2nd Ed.
Everything® Human Resource Management Book
Everything® Improve Your Credit Book
Everything® Investing Book, 2nd Ed.
Everything® Landlording Book
Everything® Leadership Book, 2nd Ed.
Everything® Managing People Book, 2nd Ed.
Everything® Negotiating Book
Everything® Online Auctions Book
Everything® Online Business Book
Everything® Personal Finance Book
Everything® Personal Finance in Your 20s & 30s Book, 2nd Ed.
Everything® Personal Finance in Your 40s & 50s Book, $15.95
Everything® Project Management Book, 2nd Ed.
Everything® Real Estate Investing Book
Everything® Retirement Planning Book
Everything® Robert's Rules Book, $7.95
Everything® Selling Book
Everything® Start Your Own Business Book, 2nd Ed.
Everything® Wills & Estate Planning Book

COOKING

Everything® Barbecue Cookbook
Everything® Bartender's Book, 2nd Ed., $9.95
Everything® Calorie Counting Cookbook
Everything® Cheese Book
Everything® Chinese Cookbook
Everything® Classic Recipes Book
Everything® Cocktail Parties & Drinks Book
Everything® College Cookbook
Everything® Cooking for Baby and Toddler Book
Everything® Diabetes Cookbook
Everything® Easy Gourmet Cookbook
Everything® Fondue Cookbook
Everything® Food Allergy Cookbook, $15.95
Everything® Fondue Party Book
Everything® Gluten-Free Cookbook
Everything® Glycemic Index Cookbook
Everything® Grilling Cookbook
Everything® Healthy Cooking for Parties Book, $15.95
Everything® Holiday Cookbook
Everything® Indian Cookbook
Everything® Lactose-Free Cookbook
Everything® Low-Cholesterol Cookbook

Everything® Low-Fat High-Flavor Cookbook, 2nd Ed., $15.95
Everything® Low-Salt Cookbook
Everything® Meals for a Month Cookbook
Everything® Meals on a Budget Cookbook
Everything® Mediterranean Cookbook
Everything® Mexican Cookbook
Everything® No Trans Fat Cookbook
Everything® One-Pot Cookbook, 2nd Ed., $15.95
Everything® Organic Cooking for Baby & Toddler Book, $15.95
Everything® Pizza Cookbook
Everything® Quick Meals Cookbook, 2nd Ed., $15.95
Everything® Slow Cooker Cookbook
Everything® Slow Cooking for a Crowd Cookbook
Everything® Soup Cookbook
Everything® Stir-Fry Cookbook
Everything® Sugar-Free Cookbook
Everything® Tapas and Small Plates Cookbook
Everything® Tex-Mex Cookbook
Everything® Thai Cookbook
Everything® Vegetarian Cookbook
Everything® Whole-Grain, High-Fiber Cookbook
Everything® Wild Game Cookbook
Everything® Wine Book, 2nd Ed.

GAMES

Everything® 15-Minute Sudoku Book, $9.95
Everything® 30-Minute Sudoku Book, $9.95
Everything® Bible Crosswords Book, $9.95
Everything® Blackjack Strategy Book
Everything® Brain Strain Book, $9.95
Everything® Bridge Book
Everything® Card Games Book
Everything® Card Tricks Book, $9.95
Everything® Casino Gambling Book, 2nd Ed.
Everything® Chess Basics Book
Everything® Christmas Crosswords Book, $9.95
Everything® Craps Strategy Book
Everything® Crossword and Puzzle Book
Everything® Crosswords and Puzzles for Quote Lovers Book, $9.95
Everything® Crossword Challenge Book
Everything® Crosswords for the Beach Book, $9.95
Everything® Cryptic Crosswords Book, $9.95
Everything® Cryptograms Book, $9.95
Everything® Easy Crosswords Book
Everything® Easy Kakuro Book, $9.95
Everything® Easy Large-Print Crosswords Book
Everything® Games Book, 2nd Ed.
Everything® Giant Book of Crosswords
Everything® Giant Sudoku Book, $9.95
Everything® Giant Word Search Book
Everything® Kakuro Challenge Book, $9.95
Everything® Large-Print Crossword Challenge Book
Everything® Large-Print Crosswords Book
Everything® Large-Print Travel Crosswords Book
Everything® Lateral Thinking Puzzles Book, $9.95
Everything® Literary Crosswords Book, $9.95
Everything® Mazes Book
Everything® Memory Booster Puzzles Book, $9.95

Everything® Movie Crosswords Book, $9.95
Everything® Music Crosswords Book, $9.95
Everything® Online Poker Book
Everything® Pencil Puzzles Book, $9.95
Everything® Poker Strategy Book
Everything® Pool & Billiards Book
Everything® Puzzles for Commuters Book, $9.95
Everything® Puzzles for Dog Lovers Book, $9.95
Everything® Sports Crosswords Book, $9.95
Everything® Test Your IQ Book, $9.95
Everything® Texas Hold 'Em Book, $9.95
Everything® Travel Crosswords Book, $9.95
Everything® Travel Mazes Book, $9.95
Everything® Travel Word Search Book, $9.95
Everything® TV Crosswords Book, $9.95
Everything® Word Games Challenge Book
Everything® Word Scramble Book
Everything® Word Search Book

HEALTH

Everything® Alzheimer's Book
Everything® Diabetes Book
Everything® First Aid Book, $9.95
Everything® Green Living Book
Everything® Health Guide to Addiction and Recovery
Everything® Health Guide to Adult Bipolar Disorder
Everything® Health Guide to Arthritis
Everything® Health Guide to Controlling Anxiety
Everything® Health Guide to Depression
Everything® Health Guide to Diabetes, 2nd Ed.
Everything® Health Guide to Fibromyalgia
Everything® Health Guide to Menopause, 2nd Ed.
Everything® Health Guide to Migraines
Everything® Health Guide to Multiple Sclerosis
Everything® Health Guide to OCD
Everything® Health Guide to PMS
Everything® Health Guide to Postpartum Care
Everything® Health Guide to Thyroid Disease
Everything® Hypnosis Book
Everything® Low Cholesterol Book
Everything® Menopause Book
Everything® Nutrition Book
Everything® Reflexology Book
Everything® Stress Management Book
Everything® Superfoods Book, $15.95

HISTORY

Everything® American Government Book
Everything® American History Book, 2nd Ed.
Everything® American Revolution Book, $15.95
Everything® Civil War Book
Everything® Freemasons Book
Everything® Irish History & Heritage Book
Everything® World War II Book, 2nd Ed.

HOBBIES

Everything® Candlemaking Book
Everything® Cartooning Book
Everything® Coin Collecting Book
Everything® Digital Photography Book, 2nd Ed.

Everything® Drawing Book
Everything® Family Tree Book, 2nd Ed.
Everything® Guide to Online Genealogy, $15.95
Everything® Knitting Book
Everything® Knots Book
Everything® Photography Book
Everything® Quilting Book
Everything® Sewing Book
Everything® Soapmaking Book, 2nd Ed.
Everything® Woodworking Book

HOME IMPROVEMENT

Everything® Feng Shui Book
Everything® Feng Shui Decluttering Book, $9.95
Everything® Fix-It Book
Everything® Green Living Book
Everything® Home Decorating Book
Everything® Home Storage Solutions Book
Everything® Homebuilding Book
Everything® Organize Your Home Book, 2nd Ed.

KIDS' BOOKS

All titles are $7.95
Everything® Fairy Tales Book, $14.95
Everything® Kids' Animal Puzzle & Activity Book
Everything® Kids' Astronomy Book
Everything® Kids' Baseball Book, 5th Ed.
Everything® Kids' Bible Trivia Book
Everything® Kids' Bugs Book
Everything® Kids' Cars and Trucks Puzzle and Activity Book
Everything® Kids' Christmas Puzzle & Activity Book
Everything® Kids' Connect the Dots
    Puzzle and Activity Book
Everything® Kids' Cookbook, 2nd Ed.
Everything® Kids' Crazy Puzzles Book
Everything® Kids' Dinosaurs Book
Everything® Kids' Dragons Puzzle and Activity Book
Everything® Kids' Environment Book $7.95
Everything® Kids' Fairies Puzzle and Activity Book
Everything® Kids' First Spanish Puzzle and Activity Book
Everything® Kids' Football Book
Everything® Kids' Geography Book
Everything® Kids' Gross Cookbook
Everything® Kids' Gross Hidden Pictures Book
Everything® Kids' Gross Jokes Book
Everything® Kids' Gross Mazes Book
Everything® Kids' Gross Puzzle & Activity Book
Everything® Kids' Halloween Puzzle & Activity Book
Everything® Kids' Hanukkah Puzzle and Activity Book
Everything® Kids' Hidden Pictures Book
Everything® Kids' Horses Book
Everything® Kids' Joke Book
Everything® Kids' Knock Knock Book
Everything® Kids' Learning French Book
Everything® Kids' Learning Spanish Book
Everything® Kids' Magical Science Experiments Book
Everything® Kids' Math Puzzles Book
Everything® Kids' Mazes Book
Everything® Kids' Money Book, 2nd Ed.
Everything® Kids' Mummies, Pharaoh's, and Pyramids
    Puzzle and Activity Book
Everything® Kids' Nature Book
Everything® Kids' Pirates Puzzle and Activity Book
Everything® Kids' Presidents Book
Everything® Kids' Princess Puzzle and Activity Book
Everything® Kids' Puzzle Book

Everything® Kids' Racecars Puzzle and Activity Book
Everything® Kids' Riddles & Brain Teasers Book
Everything® Kids' Science Experiments Book
Everything® Kids' Sharks Book
Everything® Kids' Soccer Book
Everything® Kids' Spelling Book
Everything® Kids' Spies Puzzle and Activity Book
Everything® Kids' States Book
Everything® Kids' Travel Activity Book
Everything® Kids' Word Search Puzzle and Activity Book

LANGUAGE

Everything® Conversational Japanese Book with CD, $19.95
Everything® French Grammar Book
Everything® French Phrase Book, $9.95
Everything® French Verb Book, $9.95
Everything® German Phrase Book, $9.95
Everything® German Practice Book with CD, $19.95
Everything® Inglés Book
Everything® Intermediate Spanish Book with CD, $19.95
Everything® Italian Phrase Book, $9.95
Everything® Italian Practice Book with CD, $19.95
Everything® Learning Brazilian Portuguese Book with CD, $19.95
Everything® Learning French Book with CD, 2nd Ed., $19.95
Everything® Learning German Book
Everything® Learning Italian Book
Everything® Learning Latin Book
Everything® Learning Russian Book with CD, $19.95
Everything® Learning Spanish Book
Everything® Learning Spanish Book with CD, 2nd Ed., $19.95
Everything® Russian Practice Book with CD, $19.95
Everything® Sign Language Book, $15.95
Everything® Spanish Grammar Book
Everything® Spanish Phrase Book, $9.95
Everything® Spanish Practice Book with CD, $19.95
Everything® Spanish Verb Book, $9.95
Everything® Speaking Mandarin Chinese Book with CD, $19.95

MUSIC

Everything® Bass Guitar Book with CD, $19.95
Everything® Drums Book with CD, $19.95
Everything® Guitar Book with CD, 2nd Ed., $19.95
Everything® Guitar Chords Book with CD, $19.95
Everything® Guitar Scales Book with CD, $19.95
Everything® Harmonica Book with CD, $15.95
Everything® Home Recording Book
Everything® Music Theory Book with CD, $19.95
Everything® Reading Music Book with CD, $19.95
Everything® Rock & Blues Guitar Book with CD, $19.95
Everything® Rock & Blues Piano Book with CD, $19.95
Everything® Rock Drums Book with CD, $19.95
Everything® Singing Book with CD, $19.95
Everything® Songwriting Book

NEW AGE

Everything® Astrology Book, 2nd Ed.
Everything® Birthday Personology Book
Everything® Celtic Wisdom Book, $15.95
Everything® Dreams Book, 2nd Ed.
Everything® Law of Attraction Book, $15.95
Everything® Love Signs Book, $9.95
Everything® Love Spells Book, $9.95
Everything® Palmistry Book
Everything® Psychic Book
Everything® Reiki Book

Everything® Sex Signs Book, $9.95
Everything® Spells & Charms Book, 2nd Ed.
Everything® Tarot Book, 2nd Ed.
Everything® Toltec Wisdom Book
Everything® Wicca & Witchcraft Book, 2nd Ed.

PARENTING

Everything® Baby Names Book, 2nd Ed.
Everything® Baby Shower Book, 2nd Ed.
Everything® Baby Sign Language Book with DVD
Everything® Baby's First Year Book
Everything® Birthing Book
Everything® Breastfeeding Book
Everything® Father-to-Be Book
Everything® Father's First Year Book
Everything® Get Ready for Baby Book, 2nd Ed.
Everything® Get Your Baby to Sleep Book, $9.95
Everything® Getting Pregnant Book
Everything® Guide to Pregnancy Over 35
Everything® Guide to Raising a One-Year-Old
Everything® Guide to Raising a Two-Year-Old
Everything® Guide to Raising Adolescent Boys
Everything® Guide to Raising Adolescent Girls
Everything® Mother's First Year Book
Everything® Parent's Guide to Childhood Illnesses
Everything® Parent's Guide to Children and Divorce
Everything® Parent's Guide to Children with ADD/ADHD
Everything® Parent's Guide to Children with Asperger's
    Syndrome
Everything® Parent's Guide to Children with Anxiety
Everything® Parent's Guide to Children with Asthma
Everything® Parent's Guide to Children with Autism
Everything® Parent's Guide to Children with Bipolar Disorder
Everything® Parent's Guide to Children with Depression
Everything® Parent's Guide to Children with Dyslexia
Everything® Parent's Guide to Children with Juvenile Diabetes
Everything® Parent's Guide to Children with OCD
Everything® Parent's Guide to Positive Discipline
Everything® Parent's Guide to Raising Boys
Everything® Parent's Guide to Raising Girls
Everything® Parent's Guide to Raising Siblings
Everything® Parent's Guide to Raising Your
    Adopted Child
Everything® Parent's Guide to Sensory Integration Disorder
Everything® Parent's Guide to Tantrums
Everything® Parent's Guide to the Strong-Willed Child
Everything® Parenting a Teenager Book
Everything® Potty Training Book, $9.95
Everything® Pregnancy Book, 3rd Ed.
Everything® Pregnancy Fitness Book
Everything® Pregnancy Nutrition Book
Everything® Pregnancy Organizer, 2nd Ed., $16.95
Everything® Toddler Activities Book
Everything® Toddler Book
Everything® Tween Book
Everything® Twins, Triplets, and More Book

PETS

Everything® Aquarium Book
Everything® Boxer Book
Everything® Cat Book, 2nd Ed.
Everything® Chihuahua Book
Everything® Cooking for Dogs Book
Everything® Dachshund Book
Everything® Dog Book, 2nd Ed.
Everything® Dog Grooming Book

Everything® Dog Obedience Book
Everything® Dog Owner's Organizer, $16.95
Everything® Dog Training and Tricks Book
Everything® German Shepherd Book
Everything® Golden Retriever Book
Everything® Horse Book, 2nd Ed., $15.95
Everything® Horse Care Book
Everything® Horseback Riding Book
Everything® Labrador Retriever Book
Everything® Poodle Book
Everything® Pug Book
Everything® Puppy Book
Everything® Small Dogs Book
Everything® Tropical Fish Book
Everything® Yorkshire Terrier Book

REFERENCE

Everything® American Presidents Book
Everything® Blogging Book
Everything® Build Your Vocabulary Book, $9.95
Everything® Car Care Book
Everything® Classical Mythology Book
Everything® Da Vinci Book
Everything® Einstein Book
Everything® Enneagram Book
Everything® Etiquette Book, 2nd Ed.
Everything® Family Christmas Book, $15.95
Everything® Guide to C. S. Lewis & Narnia
Everything® Guide to Divorce, 2nd Ed., $15.95
Everything® Guide to Edgar Allan Poe
Everything® Guide to Understanding Philosophy
Everything® Inventions and Patents Book
Everything® Jacqueline Kennedy Onassis Book
Everything® John F. Kennedy Book
Everything® Mafia Book
Everything® Martin Luther King Jr. Book
Everything® Pirates Book
Everything® Private Investigation Book
Everything® Psychology Book
Everything® Public Speaking Book, $9.95
Everything® Shakespeare Book, 2nd Ed.

RELIGION

Everything® Angels Book
Everything® Bible Book
Everything® Bible Study Book with CD, $19.95
Everything® Buddhism Book
Everything® Catholicism Book
Everything® Christianity Book
Everything® Gnostic Gospels Book
Everything® Hinduism Book, $15.95
Everything® History of the Bible Book
Everything® Jesus Book
Everything® Jewish History & Heritage Book
Everything® Judaism Book
Everything® Kabbalah Book
Everything® Koran Book
Everything® Mary Book
Everything® Mary Magdalene Book
Everything® Prayer Book

Everything® Saints Book, 2nd Ed.
Everything® Torah Book
Everything® Understanding Islam Book
Everything® Women of the Bible Book
Everything® World's Religions Book

SCHOOL & CAREERS

Everything® Career Tests Book
Everything® College Major Test Book
Everything® College Survival Book, 2nd Ed.
Everything® Cover Letter Book, 2nd Ed.
Everything® Filmmaking Book
Everything® Get-a-Job Book, 2nd Ed.
Everything® Guide to Being a Paralegal
Everything® Guide to Being a Personal Trainer
Everything® Guide to Being a Real Estate Agent
Everything® Guide to Being a Sales Rep
Everything® Guide to Being an Event Planner
Everything® Guide to Careers in Health Care
Everything® Guide to Careers in Law Enforcement
Everything® Guide to Government Jobs
Everything® Guide to Starting and Running a Catering Business
Everything® Guide to Starting and Running a Restaurant
Everything® Guide to Starting and Running a Retail Store
Everything® Job Interview Book, 2nd Ed.
Everything® New Nurse Book
Everything® New Teacher Book
Everything® Paying for College Book
Everything® Practice Interview Book
Everything® Resume Book, 3rd Ed.
Everything® Study Book

SELF-HELP

Everything® Body Language Book
Everything® Dating Book, 2nd Ed.
Everything® Great Sex Book
Everything® Guide to Caring for Aging Parents, $15.95
Everything® Self-Esteem Book
Everything® Self-Hypnosis Book, $9.95
Everything® Tantric Sex Book

SPORTS & FITNESS

Everything® Easy Fitness Book
Everything® Fishing Book
Everything® Guide to Weight Training, $15.95
Everything® Krav Maga for Fitness Book
Everything® Running Book, 2nd Ed.
Everything® Triathlon Training Book, $15.95

TRAVEL

Everything® Family Guide to Coastal Florida
Everything® Family Guide to Cruise Vacations
Everything® Family Guide to Hawaii
Everything® Family Guide to Las Vegas, 2nd Ed.
Everything® Family Guide to Mexico
Everything® Family Guide to New England, 2nd Ed.

Everything® Family Guide to New York City, 3rd Ed.
Everything® Family Guide to Northern California and Lake Tahoe
Everything® Family Guide to RV Travel & Campgrounds
Everything® Family Guide to the Caribbean
Everything® Family Guide to the Disneyland® Resort, California Adventure®, Universal Studios®, and the Anaheim Area, 2nd Ed.
Everything® Family Guide to the Walt Disney World Resort®, Universal Studios®, and Greater Orlando, 5th Ed.
Everything® Family Guide to Timeshares
Everything® Family Guide to Washington D.C., 2nd Ed.

WEDDINGS

Everything® Bachelorette Party Book, $9.95
Everything® Bridesmaid Book, $9.95
Everything® Destination Wedding Book
Everything® Father of the Bride Book, $9.95
Everything® Green Wedding Book, $15.95
Everything® Groom Book, $9.95
Everything® Jewish Wedding Book, 2nd Ed., $15.95
Everything® Mother of the Bride Book, $9.95
Everything® Outdoor Wedding Book
Everything® Wedding Book, 3rd Ed.
Everything® Wedding Checklist, $9.95
Everything® Wedding Etiquette Book, $9.95
Everything® Wedding Organizer, 2nd Ed., $16.95
Everything® Wedding Shower Book, $9.95
Everything® Wedding Vows Book,3rd Ed., $9.95
Everything® Wedding Workout Book
Everything® Weddings on a Budget Book, 2nd Ed., $9.95

WRITING

Everything® Creative Writing Book
Everything® Get Published Book, 2nd Ed.
Everything® Grammar and Style Book, 2nd Ed.
Everything® Guide to Magazine Writing
Everything® Guide to Writing a Book Proposal
Everything® Guide to Writing a Novel
Everything® Guide to Writing Children's Books
Everything® Guide to Writing Copy
Everything® Guide to Writing Graphic Novels
Everything® Guide to Writing Research Papers
Everything® Guide to Writing a Romance Novel, $15.95
Everything® Improve Your Writing Book, 2nd Ed.
Everything® Writing Poetry Book